MW00358870

## What the readers and trad___

"First of all, let me say that since I ordered your book, I have read it from cover to cover at least four times. It's now literally filled with highlighter and dog-eared pages, and has proven to be dollar for dollar the best investment I've made in years. You obviously have a keen grasp of your profession and your writing style communicates your expertise flawlessly. For years, I have been searching for a profitable business that I can run from home without resorting to mail order widgets, and thanks to your book I have finally found one that suits me . . . most of all, thanks for your book!"

—David V., California

"I must say that this is the best book I have ever read on the subject of futures trading. It really tells you how to get started and how not to lose money. I particularly like the concept of day-trading because, as it says in the book, lower margins are required than for overnight trading which means your capital can stretch. . . ."

—Desmond S., Jamaica

"I would first like to thank you for providing a wonderful source of encompassing information, especially for the new trader, which I am. The very up-to-date charts and examples are excellent. Also, the spirit of the book aligns with my own personality and goals, in that I've always been a knowledge seeker when first presented with something new, and my expectations are not the "retirement" trade, but rather consistent returns able to support my family."

—Kenneth G., Florida

"I am a senior research scientist and use signal processing and pattern recognition techniques . . . I am currently working in my spare time on an S&P 500 futures day-trading system; in the past I have worked on a trading system for OEX options. Your book is very informative and practically useful . . . I am reading it for the second time now. Do you mind if I call you sometimes after hours to ask your opinions?"

—Lee W., Ph.D., Washington

---

From letters on file received for a prior Internet version of this book.

"I ordered your manual which I've found to be most informative and masterfully written. It is a refreshing insight into how a person can become successful in this business using a sensible approach coupled with dedication. . . ."

—Alan J., South Dakota

"...your book is the most practical as it gets down to the real nitty-gritty of intraday trading ."

—John M., Ph.D., Astrophysics; Canada

". . . for the first time, I feel that someone has finally written a book that has provided me with information in a manner that I can understand, and act upon . . . "

—Volkmar H., Canada

"A friend of mine and I are using your workbook as the starting point in adapting the work of researchers in genetic programming for use as heuristic, real-time trading systems. This system will use a realtime feed to generate buy/sell/reversal decisions on very short term cycles."

—Mike M., California

"Already, your book has inspired a powerful paper trading methodology (that) has managed to generate approximately $25,000 (in the S&P 500) in the last three weeks!"

—Alan G., Canada

"Thanks for a software package that really does what it is supposed to and a book that puts it all together."

—Beth A., Maine

". . . I could go on and on telling you how good your book is but I'm quite sure you already know that. Unlike other books on the markets, it is evident that you know how to write. The book is well organized in a logical and even beautiful sequence. In addition, there is a good bit of lightheartedness and humor to be found in its pages. . . In summary, you deserve a BIG THANK YOU! for taking the time to write this book and for caring about the new trader."

—Peter S., Hawaii

"... there is so much information, have to stop to allow it to soak in! Didn't realize how much I did not know about futures trading. Now I understand that my financial loss in the market was a stupid move on my part, and wish I had known about your book before I threw away (literally) my money . . . Your book may well be the turning point in my life . . . the price of your book is a 'Bargin'."

—Bruce L., Texas

"Thanks for the manual . . . I have read and am continuing to read various source material on the subject — and consider your manual the best learning material so far. I am treating it as a bible to be revisited often . . . I have been involved in the physical metal markets for over 20 years and my only regret is that my fascination with physical trading kept me from exploring the futures — until now!"

—Hugo K., Massachussetts

"I think your book is an excellent illustration and learning tool."

—Rudy H., Missouri

"... I am an admitted skeptic. I have sent away and spent money on a variety of business opportunities. Some areas I am familiar with, others new to me. Over the past two years I have spent a few hundred dollars trying to learn futures trading. Your book for the money is worth its weight in futures contracts. I finished about an hour ago. I will spend time re-reading the technical tools. The layout is methodical and easy reading. I feel closer to defining what type of trader I am and the tools I need to trade. You helped me realize the way I would like to trade is realistic."

—Scott A., Hawaii

"I've just finished reading your guide on commodity trading from home. You have my congratulations. First-rate information. Fascinating. I have plans to build my own trading system based on neural nets and non-linear optimization. Your guide has opened up to me a whole new range of opportunities . . ."

—Nelson C., Portugal

*How to Become a*

# Real-Time Commodity Futures Trader

*from Home*

*How to Become a*

# Real-Time Commodity Futures Trader
## *from Home*

### LIVING THE ULTIMATE ENTREPRENEURIAL DREAM

Scott A. Krieger

**The Futures Group**
Leeds, Massachusetts

www.futures-trader.com

This publication is designed to provide accurate and authoritative information in regard to the subject matter covered. It is sold with the understanding that the publisher is not engaged in rendering legal, accounting, or any other professional service. If legal advice or other expert assistance is required, the services of a competant professional person should be sought.

*From a Declaration of Principles Jointly Adopted by*
*a Committee of the American Bar Association and*
*a Committee of Publishers and Associations.*

PLEASE NOTE: This book is presented for educational purposes only. Trading futures has large potential rewards and large risks, and is not for everybody. Investors in the futures markets need to understand and accept the risks of loss, and they should not invest money that they cannot afford to lose. That trading methods made money in the past does not guarantee that they will make money in the future. Hypothetical performance results do not represent actual trading but are calculated from an analysis of back data. In actual trading, live market factors can affect those results positively or negatively. Nothing in this book constitutes a solicitation to buy or an offer to sell commodities, and no claims are being made that the same or similar results will be experienced by users of this information.

*TradeStation* is a registered trademark of Omega Research, Inc. *EasyLanguage* is a trademark of Omega Research, Inc. *MAG Innovision* is a registered trademark of MAG Technology Co., Ltd. *A Guide to Futures and Options Market Terminology* is used with permission from the Center for Futures Education.

Cover design concept and autumn scene photo by Scott A. Krieger
Design consultation with CHC/studioIGS
Design composition: Yamaraj dasa/Computer production: Beverly Symes
Trading desk photo and portrait by Jose Ramon Garcia

This book is manufactured with the special *Otabind*™ process for the convenience of "lay-flat" reading and study.

Copyright © 1997 by Scott A. Krieger
All Rights Reserved. No part of this book may be reproduced in any form or by any means whatsoever without permission in writing from the publisher. For information contact: The Futures Group, P.O. Box 131, Leeds, MA 01053.

**The Futures Group**
Leeds, Massachusetts

www.futures-trader.com

Library of Congress Catalog Card Number: 96-91002

**Cataloging in Publication**
(Quality Books, Inc. follows Library of Congress guidelines)

Krieger, Scott A.
  How to become a real-time commodity futures trader from home:
living the ultimate entrepreneurial dream / Scott A. Krieger. — 1st printed ed.
    p. cm.
    Includes bibliographical references and index.
    Preassigned LCCN: 96-91002
    ISBN 0-9650353-7-9

    1. Commodity futures.  2. Investments  3. Entrepreneurship
    4. Home-based businesses  I. Title.

  HG6046.K74 1997              332.63 '28
                              QBI97-40031

# Dedication

To the great and wise personality known as Srila Prabhupada who once traversed this planet, freely distributing wealth beyond all measure. From the ancient *Vedas* of India he taught that if we really wish to find fortune, we must ever strive to please the Goddess of Learning (Saraswati devi) more than we do the somewhat jealous Goddess of Fortune (Lakshmi devi). In this way we will receive not only the highest knowledge from Saraswati devi, but gifts in abundance from Lakshmi devi, who will ever strive to win back our attention.

(Translation: Strive first for knowledge. Fortune will surely follow!)

# Acknowledgments

I would like to thank the Chicago Mercantile Exchange and the Chicago Board of Trade for general industry information plus the use of the illustrations which depict the "method in the madness" trading process taking place daily on their exchange floors. I deeply appreciate the Center for Futures Education's enthusiastic permission to print their contract and government report spec lists, as well as their excellent guide to futures and options market terminology. I would also like to thank Steve Nison for introducing the ancient art of Japanese Candlesticks to the western world.

# Contents

# INTRODUCTION

Years back, before I got determined to scour the earth and dig up what I needed simply to begin to comprehend "what the heck is this all about anyway!?," I heard about futures trading only rarely—so respectful here, so terrified there—in novels, TV shows, and in the movies. It was obviously a high-stakes game open only to billionaires and gamblers. Or billionaire gamblers. At first glance the subject appeared tailor-made for Hollywood. Up there on the marquis: *Futures!* That most rarified of financial instruments; the darling of the Chicago financial world, Wall Street, and global high finance: ever elusive, impossible to understand (by mortals certainly) and ever so exotic![1] Hollywood has indeed tried to capitalize on the mystique of high finance futures trading, and while a number of films just mention the word "futures" to lend a wealthy air to their plot, there is one movie that not only mentioned the subject but pretty much tackled it head-on. You've probably seen it. *Trading Places*, a comedy starring Dan Aykroyd, Eddie Murphy, and Jamie Lee Curtis, used the futures industry and its players as the main background motif. Since general knowledge of futures trading is virtually nonexistent for the common movie viewer, the screen writers of *Trading Places* wound up having to research and artfully explain the basics of futures trading throughout the course of the film. Along with Eddie Murphy we are taught about commodities and given a tour of the floor of a futures exchange (Note: The trading scenes were filmed at the New York Cotton Exchange where "FCOJ" [Frozen Concentrated Orange Juice] futures are traded.) Ultimately we're treated to a wild scene of pit trading where leaked insider knowledge of a Department of Agriculture harvest report enables Dan and Eddie to make a fortune in the selling panic — that they initiate. Through their illegal knowledge of that report plus their understanding of the effect it would have on subsequent market action, they are enabled to completely dominate and manipulate the fear, the greed, and the profits in the pit. (Note: How they opened up a personal account of such size and margin to handle the many thousands of contracts needed to make such a fortune is a detail of cinematic justice. It must have been Eddie's good looks.) The credits roll on the three sipping piña coladas on their own tropical island after having won over $300,000,000 in a few hours of trading. Hurray for Hollywood!

And that pretty much is the Hollywood take on commodity futures trading: it's either utter annihilation or rulership over the universe. Nothing in between. What is interesting is that this view has virtually become *the* view. Not only is basic knowledge of trading in futures obscure to the common movie viewer, but it is also a mystery to the common investor in stocks, bonds and funds. In this absence of knowledge, the mythmakers have rushed to fill the vacuum with illusion. Consciously or unconsciously, the Hollywood version has done much to define and shape popular opinion of the industry (Note: But even Hollywood could do only so much with the subject; there have been many movies dealing with ruthless Wall Street moguls and corporate takeovers — the "stock stuff" most folks can grasp — but Hollywood hasn't seriously touched commodity trading since *Trading Places*. After all, how often can you turn lessons and education on commodity trading into entertainment?) Life has clearly followed "art" in this case. Ask anyone not in the business to tell you what he thinks about commodity futures trading, and if you don't get a blank stare or shrug, you'll hear echoes of the contrived myth that commodity futures trading is nothing but a high-stakes crap shoot. Of course it doesn't help its reputation any that many traders have also bought into that myth and therefore treat futures trading not as a lucrative business opportunity, if intelligently managed, but as a casino roll of the dice. And of course, any business can be mistreated in this fashion. But if that's what someone wants, then futures trading can become one of the most exciting (read: *terrifying*) high-tech global casino rolls imaginable, ultimately with devastating Hollywood-style results. In fact, if trading is approached as a game of chance, one will do far worse than at a real game of chance. The power of leverage (discussed later) will see to that. Trading is, in reality, very much a game of skill, and if I misread this high-stakes game of skill to be a high-stakes game of chance, I will lose—consistently. Not all games are the same! Let's look at an example.

Take chess. Everyone knows that chess is a game of skill and not a game of chance. Let's say I don't know this. Let's say I know absolutely nothing about the game except what I "learned" about it in a Hollywood fiction. A well-directed movie convinces me that this legitimate and generally highly-regarded pastime is nothing but a wild casino game, requiring as much intellectual prowess to play as it takes to play the well-named one-arm bandit.

Now let's say that with this image in my mind, I try to play the game of chess. How do you think I would fare pitted against someone who knows that chess is actually a game of skill, and who took the time to first learn the rules and then perhaps a bit of strategy? Like driving blind, I factually would not have a chance! If chess (or trading) were just a game of chance, then I'd have about the same 50% odds of winning as I would by calling heads or tails on the flip of a coin. But since these are games won instead through the application of learned rules, tested strategies, and artful and creative skill (which, by the way, also sounds like a pretty good success formula for a business, doesn't it?), my chances of winning based solely on emotion or hope approach not 50%, but 0%! While this might lead to embarrassment in the game of chess, it quickly leads to financial ruin in the business of futures trading.

In chess and in trading it is the superior player possessing the requisite skills and strategic ability who wins, and wins practically every time. Traders who are too impatient—whose eyes are filled with images of that single blockbuster "retirement trade" with all those fabulous mansions, Lambourginis, and tropical island homes riding on it, and who are ultimately unwilling to take the time and effort required to really learn the essentials and go forth into each trading day armed with *knowledge*—these traders have a very fast and short half-life at their imagined casino.

Bottom line: Futures trading is a business, number one, and game of skill, number two. Success is directly proportionate to our ability to manage the business end; learn the rules, tools, and strategies of the game end; then blend it all together with our individual psychology, creativity, and personal trading style. This is the direction toward profitable trading. And fun trading!

Futures trading is a zero-sum world. At the end of every day, without exception, there's a dollar won for every dollar lost; or a dollar lost for every dollar won, depending on which side you are standing. And at the end of every trading day, in every market, there are consistent losing traders who don't know what they are doing (or who psychologically can't do what they know they should do), who simply hand over their money to the consistent winners who have taken the time and effort required to create a successful mind-set and really learn the business.

You can—most definitely—be the latter.

This book is designed to be a practical and profitable guide to futures trading for both new and experienced traders. While the subject of trading in its entirety encompasses libraries of information, this guide does serve its niche purpose. It may be the only practical "how to" guide to getting physically set up to trade from home, hardware-wise and software-wise. On the other side of the spectrum, it gives valuable time-tested strategies and advanced information, beyond theory, that can improve anyone's trading methodology. Charts, tables, and figures are provided to give visual support and to bring clarity to technical points. As for any art or science (and futures trading has been called both) the futures industry has evolved its own lingo or "futures-speak," and such terminology is placed in italics throughout the guide and defined in context. A comprehensive guide to futures and options market terminology is included as well, and we think you will find this an education in itself. Excellent sources for further study are provided in the Appendixes since (and it can never be repeated enough) knowledge is everything. Your determination to first get yourself firmly rooted in the basics and then keep yourself up-to-date will define the type of trader you become. Futures trading is a fascinating vocation or avocation and can be enormously lucrative (more than anything *I* know of). Your success in this field is most definitely in your hands—not the house's!

With the exponential development of high-performance personal computers, real-time charting software, real-time data vendors, and home cable/satellite feeds, the private trader[2] can do from home in real-time what could have only been done "by being there" just a few years back. So let's get beyond the glamour and the terror, trash the myths, realize once again that knowledge is everything, keep our minds open, get determined, and begin . . . .

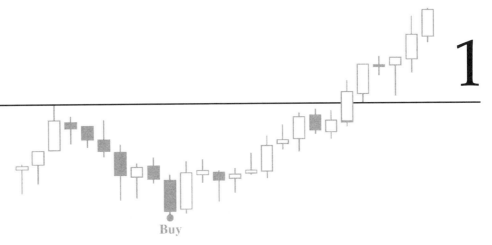

# A Brief History Of Futures Trading

In the research of Glamann[3] and Haccou[4] there is some evidence that futures trading started in late seventeenth-century Amsterdam in various popular commodities like coffee, grains, brandy, and whale oil. John Cary writes of the trading of the time: "They invest in new ways of trade, great quantities of brandy being disposed of every year, which are never intended to be delivered, only the buyer and seller get or lose according to the rates it bears at the time agreed upon to make good the bargains."

However, there appears to be more compelling evidence[5] that the actual mechanics of futures trading via standardized futures contracts—the backbone of modern futures trading worldwide—began to take shape even earlier in feudal Japan. This is the Japan made popular to the world, and endearingly so, in the novels of the late and great storyteller, James Clavell. The most famous of these, *Shogun*, was later made into one of the longest TV sagas (Paramount called it a maxi-series) ever produced. If you've either read the novel or seen the TV production, you may recall the name of the powerful *daimyo* (feudal lord) who, through sheer power of personality, psychological control, and brilliantly ruthless war strategy, masterminded himself into the position of *shogun,* supreme lord of all Nippon, Japan. His name in Clavell's epic was Toranaga Sama, or Lord Toranaga. It is no coincidence that the name of the real shogun of Japan who defeated all the other warlords at the end of the terrible war (the *sengoku jidai* or "Age of Country at War," lasting from the fifteenth to sixteenth century) was Tokugawa Sama, or Lord Tokugawa.

During the period of the Tokugawa shogunate, which lasted from approximately 1600 to 1870, the city of Osaka became the natural site for developing into the primary commercial region for the country. It was well-situated in the center of Japanese cultural development and had easy access to water transport. Rice supplies were initially warehoused there starting from the time of Toyotama Hideyoshi in 1582. Lord Tokugawa defeated Toyotama and gained full control by 1615, and with no opposition to his control the revenue base of rice supplies was expanded greatly throughout the region.

As the rice trade continued to bloom the markets became organized by a rising merchant class, flourishing in the peaceful atmosphere which finally blessed the country under the powerful Tokugawa shoganate. By 1626 there were 111 daimyo rice warehouses in the city and the primary rice market was regulated at the Dojima Rice Exchange in Osaka.

Trade in rice ultimately became so ubiquitous that it was eventually used as the primary currency and standard of exchange throughout Japan (currency exchanges based on gold and other precious metals failed due to widespread counterfeiting and degrading of the metals). Rice coupons were created as the common medium to be exchanged for bales of rice that were stocked in warehouses in the owner's name. By the beginning of the 1700s, the use of these coupons grew enormously and especially as sold against future rice deliveries. Used in this way, rice coupons became the world's first futures contracts, and the Dojima Rice Exchange became the world's first futures exchange, where these coupons were daily and very actively traded.

The nineteenth century saw the development of modern-type futures exchanges in Chicago, New York, Liverpool, London, Berlin, and elsewhere. Along with this proliferation of exchanges grew the methodology of trading regulation and control, such as the concept of the clearing house (described later) and the settlement of disputes via arbitration committees. The oldest commodities exchange in the US is the Chicago Board of Trade (CBOT). It started operations in 1848 as the primary grain exchange in the nation and became a model for the development of other exchanges, not only in the US. As the decades passed, more and more exchanges opened up worldwide as trade grew in different varieties of commodities. Today there is an ever-increasing development of new commodity products, including sophisticated financial products, available for trade in more and more exchanges around the globe.

Futures trading has certainly had a fascinating history, and it has grown to become a critical and indispensable enabler of trade and commerce in today's global economy. As far as the individual futures trader is concerned, it all translates into job security—being your own boss in a lucrative business that is very much here to stay!

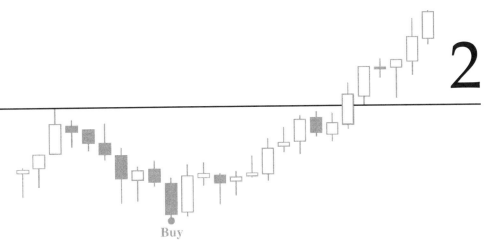

# THE MECHANICS OF FUTURES TRADING

## The Futures Contract

"Futures" is a term that can refer to both the commodity futures industry and to the commodity markets daily traded at commodity exchanges worldwide. To get an idea how futures actually work, we have to look at the single most essential element of futures trading that makes it all possible: the futures contract. Simply put, a *futures contract* is a formalized agreement for the later purchase or sale of a commodity. Whether the specific commodity is a single contract unit of 50,000 lbs. of copper, 5,000 bushels of soybeans, or $125,000 in Swiss Francs, this contract between buyer and seller is based on future delivery of an exact standardized quantity and, if applicable, standardized type and grade of the commodity. The commodity itself may not even exist at the time the contract is purchased/sold, and often doesn't. A somewhat oversimplified example of futures trading (or how you can buy or sell something that does not actually exist via a futures contract) is found in the buyer-seller relationship found at any functioning car dealership. It goes something like this:

Buyer wants a new car and goes to the dealership, picks out the model he wants on the floor or lot, hopefully takes it for a test drive, chooses the options and interior/exterior color, haggles the price, and, when satisfied, decides to buy it at the agreed-upon price and delivery date. Dealer (as the seller) checks out Buyer, takes Buyer's credit for a test drive, haggles the price, and, when satisfied, decides to sell the car at the agreed-upon price and delivery date. A formalized contract is signed, stipulating all of the standards, specifications, and prices agreed upon, including a future delivery date and place for this precisely specified automobile. A deposit is usually put down as a monetary guarantee of performance by Buyer. Of course this particular car, with its detailed options, specs, colors, etc. may not, and probably does not, even exist at the time the contract is signed. In futures terms, a futures contract of a currently non-existent automobile (*commodity*) is being traded now according to precise specifications for future delivery on a fixed date, using the advance deposit as the *margin* requirement guaranteeing full payment upon maturation and settlement of the contract. The Dealer is *short* one Scamper: he owes it; and the Buyer is *long* one Scamper: he's buying it. On the delivery date, when the contract reaches maturity, if all details of the contract are met, the auto commodity and the cash change hands, and the trade is completed or offset.

And that is pretty much where the similarity between actual futures trading and the above example ends. In fact, the similarity in this case ended before the commodity changed hands. In approximately 98% of all futures trading, the participants would never purposefully wait until maturation of the contract (until the delivery date of the futures contract was reached). In nearly every case, futures traders who are speculating in the marketplace have neither the desire nor the ability to either provide for, or take possession of, the physical commodity, and so they make sure to offset their purchase or sale with the opposite trade before the delivery of the commodity comes due. Their only desire is to profit from the difference in price from the moment of purchase of the futures contract to the moment of sale of the futures contract. I want to buy (go long) December Corn when the price is low and sell it (go short) when the price is higher. I also want to go short December Corn when the price is high and go long when the price is lower, which really is the same thing, except for which happens first. Both bring me profits, and their opposite brings me losses. How can I initiate a trade by selling 5,000 bushels of December Corn if I happen to be living in Brooklyn or Liverpool and don't happen to be a farmer or know any farmers? The same way that I can buy it: Through the *promised* delivery or purchase of the commodity on the delivery date, based on an ironclad futures contract. Even though the vast majority of futures contracts are offset by the opposite trade before the delivery date is reached, the contract itself is absolutely binding, in that it specifies that delivery will take effect. When the delivery date is reached, the contract will be enforced upon the last holders of the contract. This means that if you've gone long one contract of November soybean meal, you'd better go short one contract of November soybean meal before the actual delivery date in November—unless you really want a lot of soybean meal and are looking forward to receiving that warehouse receipt notifying you that your meal has arrived. Delivery on one contract of soybean meal would get you 100 tons of the stuff (which, yes, you'd also be expected to pay for).

## The Players

We have discussed some of the basic ideas of trading and the futures contract. But what is the actual motivation, the engine behind the trading? Profit? Of course, but that is not the cause of trading; it is a result of trading. Futures trading was created to fill a specific commercial need, a need that is fulfilled perfectly by the unique relationship existing between the two primary categories of traders themselves: the speculator and the hedger.

In the early development of commerce in commodities, a method had to be developed by which the merchants or owners of cash commodities could shift the inherent risks of ownership from themselves onto others. The often perishable and time-sensitive nature of commodities and inventories, the variance in price over time, and the large sums of capital involved, all contributed to the need for someone to assume the huge financial ownership risks that the merchants and the financing banks were both unwilling to take.

Enter the system of hedging. Every future has its underlying cash commodity. *Hedging* takes advantage of this by offsetting one's position in the cash commodity with an equal and opposite futures position in the same commodity. If, for example, a grain merchant has 200,000 bushels of wheat in stock, he is long cash wheat. He is at direct risk of downward price movement in the commodity. By selling 200,000 bushels of futures contracts, he becomes short wheat futures: his long cash position is offset by his short futures position. And he has become the first player in the futures game: the hedger. If cash wheat and wheat futures both go up and down together (which, in most cases, they tend to do), he will neither gain nor lose from a change in price over time; i.e. when the price of his cash commodity goes down he loses money and, simultaneously, when the price of his short futures goes down he makes money. Until he sells the physical commodity, his short futures position will protect the differences in price. When the time comes for the merchant to sell his cash wheat, he also buys back his short futures. He thus completes the entire transaction: buying cash grain/selling grain futures and then selling cash grain/buying grain futures. He has protected himself from loss in the price change of his commodity over time by shifting the risk (through his futures trade) to others. In other words, he has successfully hedged his risk. (Note: Due to the complexities of hedging, including carrying charges and other factors, the perfect hedge, i.e. net zero price gain or loss over time, is rarely achieved. Instead the hedger generally winds up either making some money or losing some money, but if he loses, the loss will be greatly minimized due to the hedged trade). When the owners of physical commodities need to export their goods, they can also hedge against the risk in the variance of price in the rate of exchange between their currency and the foreign currency. In this case, they are not only hedging the change in price of the physical commodity itself, but are also hedging any rate changes in the actual foreign paper currency that they plan to use to exchange for those hard goods. For example, say a US firm agrees to ship goods to Germany in three months. When payment is made after three months, the U.S. firm will convert the Deutsche marks received to U.S. dollars. To hedge against the risk that the value of the dollar will go up against the mark over that time (thus making the value of DM to be received in three months less than they are now), the firm sells DM futures now in an amount equal to the payment in DM cash currency that they will receive in three months. If the DM goes down in value in the cash (spot) market, it will also tend to go down in the futures market. Since the firm has gone short DM futures, and since one makes money on a short sale as the price goes down, their long spot currency loss will be neutralized by their short futures currency gain. When payment is finally made, the firm buys back the DM futures and is protected against loss in the exchange rate. Again we have a successfully hedged risk.

Hedgers encompass a wide spectrum of commercial interests that are concerned with maintaining profitability, and this certainly involves financial protection and risk reduction. The list of commercial hedgers includes farmers, warehousers, multinational corporations, pension funds, insurance companies, and food processors.

And so, who are the poor souls who get strapped with all this risk? Who buys all those grain futures and Deutsche marks from the merchants just to sell them back (to the clearing house) later? The answer is that the risk is shifted on to individuals, institutions, governments and other assorted entities (many of whom are far from poor) who are more than willing to take on that risk, with the goal of managing it skill-fully enough to profit from the difference in the futures prices over time. For this huge profit potential, they (and we) willingly assume the risk that exists for the producer and user of the commodity. This second vital partner in the process is the trader or speculator. Speculators also come in many forms, and some of their basic categories can give you an idea of their trading style and financial situation, if not their demeanor:

*Scalpers* are a class of trader that try to get in and out of a large volume of trades in a lightning fast manner. The scalper looks to profit from small differences in price in any market. By committing themselves to trade many times each day, such small differences in price add up to large profits quickly (or large losses —therefore the need for speed). Scalpers also do a brisk business in spread trading, where differences in price between the front or nearby month (nearest delivery month) of the commodity and the current price for the same commodity at a more distant month are taken advantage of. The difference is the profit (or loss). Since scalping requires a highly specialized level of skill and instant reaction time, it is a type of trading almost always associated with direct pit action at the physical exchange, and not something to be attempted from home.

*Pit traders* take larger positions (trade more contracts) than scalpers and stay with the trade for a longer period of time. They are, in virtually every case, daytraders. They take advantage of intraday price changes and close out their positions at the end of the day, i.e. offset each trade with the opposite trade. Pit traders are the folks you saw in *Trading Places*; they are an excitable lot. They may react with terror one moment and ecstacy the next, based on hope, rumor, news (real or imagined), or in anticipation of what the trader next to them or across the pit is about to do. Using the age-old open outcry method, each trader acts as his own auctioneer and makes bids and offers of prices with loud shouts and wild gesticulations of hand signals, which are actually a scientific language of numbers and buy/sell intentions. If and when they get a tip, or a feeling, about a large order just above or below the current market price, they may attempt to vigorously buy or sell contracts in quantity to move the market to that order (the price stop of that order) and take advantage of the fast move of the market if that order is hit. This is sometimes called "running the stops" (more on stops later). This is something that pit traders might not admit to, but usually hope to accomplish.

*Floor traders* often take on large positions and are seen wandering from pit to pit, generally appearing more relaxed than some of their red-in-the-face counterparts in the pits. Unlike the scalpers or pit traders, they may be involved in more than one market at the same time and may simultaneously be placing trades through brokers. They are the "commentators from the floor" for each market period: the pre-session, the market open, the morning session, midsession, afternoon session, and the closing market. They offer opinions on what current market forces and trading sentiments might affect today's trading. Specialized news services furiously type out these comments and beam them to subscribers around the world instantly via satellite (more on this later). As their trading positions are generally large, many floor traders represent financial institutions and commodity funds. Others may be large individual speculators. And unlike scalpers and pit traders, they may hold their trades for days, weeks, or months, in addition to any day trading activity.

*Brokers* execute the tens of thousands of orders that come in from the outside world, including yours and mine, in addition to those given to them by the floor traders. Therefore they tend to be the largest trading group. They act as agents for principals: exchange members, commercial hedgers, and FCMs (Futures Commission Merchants), who are our link to the brokers. They receive a commission for each trade executed (each *round-turn:* a buy order and the sell order that offsets it, or a sell order and the buy order that offsets it). Brokers can trade on their own accounts besides carrying on their brokerage business, although to avoid a conflict of interest, their clients' business is supposed to take precedence over their own. They can carry on large amounts of commercial business for the hedgers, as well as worldwide business for individual speculators, through the FCM intermediaries. When trading their own accounts they often specialize in certain markets. In every case, their expertise rests in their knowledge of the pits they are involved with, their speed in execution and management of orders, and the success of their trading tactics in relationship to what the other brokers, scalpers, pit traders, and floor traders are doing.

## The Intermediaries

*Futures Commissions Merchant* (FCM): For us, the traders from home, the FCM is our most cost-effective direct interface with the real-time world of futures trading[6]. Outside of being physically present at the exchange, our FCM (usually called "the commission house") is our proxy presence in the pit. Actually, the

FCM is the intermediary between the broker in the pit and ourselves. Although the arrangement sounds complicated, our orders should be able to be executed within seconds. The ability of our account executive (our personal "rep" at the FCM) to think and act fast, work closely with us, and, if necessary, "go to bat" for us should we get a bad fill (order execution), becomes an essential part of our success as a trader.

Amidst all the screaming and apparent chaos on the exchange floor, every individual and element that is supposed to work together does so nearly flawlessly, making futures trading happen in a highly efficient and fully accountable manner many thousands of times each trading day. Figure 1 shows the broad outline for making a trade; Figure 2 details the order process.

*Clearing houses* are corporations set up within the exchanges to reconcile all futures transactions and the financial integrity of those transactions. Clearing houses deal only with clearing members (which may be an FCM); they interpose between member firms and guarantee the contractual obligations of each transaction. The member firms also act as guarantors to the clearing house. The clearing house becomes the seller for every buyer and buyer for every seller, thus making the need to match actual buyers with sellers unnecessary.

The trade guarantee is made through a margin deposit made by the member firm to the clearing house. This margin (like the deposit made by our buyer at the car dealership) is a performance bond to assure settlement of the contracts. The buyers and sellers, in turn, have made their margin deposits which ultimately guarantee performance to the member firms. The margin requirements depend upon the number of open contracts

# How a Trade is Made

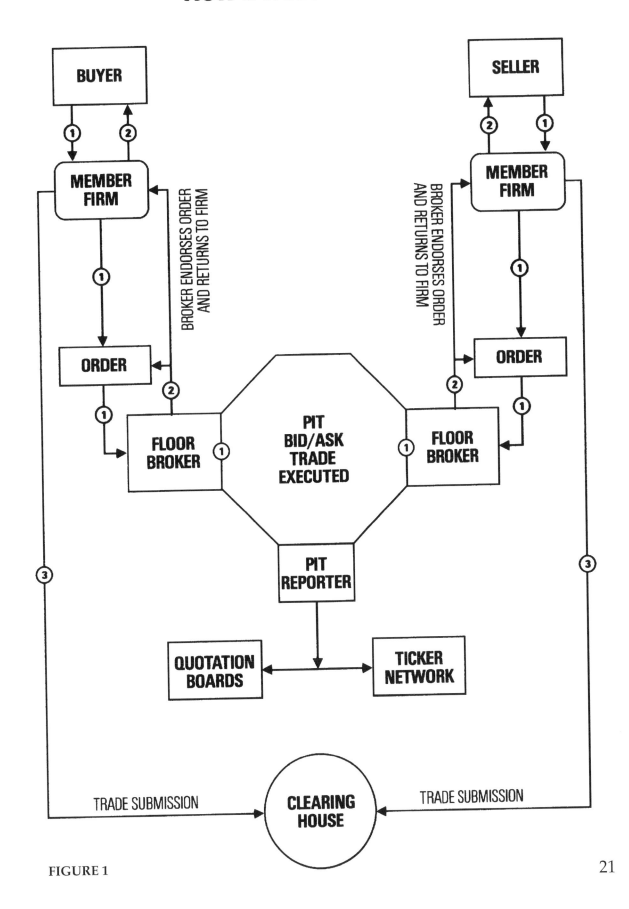

FIGURE 1

21

# The Order Process

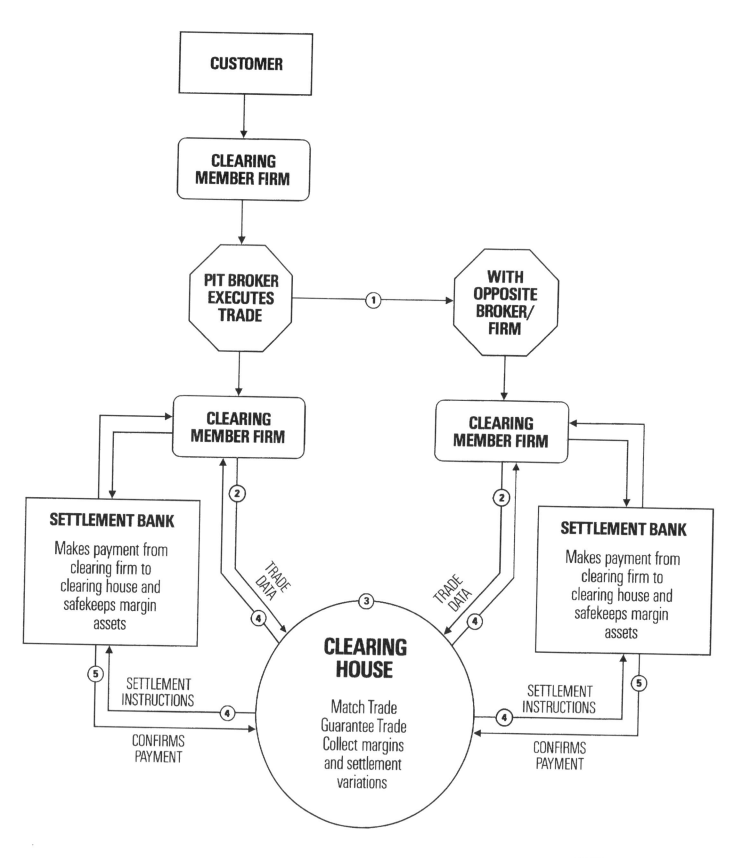

FIGURE 2

(unsettled, not yet offset, trades) and is kept as low as possible for the security of the contracts. If market conditions move against the member's position, so much so that their standing margin is not enough to cover the extent of the price change, the clearing house can demand additional margin, at any time, to cover the position. This is known as a "margin call" and is not particularly welcome, since the member must pay the amount by certified check within one hour. Naturally the buyers and sellers whose positions were affected by the price move receive a margin call as well. All accounts must be settled by the end of the day, and there is virtually no record of a default on a transaction cleared through a clearing house.

## Oversight

Over the many decades of its development, the futures industry has seen nearly every scam and scam artist imaginable. During the same period, there has occurred every possible variety of legitimate dispute in the course of trading as well. Therefore, out of the necessity born from its critical function in global trade and commerce, the industry has evolved into a highly sophisticated entity, more than able to protect itself and its tight family of honest participants. The regulatory process of the futures industry in the United States—put quite simply—works, and works extraordinarily well. For example, in the history of the Chicago Mercantile Exchange, the exchange ranked second in the world: (a) no customer has lost money due to the financial insolvence of a clearing member; (b) no clearing member has failed to meet a margin call to the clearing House, and

(c) no clearing member has failed to satisfy delivery obligations. The industry is both self-regulated through the National Futures Association (NFA), which among other things deals with out-of-court arbitration of disputes, and Federally regulated through the Commodity Futures Trading Commission (CFTC). Figure 3 shows these interlocking regulatory agencies, using the CME as an example. The major exchanges around the world also regulate themselves well, and, as a rule, any major exchange able to

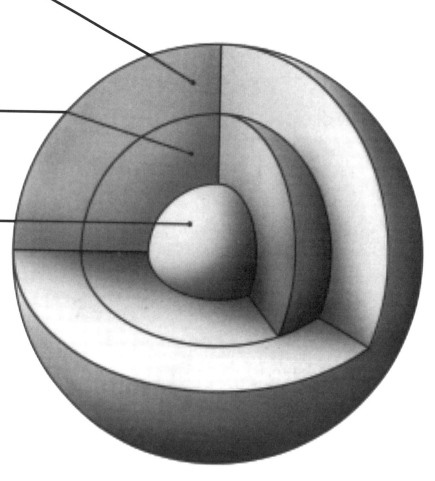

**Commodity Futures Trading Commision**
A Federal Regulatory Agency

**National Futures Association**
The Industry's Self-regulatory Group

**Chicago Mercantile Exchange**
Customer protection is a CME priority; its safeguards include ensuring the fulfillment of every trade, monitoring its clearing member firms to insure they comply with CME rules, and employing circuit breakers to maintain orderly markets for investors.

FIGURE 3

be a player in international trade knows what it is doing and has earned its place in the global trading community.

## The Marketplace

Now that we've taken a look at the futures contract and who's involved in trading it, let's see exactly what is being traded and where. The basic prerequisites for commodities being traded on exchanges are: (1) homogeneity so that commercial units are exchangeable, (2) durability or minimum degree of perishability, and (3) an adequate supply of the actual commodity flowing to or through the terminal market where the futures market is established. Two other important points are that supply and demand must be of sufficient size to allow for a natural marketplace free of the possibility of monopoly control, and that the commodity must be susceptible to standardization and grades.

Tables 1 through 13 comprise the complete listing of the world's actively traded commodities as of November, 1996. "Min. Fluctuation" refers to the minimum price fluctuation—i.e. the smallest price change (tick value) or price movement that can occur in the commodity as arranged by the exchange and the amount of money it represents. "Daily Limit" is the normal trading limit or maximum price movement allowed up or down from the previous day's close, as a protective measure for the market involved. Many markets have no limit, and many that do, vary it during volatile times. When a market has gone or locked *limit up* or *limit down*, the daily limit has been reached, and no more orders in the direction of the limit will be considered until the market comes off limit. Abbreviations for the exchanges at which each commodity is traded are shown as well.

| Rank | Exchange | Established | Location |
|------|----------|-------------|----------|
| 1 | Chicago Board of Trade (CBOT) | 1848 | Chicago |
| 2 | Chicago Mercantile Exchange (CME) | 1919 | Chicago |
| 3 | London International Financial Futures Exchange (LIFFE) | 1982 | London |
| 4 | Chicago Board of Options Exchange (CBOE) | 1973 | Chicago |
| 5 | Bolsa de Mercadorias & Futuros (BM&F) | 1991 | São Paulo |
| 6 | Marché à Terme International de France (MATIF) | 1986 | Paris |
| 7 | New York Mercantile Exchange (NYMEX) | 1872 | New York |
| 8 | Deutsche Terminboërse AG (DTB) | 1988 | Frankfort |
| 9 | London Metal Exchange (LME) | 1877 | London |
| 10 | Tokyo International Financial Futures Exchange (TIFFE) | 1989 | Tokyo |
| 11 | MEFF RENTA VARIABLE (MEFF-V) | 1988 | Madrid |
| 12 | Sydney Futures Exchange (SFE) | 1960 | Sydney |
| 13 | Tokyo Commodity Exchange (TOCOM) | 1984 | Tokyo |
| 14 | Singapore International Monetary Exchange (SIMEX) | 1991 | Singapore |
| 15 | OM Stockholm | 1985 | Stockholm |

**Here are a few of the smallest exchanges:**

| Rank | Exchange | Established | Location |
|------|----------|-------------|----------|
| 54 | Toyahashi Dried Cocoon Exchange (TDCE) | 1937 | Toyahashi |
| 56 | Toronto Futures Exchange (TFE) | 1861 | Toronto |
| 62 | Irish Futures & Options Exchange (IFOX) | 1988 | Dublin |

As recently reported by the Futures Industry Association (FIA), the above were the fifteen largest exchanges in the world ranked by volume of contracts traded annually:

It should be noted that some of the fastest-growing exchanges in the world are outside of the United States. For

TABLE 1

# ACTIVE FUTURES CONTRACT SPECIFICATIONS

| FUTURES | EXCH | CONTRACT SIZE | LOCAL TRADING HOURS | MIN. FLUCTUATION | DAILY LIMIT |
|---|---|---|---|---|---|
| **Currencies:** | | | | | |
| Austr. Dollar | CME | A$100,000 | 7:20–14:00; Globex 14:30–7:04+ | .01¢/AD = $10.00 | Please consult exchange |
| Austr. Dollar | MACE | A$50,000 | 7:20–14:15 | .01¢/AD = $5.00 | None |
| Brazilian Real | BBF | US$10,000 | 9:45–16:30 | R$.01/US$1000=R$.01 | Please consult exchange |
| British Pound | CME | £62,500 | 7:20–14:00; Globex 14:30–7:04+ | .02¢/£ = $12.50 | Please consult exchange |
| British Pound | CTN | £125,000 | 19:00–22:00; 3:00–8:00; 8:05–15:00** | .01¢/£ = $12.50 | None |
| British Pound | MACE | £12,500 | 7:20–14:15 | .02¢/£ = $2.50 | None |
| £ Rolling Spot | CME | £250,000 | 7:20–14:00 | .0001 = $25.00 | None |
| £/DMark | CTN | £125,000 | 19:00–22:00; 3:00–9:00; 9:05–15:00** | .0001 = DM12.50 | None |
| Canad. Dollar | CME | C$100,000 | 7:20–14:00; Globex 14:30–7:04+ | .01¢/CD = $10.00 | Please consult exchange |
| Canad. Dollar | MACE | C$50,000 | 7:20–14:15 | .01¢/CD = $5.00 | None |
| Deutsche Mark | CME | DM125,000 | 7:20–14:00; Globex 14:30–7:05+ | .01¢/DM = $12.50 | Please consult exchange |
| Deutsche Mark | MACE | DM62,500 | 7:20–14:15 | .01¢/DM = $6.25 | None |
| Deutsche Mark | PBOT | DM125,000 | 2:30–14:30 | .01¢/DM = $12.50 | None |
| DM Rolling Spot | CME | US$250,000 | 7:20–14:00; Globex 14:30–7:05+ | .0001 = DM25.00 | Please consult exchange |
| DMark/FF | CTN | DM500,000 | 19:00–22:00; 3:00–9:00; 9:05–15:00** | .0001 = FF50.00 | None |
| DMark/ITL | CTN | DM250,000 | 19:00–22:00; 3:00–9:00; 9:05–15:00** | .05 = ITL12,500 | None |
| DMark/SF | CTN | DM125,000 | 19:00–22:00; 3:00–9:00; 9:05–15:00** | .0001 = SF12.50 | None |
| DMark/Yen | CTN | DM125,000 | 19:00–22:00; 3:00–9:00; 9:05–15:00** | .01 = ¥1,250.00 | None |
| ECU | PBOT | 125,000 ECU | 2:30–14:30 | .01¢/ECU = $12.50 | None |
| French Franc | CME | FF500,000 | 7:20–14:00; Globex 14:30–7:04+ | .002 = $10.00 | Please consult exchange |
| French Franc | PBOT | FF500,000 | 2:30–14:30 | .002¢/FF = $10.00 | None |
| Japanese Yen | CME | ¥12,500,000 | 7:20–14:00; Globex 14:30–7:05+ | .0001¢/¥ = $12.50 | Please consult exchange |
| Japanese Yen | MACE | ¥6,250,000 | 7:20–14:15 | .0001¢/¥ = $6.25 | None |
| Japanese Yen | PBOT | ¥12,500,000 | 2:30–14:30 | .0001¢/¥ = $12.50 | None |
| Jap Yen Rlng spot | CME | US$250,000 | 7:20–14:00; Globex 14:30–7:05+ | .01 = ¥2,500.00 | Please consult exchange |

**During DST, evening hours are 20:00–23:00; 3:00–8:00 (9:00) on Dublin Floor. + Globex Mon.–Thurs. & 17:30–normal close Suns. and holidays.

TABLE 2

| FUTURES | EXCH | CONTRACT SIZE | LOCAL TRADING HOURS | MIN. FLUCTUATION | DAILY LIMIT |
|---|---|---|---|---|---|
| **Currencies (cont.):** | | | | | |
| New Mexican Peso | CME | N.M.P.500,000 | 8:00–14:00; Globex 14:30–7:04@@ | .0025¢/NMP = $12.50 | Please consult exchange |
| Swiss Franc | CME | SF125,000 | 7:20–14:00; Globex 14:30–7:05@@ | .01¢/SF = $12.50 | Please consult exchange |
| Swiss Franc | MACE | SF62,500 | 7:20–14:15 | .01¢/SF = $6.25 | None |
| Swiss Franc | PBOT | SF125,000 | 2:30–14:30 | .01¢/SF = $12.50 | None |
| US$/DMark | CTN | $200,000 | 19:00–22:00; 3:00–8:00; 8:05–15:00** | .0001 = DM20.00 | None |
| US$/Japan. Yen | CTN | $200,000 | 19:00–22:00; 3:00–8:00; 8:05–15:00** | .01 = ¥2,000.00 | None |
| US$/Japan. Yen | TIFFE | US$50,000 | 9:00–11:30; 12:30–15:30 | .05 = ¥2,500.00 | None |
| US$/Swiss Franc | CTN | $200,000 | 19:00–22:00; 3:00–8:00; 8:05–15:00** | .0001 = SF20.00 | None |
| **Energy:** | | | | | |
| Brent Crude Oil | IPE | 1,000 barrels | 10:02–20:15 | US1¢/bbl. = $10.00 | None |
| Crude Oil | NYM | 1,000 barrels | 9:45–15:10; ACCESS+ | 1¢/bbl. = $10.00 | $1.50/barrel = $1,500* |
| Elect. PV & COB | NYM | 736 Mwh | 10:30–15:30; ACCESS++ | 1¢/Mwh = $7.36 | $3.00/Mwh = $2.208* |
| Gas Oil | IPE | 100 metric tons | 9:15–17:27 | US25¢/ton= $25.00 | None |
| Gasoline NYH | NYM | 42,000 gallons | 9:50–15:10; ACCESS+ | .01¢/gallon = $4.20 | 4¢/gallon = $1,680* |
| Heating Oil | NYM | 42,000 gallons | 9:50–15:10; ACCESS+ | .01¢/gallon = $4.20 | 4¢/gallon = $1,680* |
| Natural Gas | KCBT | 10,000 MMBtu | 8:30–14:30 | .1¢/MMBtu = $10.00 | 15¢/MMBtu = $1,500* |
| Natural Gas | NYM | 10,000 MMBtu | 10:00–15:10; ACCESS@ | .1¢/MMBtu = $10.00 | 15¢/MMBtu = $1,500* |
| Propane | NYM | 42,000 gallons | 9:55–15:00; ACCESS# | .01¢/gallon = $4.20 | 4¢/gallon = $1,680* |
| Sour Crude Oil | NYM | 1,000 barrels | 9:35–15:20 | 1¢/barrel = $10.00 | $1.50/barrel = $1,500* |
| Unleaded Gas-GC | NYM | 42,000 gallons | 9:40–15:10 | .01¢/gal. = $4.20 | 4¢/gallon = $1,680* |
| **Food and Fiber:** | | | | | |
| Butter | CME | 40,000 lbs. | 8:00–13:10 | 2.5¢/cwt. = $10.00 | 2.5¢/lb. = $1,000* |
| Cheddar Chs. | CSCE | 10,500 lbs. | 9:00–14:00 | .1¢/lb. = $10.50 | 6¢/lb. = $630* |
| Cocoa | CSCE | 10 metric tons | 9:00–14:00 | $1/ton = $10.00 | $88/ton = $880* |
| Coffee 'C' | CSCE | 37,500 lbs. | 9:15–13:35 | .05¢/lb. = $18.75 | 6¢/lb. = $2,250* |
| Coffee Brazil Diff | CSCE | 37,500 lbs. | 9:05–13:58 | .05¢/lb. = $18.75 | None |

*Expanded limits at times. **DST evening hrs. 20:00–23:00; 3:00–8:00 (9:00) on Dublin Floor. +ACCESS hrs. Sun 19:00–8:00 & Mon.–Thur. 16:00–8:00. ++ACCESS hrs. Mon.–Thur. 16:15–19:15. #ACCESS hrs. Mon.–Thur. 17:00–19:00. @ACCESS hrs. Mon.–Thur. 16:00–19:00. @@Globex Mon.–Thur. & 17:30–normal close Suns. & holidays.

TABLE 3

| FUTURES | EXCH | CONTRACT SIZE | LOCAL TRADING HOURS | MIN. FLUCTUATION | DAILY LIMIT |
|---|---|---|---|---|---|
| **Food and Fiber (cont.):** | | | | | |
| Cotton | CTN | 50,000 lbs. | 10:30-14:40 | .01¢/lb. = $5.00## | 3¢/lb. = $1,500* |
| Nonfat Dry Milk | CSCE | 11,000 lbs. | 9:00-14:00 | .1¢/lb. = $11.00 | 6¢/lb. = $660* |
| O.J., Frozen | CTN | 15,000 lbs. | 10:15-14:15 | .05¢/lb. = $7.50 | 5¢/lb. = $750* |
| Shrimp—Blk Tiger | MPLS | 5,000 lbs. | 9:40-13:30 | ¼¢/lb. = $12.50 | 20¢/lb. = $1,000* |
| Shrimp—White | MPLS | 5,000 lbs. | 9:40-13:30 | ¼¢/lb. = $12.50 | 20¢/lb. = $1,000* |
| Sugar #11 | CSCE | 112,000 lbs. | 9:30-13:20 | .01¢/lb. = $11.20 | .5¢/lb. = $560* |
| Sugar #14 | CSCE | 112,000 lbs. | 9:10-13:15 | .01¢/lb. = $11.20 | .5¢/lb. = $560* |
| Sugar Wld Wht | CSCE | 50 metric tons | 9:15-13:20 | 20¢/ton = $10.00 | $10.00/ton = $500* |
| **Grains and Oilseeds:** | | | | | |
| Anhydrous Ammonia | CBT | 100 tons | 9:05-12:20; Project A+ | 10¢/ton = $10.00 | $10/ton = $1,000* |
| Barley | MPLS | 180,000 lbs. | 9:45-13:25 | .5¢/cwt. = $9.00 | 25¢/cwt. = $450* |
| Barley | WPG | 20 metric tons | 9:30-13:15 | C$.10/ton = C$2.00 | C$5/ton = C$100 |
| Canola | WPG | 20 metric tons | 9:30-13:15 | C$.10/ton = C$2.00 | C$10/ton = C$200 |
| Corn | CBT | 5,000 bu. | 9:30-13:15; Project A+ | ¼¢/bu. = $12.50 | 12¢/bu. = $600* |
| Corn | MACE | 1,000 bu. | 9:30-13:45 | 1/8¢/bu. = $1.25 | 12¢/bu. = $120* |
| Diammonium Phos. | CBT | 100 tons | 9:00-12:15; Project A+ | 10¢/ton = $10.00 | $10/ton = $1,000* |
| Feed Peas | WPG | 20 metric tons | 9:30-13:15 | US$.10/ton = US$2.00 | US$5/ton = US$100 |
| Flaxseed | WPG | 20 metric tons | 9:30-13:15 | C$.10/ton = C$2.00 | C$10/tonne = C$200 |
| Oats | CBT | 5,000 bu. | 9:30-13:15; Project A+ | ¼¢/bu. = $12.50 | 10¢/bu. = $500* |
| Oats | MACE | 1,000 bu. | 9:30-13:45 | 1/8¢/bu. = $1.25 | 10¢/bu. = $100* |
| Oats | WPG | 20 metric tons | 9:30-13:15 | C$.10/ton = C$2.00 | C$5.00/ton = C$100 |
| Rice, Rough | CBT | 2,000 cwt. | 9:15-13:30; Project A+ | .5¢/cwt. = $10.00 | 30¢/cwt. = $600* |
| Soybeans | CBT | 5,000 bu. | 9:30-13:15; Project A+ | ¼¢/bu. = $12.50 | 30¢/bu. = $1,500* |
| Soybeans | MACE | 1,000 bu. | 9:30-13:45 | 1/8¢/bu. = $1.25 | 30¢/bu. = $300* |
| Soybean Meal | CBT | 100 tons | 9:30-13:15; Project A+ | 10¢/ton = $10.00 | $10/ton = $1,000* |
| Soybean Meal | MACE | 50 tons | 9:30-13:45 | 10¢/ton = $5.00 | $10/ton = $500* |

* Expanded limits go into effect under certain conditions. + Project A hours are 22:30-4:30 Sun.-Thurs. ##Below 95¢/lb. Prices at or above 95¢/lb.: .05¢/lb. = $25.00.

29

TABLE 4

| FUTURES | EXCH | CONTRCT SIZE | LOCAL TRADING HOURS | MIN. FLUCTUATION | DAILY LIMIT |
|---|---|---|---|---|---|
| **Grains/Oilseeds (cont.):** | | | | | |
| Soybean Oil | CBT | 60,000 lbs. | 9:30–13:15; Project A++ | .01¢/lb. = $6.00 | 1¢/lb. = $600* |
| Soybean Oil | MACE | 30,000 lbs. | 9:30–13:45 | .01¢/lb. = $3.00 | 1¢/lb. = $300* |
| Wheat | CBT | 5,000 bu. | 9:30–13:15; Project A++ | ¼¢/bu. = $12.50 | 20¢/bu. = $1,000* |
| Wheat | KCBT | 5,000 bu. | 9:30–13:15 | ¼¢/bu. = $12.50 | 25¢/bu. = $1,250 |
| Wheat | MACE | 1,000 bu. | 9:30–13:45 | ⅛¢/bu. = $1.25 | 20¢/bu. = $200* |
| Wheat | WPG | 20 metric tons | 9:30–13:15 | C$.10/ton = C$2.00 | C$5.00/ton = C$100 |
| Wheat, Spring | MPLS | 5,000 bu. | 9:30–13:15 | ¼¢/bu. = $12.50 | 20¢/bu. = $1,000* |
| Wheat, White | MPLS | 5,000 bu. | 9:30–13:15 | ¼¢/bu. = $12.50 | 20¢/bu. = $1,000* |
| **Indexes:** | | | | | |
| All Ordinaries | SFE | A$25 x index | 9:50–12:30; 14:00–16:10; SYCOM** | 1.0 = A$25.00 | None |
| CAC-40 Index | MATIF | FF200 x index | 10:00–17:00; Globex 17:00–10:00 | .005 = FF100.00 | 120 pts. = FF24,000 |
| DAX | DTB | DM100 x index | 9:00–17:00 | .5 = DM50.00 | None |
| Emerg Mkts Debt | CTN | $1,000 x index | 8:20–15:00 | .025 = $25.00 | None |
| Eurotop 100 | CMX | $100 x index | 5:30–11:30 | .1 = $10.00 | None |
| FT-SE 100 Index | CME | $50 x index | 8:30–15:15 | .5 = $25.00 | None |
| FT-SE 100 Index | LIFFE | £25 x index | 8:35–16:10; APT 16:32–17:30 | .5 = £12.50 | None |
| FT-SE 250 Index | LIFFE | £10 x index | 8:30–16:05 | .5 = £5.00 | None |
| GSCI | CME | $250 x index | 8:15–14:15; Globex 14:45–8:00# | .10 = $25.00 | None (Globex = 30.00) |
| Corn Yld. Ins. | CBT | $100 x Yld Est | 10:30–12:45 | 1/10 bu./acre = $10.00 | 15 bu./acre = $1,500 |
| Hang Seng Index | HKFE | HK$50 x index | 10:00–12:30; 14:30–16:00 | 1 pt. = HK$50.00 | 500 pts. = HK$25,000 |
| IPC Stock Index | CME | $25 x index | 8:30–15:15; Globex 15:45–8:15# | .01 = $25.00 | Pls consult exchange |
| KR-CRB Index | NYFE | $500 x index | 9:40–14:45 | .05 = $25.00 | None |
| MMI | CME | $500 x index | 8:30–15:15; Globex 15:45–8:15# | .05 = $25.00 | Pls consult exchange |
| Mini Value-Line | KCBT | $100 x index | 8:30–15:15 | .05 = $5.00 | Pls consult exchange |
| Muni-Bond Index | CBT | $1,000 x index | 7:20–14:00; Project A + | 1/32 = $31.25 | 3 pts. = $3,000* |
| NASDAQ 100 | CME | $100 x index | 8:30–15:15; Globex 15:45–8:15# | .05 = $5.00 | Pls consult exchange |

* Expanded limits sometimes. **SYCOM hours are 16:40–6:00. +Project A hours are 14:30–16:30 Mon.–Thurs. and 22:00–6:00 Sun.–Thurs. #Globex hours are Mon–Thur and 17:30–normal close Suns. and holidays. ++Project A hours are 22:30–4:30 Sun.–Thurs.

TABLE 5

| FUTURES | EXCH | CONTR. SIZE | LOCAL TRADING HOURS | MIN. FLUCT. | DAILY LIMIT |
|---|---|---|---|---|---|
| **Indexes (cont.):** | | | | | |
| Nikkei 225 | CME | $5 x average | 8:00–15:15 | 5 pts. = $25.00 | Pls consult exchange |
| Nikkei 225 | SIMEX | ¥500 x index | 7:55–10:15; 11:15–14:15@ | 5 pts. = ¥2,500 | Pls consult exchange |
| NYSE Compos Index | NYFE | $500 x index | 9:30–16:15 | .05 = $25.00 | Pls consult exchange |
| PSE Technology Index | NYFE | $500 x index | 9:30–16:15 | .05 = $25.00 | Pls consult exchange |
| Russell 2000 | CME | $500 x index | 8:30–15:15; Globex 15:45–8:15++ | .05 = $25.00 | Pls consult exchange |
| S&P 500 Index | CME | $500 x index | 8:30–15:15; Globex 15:45–8:15++ | .05 = $25.00 | Pls consult exchange |
| S&P MidCap 400 | CME | $500 x index | 8:30–15:15; Globex 15:45–8:15++ | .05 = $25.00 | Pls consult exchange |
| Toronto 35 | TFE | $500 x index | 9:15–16:15 | .02 = $10.00 | 13.50 = $6,750* |
| US$ Index | CTN | $1,000 x index | 19:00–22:00; 3:00–8:00, 8:05–15:00** | .01 = $10.00 | 2.00 = $2,000* |
| Value-Line Index | KCBT | $500 x index | 8:30–15:15 | .05 = $25.00 | Pls consult exchange |
| Yield Curve Spread | CBT | $25000x100+sprd | 7:20–14:00 | 1/8 = $31.25 | None |
| **Interest Rates** | | | | | |
| Austrl. Gov Bond–10Yr | SFE | A$100,000 | 8:30–12:30; 14:00–16:30; SYCOM# | .005%/Annum | None |
| Austrl. Gov Bond–3Yr | SFE | A$100,000 | 8:30–12:30; 14:00–16:30; SYCOM # | .01%/Annum | None |
| Bank Bill, 90-day | NZFOE | NZ$500,000 | 21:30–7:00; 8:00–12:00, 13:00–16:30 | .01%/Annum | None |
| Bank Bill, 90-day | SFE | A$1,000,000 | 8:30–12:30; 14:00–16:30; SYCOM # | .01%/Annum | None |
| Bobl Med-Term Bond | DTB | DM250,000 | 8:00–17:30 | .01 = DM25.00 | None |
| Brazil Avg Interbank Rt | BBF | R$50,000 | 9:45–13:00; 15:00–16:30 | .01 = R$0.05 | Pls consult exchange |
| Can 3-mo.Bnkrs Accpt | ME | C$1,000,000 | 8:00–15:00 | .01 = C$25.00 | None |
| Canad. Govt. Bond | ME | C$100,000 | 8:20–15:00 | .01 = C$10.00 | 3 pts. = C$3,000 |
| ECU Bond | MATIF | ECU100,000 | 9:00–16:30; Globex 16:30–9:00 | .02 = ECU20.00 | 2.00 = ECU2,000 |
| ECU Interest Rate | LIFFE | ECU1,000,000 | 8:05–16:05 | .01 = ECU25.00 | None |
| Euro$ Time Dep | CME | $1,000,000 | 7:20–14:00; Globex 14:45–7:05++ | .01 = $25.00 | None (Globex = 200 pts.) |
| Euro$ Time Dep | MACE | $500,000 | 7:20–14:15 | .01 = $12.50 | None |
| Euro$ Time Dep | SIMEX | US$1,000,000 | 7:45–19:00@ | .01 = US$25.00 | None |
| Euro$ Time Dep | TIFFE | $1,000,000 | 9:00–11:30; 12:30–15:30 | .01 = $25.00 | None |

++Globex hrs. are Mon.–Thurs. and 17:30–normal close Suns. and holidays. @ Traded in other places at different times. # SYCOM hrs. are 16:40–6:00. **Evening hrs. during DST are 20:00–23:00; 3:00–8:00 on Dublin Floor.

## TABLE 6

| FUTURES | EXCH | CONTRACT SIZE | LOCAL TRADING HOURS | MIN. FLUCT. | DAILY LIMIT |
|---|---|---|---|---|---|
| **Interest Rates (cont.):** | | | | | |
| Eurolira Int. Rate | LIFFE | ITL 1 billion | 7:55–16:10; APT 16:23–17:58 | .01 = ITL25,000 | None |
| EuroMark Int. Rate | CME | DM1,000,000 | 7:20–14:00 | .01 = DM25.00 | None |
| EuroMark Int. Rate | LIFFE | DM1,000,000 | 8:00–16:10; APT 16:25–17:59 | .01 = DM25.00 | None |
| EuroMark (3 mo.) | SIMEX | DM1,000,000 | 10:00–19:10; 19:35–1:00 | .01 = DM25.00 | None |
| EuroSF Int. Rate | LIFFE | SF1,000,000 | 8:10–16:05; APT 16:24–17:55 | .01 = SF25.00 | None |
| EuroYen | CME | ¥100,000,000 | 7:20–14:00 | .01 = ¥2,500.00 | None |
| EuroYen | SIMEX | ¥100,000,000 | 7:58–20:05; Elct 19:35–1:00; MOS 21:20–4:00@ | .01 = ¥2,500.00 | None |
| EuroYen (3 mo.) | TIFFE | ¥100,000,000 | 9:00–11:30; 12:30–15:30; 16:00–18:00 | .01 = ¥2,500.00 | None |
| EuroYen (1 Yr.) | TIFFE | ¥100,000,000 | 9:00–11:30; 12:30–15:30; 16:00–18:00 | .01 = ¥10,000.00 | None |
| Fed Funds Rate | CME | $3,000,000 | 7:20–14:00; Globex 14:45–7:05** | .005 = $12.50 | None (Globex = 200 pts.) |
| FIBOR | DTB | DM1,000,000 | 8:45–17:15 | .01 = DM25.00 | None |
| Fr Govt Notl Bond | MATIF | FF500,000 | 9:00–16:30; Globex 16:30–9:00 | .02 = FF100.00 | 2.00 = FF10,000 |
| German Govt. Bund | DTB | DM250,000 | 8:00–17:30 | .01 = DM25.00 | None |
| German Govt. Bund | LIFFE | DM250,000 | 7:30–16:15; APT 16:20–17:55 | .01 = DM25.00 | None |
| Italian Govt Bond | LIFFE | ITL200,000,000 | 8:00–16:10; APT 16:21–17:58 | .01 = ITL20,000 | None |
| Japan. Govt Bond | LIFFE | ¥100,000,000 | APT 7:00–16:00 | .01 = ¥10,000.00 | Pls. consult exchange |
| LIBOR (1 month) | CME | $3,000,000 | 7:20–14:00; Globex 14:45–7:05** | .01 = $25.00 | None |
| Long Gilt | LIFFE | £50,000 | 8:00–16:15; APT 16:30–18:00 | 1/32 = £15.625 | None |
| PIBOR (3 month) | MATIF | FF5,000,000 | 8:30–16:00; Globex 16:00–8:30 | .01 = FF125.00 | 0.60 = FF7,500 |
| Portuguese Notl Bond | BDP | PTE10,000,000 | 9:00–16:45 | .01 = PTE1,000.00 | 1.40 = PTE140,000 |
| Short Sterling | LIFFE | £500,000 | 8:05–16:05; APT 16:22–17:57 | .01 = £12.50 | None |
| 30-day Fed. Funds | CBT | $5,000,000 | 7:20–14:00; Project A # | .01 = $41.67++ | 150 pts. = $6,250.50* |
| U.S. T-Bills | CME | $1,000,000 | 7:20–14:00; Globex 14:45–7:05** | .01 = $25.00 | None (Globex = 200 pts.) |
| U.S. T-Bills 1Yr | CME | $500,000 | 7:20–14:00; Globex 14:45–7:05** | .005 = $25.00 | None (Globex = 200 pts.) |
| U.S. T-Bills | MACE | $500,000 | 7:20–14:15 | .01 = $12.50 | None |
| U.S. T-Bonds | CBT | $100,000 | 7:20–14:00; 17:20–20:05; Project A # | 1/32 = $31.25 | 3 pts. = $3,000* |

\* Expanded limits sometimes. ** Globex hrs. Mon.–Thurs. & 17:30–normal close Suns. and holidays. # Evening hours are CST. Project A hours from 14:30–16:30 Mon.–Thurs. and 22:00–6:00 Sun.–Thurs. ++ .005 = $20.835 in spot Month only. Subject to change. @Traded in other locations at different times.

TABLE 7

| FUTURES | EXCH | CONTRACT SIZE | LOCAL TRADING HOURS | MIN. FLUCTUATION | DAILY LIMIT |
|---|---|---|---|---|---|
| **Interest Rates (cont.):** | | | | | |
| U.S. T-Bonds | MACE | $50,000 | 7:20–15:15 | $1/32 = $15.62 | 3 pts. = $1,500* |
| U.S. T-Notes 10 Yr | CBT | $100,000 | 7:20–14:00; 17:20–20:05; Project A # | $1/32 = $31.25 | 3 pts. = $3,000* |
| U.S. T-Notes 10 Yr | MACE | $50,000 | 7:20–15:15 | $1/32 = $15.62 | 3 pts. = $1,500* |
| U.S. T-Notes 2 Yr | CBT | $200,000 | 7:20–14:00; 17:20–20:05; Project A # | $1/4$ of $1/32 = $15.625 | 1 pt. = $2,000* |
| U.S. T-Notes 2 Yr | CTN | $500,000 | 8:20–15:00 | .005 = $50.00 | None |
| U.S. T-Notes 5 Yr | CBT | $100,000 | 7:20–14:00; 17:20–20:05; Project A # | $1/2$ of $1/32 = $15.625 | 3 pts. = $3,000* |
| U.S. T-Notes 5 Yr | CTN | $250,000 | 8:20–15:00 | .005 = $50.00 | None |
| U.S. T-Notes 5 Yr. | MACE | $50,000 | 7:20–15:15 | $1/2$ of $1/32 = $7.81 | 3 pts. = $1,500* |
| **Livestock:** | | | | | |
| Feeder Cattle | CME | 50,000 lbs. | 9:05–13:00 | 2.5¢/cwt. = $12.50 | 1.5¢/lb. = $750 |
| Live Cattle | CME | 40,000 lbs. | 9:05–13:00 | 2.5¢/cwt. = $10.00 | 1.5¢/lb. = $600 |
| Cattle | MACE | 20,000 lbs. | 9:05–13:15 | .025¢/lb. = $5.00 | 1.5¢/lb. = $300* |
| Lean Hogs | CME | 40,000 lbs. | 9:10–13:00 | 2.5¢/cwt. = $10.00 | 2.0¢/lb. = $800 |
| Hogs | MACE | 20,000 lbs. | 9:10–13:15 | .025¢/lb. = $5.00 | 1.5¢/lb. = $300* |
| Pork Bellies | CME | 40,000 lbs. | 9:10–13:00 | 2.5¢/cwt. = $10.00 | 3¢/lb. = $1,200 |
| **Metals:** | | | | | |
| H.G. Primary Aluminium | LME | 25 tonnes | 11:55–12:00; 12:55–13:00; 15:35–15:40; 16:15–16:20; Kerb 13:15–13:30; 16:35–17:00 | US50¢/tonne = $12.50 | None |
| Copper—Grade 1 | CMX | 25,000 lbs. | 8:10–14:00; ACCESS+ | .05¢/lb. = $12.50 | $.20/lb. = $5,000 |
| Copper—Grade A | LME | 25 tonnes | 12:00–12:05; 12:30–12:35; 15:30–15:35; 16:10–16:15; Kerb 13:15–13:30;16:35–17:00 | US$.50/tonne = $12.50 | None |
| Gold | CMX | 100 troy ozs. | 8:20–14:30; ACCESS+ | 10¢/oz. = $10.00 | $75/troy oz. = $7,500 |
| Gold | CBT | 1 kilo | 7:20–13:40 | 10¢/oz. = $3.22 | $50/oz. = $1,607.50* |
| Gold | CBT | 100 troy ozs. | 7:20–13:40; 17:20–20:05** | 10¢/oz. = $10.00 | $50/oz. = $5,000* |
| Gold, New York | MACE | 33.2 troy ozs. | 7:20–13:40 | 10¢/oz. = $3.32 | None |
| Gold | SIMEX | 100 troy ozs. | 9:00–17:13; 19:35–1:00@ | US5¢/oz. = US$5.00 | None |

* Expanded limits sometimes. ** Evening hrs. CST Sunday–Thursday. +ACCESS hrs. are Sun. 19:00–8:00 and Mon.–Thurs. 16:00–8:00. @Trades in other places at different times. #Evening hours are CST. Project A hours are 14:30–16:30 Mon.–Thurs. and 22:00–6:00 Sun.–Thurs.

TABLE 8

| FUTURES | EXCH | CONTRACT SIZE | LOCAL TRADING HOURS | MIN. FLUCT. | DAILY LIMIT |
|---|---|---|---|---|---|
| **Metals (cont.):** | | | | | |
| Palladium | NYM | 100 troy ozs. | 8:10–14:20 | 5¢/oz. = $5.00 | $6/troy oz. = $600* |
| Platinum | NYM | 50 troy ozs. | 8:20–14:30; ACCESS+ | 10¢/oz. = $5.00 | $25/oz. = $1,250* |
| Platinum | MACE | 25 troy ozs. | 7:20–13:40 | 10¢/oz. = $2.50 | $25/troy oz. = $625* |
| Silver | CMX | 5,000 tr. ozs. | 8:25–14:25; ACCESS+ | .5¢/oz. = $25.00 | $1.50/oz. = $7,500 |
| Silver | CBT | 1,000 tr. ozs. | 7:25–13:25 | .1¢/oz. = $1.00 | $1/troy oz. = $1,000* |
| Silver | CBT | 5,000 troy oz. | 7:25–13:25; 17:20–20:05++ | .1¢/oz. = $5.00 | $1/troy oz. = $5,000* |
| Silver, New York | MACE | 1,000 troy oz. | 7:25–13:40 | .1¢/oz. = $1.00 | None |
| H.G. Zinc | LME | 25 tonnes | 12:10–12:15; 12:50–12:55; 15:25–15:30; 16:05– 16:10: Kerb 13:15–13:30; 16:35–17:00 | US50¢/tonne = $12.50 | None |
| **Wood:** | | | | | |
| Randm Lngth Lumber | CME | 80,000 bd. ft. | 9:00–13:05 | 10¢/1000bd. ft. = $8 | Pls consult exchange |
| OSB Board | CME | 100,000 sq. ft. | 9:00–13:05 | 10¢/1000 sq ft =$10.00 | $10/1000 sq ft = $1,000* |

## ACTIVE FUTURES OPTION SPECIFICATIONS

| OPTION | EXCH | CONTRACT SIZE | LOCAL TRADING HRS | MIN. FLUCTUATION | DAILY LIMIT |
|---|---|---|---|---|---|
| **Agricultural:** | | | | | |
| Barley | MPLS | 1 MPLS Barley contract | 9:50–13:30 | .5¢/cwt. = $9.00 | 25¢/cwt. = $450* |
| Butter | CME | 1 CME Butter contract | 8:00–13:10 | 2.5¢/cwt. = $10.00 | None |
| Cheddar Cheese | CSCE | 1 CSCE Cheddar Cheese contract | 9:00–14:00 | .01¢/lb. = $1.05 | None |
| Cocoa | CSCE | 1 CSCE Cocoa contract | 9:00–14:00 | $1/ton = $10.00 | None |
| Coffee 'C' | CSCE | 1 CSCE Coffee contract | 9:15–13:35 | .01¢/lb. = $3.75 | None |
| Corn | CBT | 1 CBT Corn contract | 9:30–13:15; Project A** | 1/8¢/bu. = $6.25 | 12¢/bu. = $600* |
| Corn | MACE | 1 MACE Corn contract | 9:30–13:45 | 1/8¢/bu. = $1.25 | 12¢/bu. = $120* |
| Cotton | CTN | 1 CTN Cotton contract | 10:30–14:40 | .01¢/lb. = $5.00 | None |
| Diammonium Phos. | CBT | 1 CBT Diammonium Phosphate contr. | 9:00–12:15 | 5¢/ton = $5.00 | $10/ton = $1,000 |

* Expanded limits sometimes. ** Project A hours 22:30–4:30 Sun.–Thurs. +ACCESS hrs. are Sun. 19:00–8:00 and Mon.–Thurs. 16:00–8:00. ++ Evening hrs. CST Sunday–Thursday.

TABLE 9

| OPTION | XCH | CONTRACT SIZE | LOCAL TRADING HRS | MIN. FLUCTUATION | DAILY LIMIT |
|---|---|---|---|---|---|
| **Agricultural (cont.):** | | | | | |
| Feeder Cattle | CME | 1 CME Feeder Cattle contract | 9:05–13:00 | 2.5¢/cwt. = $12.50 | None |
| Lean Hogs | CME | 1 CME Lean Hog contract | 9:10–13:00 | 2.5¢/cwt. = $10.00 | None |
| Live Cattle | CME | 1 CME Live Cattle contract | 9:05–13:00 | 2.5¢/cwt. = $10.00 | None |
| Nonfat Dry Milk | CSCE | 1 CSCE Nonfat Dry Milk contr. | 9:00–14:00 | .01¢/lb. = $1.10 | None |
| Oats | CBT | 1 CBT Oat contract | 9:30–13:15; Project A** | ¹/₈¢/bu. = $6.25 | 10¢/bu. = $500* |
| Orange Juice | CTN | 1 CTN Orange Juice contract | 10:15–14:15 | .05¢/lb. = $7.50 | None |
| Pork Bellies | CME | 1 CME Pork Belly contract | 9:10–13:00 | 2.5¢/cwt. = $10.00 | None |
| Rice, Rough | CBT | 1 CBT Rough Rice contract | 9:15–13:30; Project A** | ¼¢/cwt. = $5.00 | 30¢/cwt. = $600* |
| Shrimp, Black Tiger | MPLS | 1 MPLS Blck Tiger Shrimp contr | 9:45–13:40 | ¹/₈¢/lb. = $6.25 | 20¢/lb. = $1,000* |
| Shrimp, White | MPLS | 1 MPLS White Shrimp contract | 9:45–13:40 | ¹/₈¢/lb. = $6.25 | 20¢/lb. = $1,000* |
| Soybeans | CBT | 1 CBT Soybean contract | 9:30–13:15; Project A** | ¹/₈¢/bu. = $6.25 | 30¢/bu. = $1,500* |
| Soybeans | MACE | 1 MACE Soybean contract | 9:30–13:45 | ¹/₈¢/bu. = $1.25 | 30¢/bu. = $300* |
| Soybean Meal | CBT | 1 CBT Soybean Meal contract | 9:30–13:15; Project A** | 5¢/ton = $5.00 | $10/ton = $1,000* |
| Soybean Oil | CBT | 1 CBT Soybean Oil contract | 9:30–13:15; Project A** | .005¢/lb. = $3.00 | 1¢/lb. = $600* |
| Soybean Oil | MACE | 1 MACE Soy Oil contract | 9:30–13:45 | .01¢/lb. = $3.00 | 1¢/lb. = $300* |
| Sugar #11 | CSCE | 1 CSCE Sugar #11 contract | 9:30–13:20 | .01¢/lb. = $11.20 | None |
| Wheat | CBT | 1 CBT Wheat contract | 9:30–13:15; Project A** | ¹/₈¢/bu. = $6.25 | 20¢/bu. = $1,000* |
| Wheat | KCBT | 1 KCBT Wheat contract | 9:30–13:20 | ¹/₈¢/bu. = $6.25 | 25¢/bu. = $1,250 |
| Wheat | MACE | 1 MACE Wheat contract | 9:30–13:45 | ¹/₈¢/bu. = $1.25 | 20¢/bu. = $200* |
| Wheat, Spring | MPLS | 1 MPLS Spring Wheat contract | 9:35–13:25 | ¹/₈¢/bu. = $6.25 | 20¢/bu. = $1,000* |
| Wheat, White | MPLS | 1 MPLS White Wheat contract | 9:35–13:25 | ¹/₈¢/bu. = $6.25 | 20¢/bu. = $1,000* |
| **Currencies:** | | | | | |
| Austral. Dollar | CME | 1 CME Australian $ contract | 7:20–14:00 | .01¢/AD = $10.00 | None++ |
| Brazilian Real | BBF | 1 BBF Brazilian Real contract | 9:45–16:30 | R$.01/US$1000=R$0.010 | None |
| British Pound | CME | 1 CME British £ contract | 7:20–14:00; Globex 14:30–7:01+ | .02¢/£ = $12.50 | None++ |

* Expanded limits sometimes. +Globex hours are Mon.–Thurs. & 17:30–normal close Suns. & holidays. **Project A hours 22:30–4:30 Sun.–Thurs. ++ Trading on options stops when underlying futures are locked limit-up or -down.

35

TABLE 10

| OPTION | EXCH | CONTRACT SIZE | TRADING HOURS | MIN. FLUCTUATION | DAILY LIMIT |
|---|---|---|---|---|---|
| **Currencies (cont.):** | | | | | |
| Brit £ Ring Spt | CME | 1 CME £ Ring Spot contr. | 7:20–14:00 | .0001 = $25.00 | None |
| Canadian Dollar | CME | 1 CME Canadian $ contract | 7:20–14:00; Globex 14:30–7:00+ | .01¢/CD = $10.00 | None++ |
| Deutsche Mark | CME | 1 CME DMark contract | 7:20–14:00; Globex 14:30–7:01+ | .01¢/DM = $12.50 | None++ |
| DM Rolling Spot | CME | 1 CME DMark Ring Spot contr | 7:20–14:00 | .0001 = DM25.00 | None |
| DM/SF | CTN | 1 CTN DM/SF contract | 19:00–22:00; 3:00–9:00; 9:05–15:00** | .0001 = SF12.50 | None |
| Dmark/Yen | CTN | 1 CTN DMark/Yen contract | 19:00–22:00; 3:00–9:00; 9:05–15:00** | .01DM = ¥1,250.00 | None |
| Japanese Yen | CME | 1 CME Japanese Yen contract | 7:20–14:00; Globex 14:30–7:01+ | .0001¢/¥ = $12.50 | None++ |
| French Franc | CME | 1 CME Fr. Franc contract | 7:20–14:00; Globex 14:30–7:00+ | .002¢/FF = $10.00 | None++ |
| New Mex. Peso | CME | 1 CME Mexican Peso contract | 8:00–14:00; Globex14:30–7:00+ | .0025¢/NMP = $12.50 | Pls consult exchg |
| Sterling/Mark | CTN | 1 CTN Sterling/Mark contr. | 19:00–22:00; 3:00–9:00; 9:05–15:00** | .0001DM = DM12.50 | None |
| Swiss Franc | CME | 1 CME Swiss Franc contract | 7:20–14:00; Globex 14:30–7:01+ | .01¢/SF = $12.50 | None++ |
| **Energy:** | | | | | |
| Brent Crude | IPE | 1 IPE Brent Crude contract | 10:02–20:15 | US1¢/bbl. = $10.00 | None |
| Crude Oil | NYM | 1 NYM Crude Oil contract | 9:45–15:10; ACCESS@ | $.01/bbl. = $10.00 | None |
| Elect-PV & COB | NYM | 1 Elect. PV & COB contract | 10:30–15:30 | 1¢/Mwh = $7.36 | None |
| Gas Crack | NYM | 1 ea. NYM Gas & Crude contr | 9:50–15:10 | $.01/bbl. = $10.00 | None |
| Gas Oil | IPE | 1 IPE Gas Oil Contract | 9:15–17:29 | US5¢/tonne = $5.00 | None |
| Gasoline (NYH) | NYM | 1 NYM Gasoline contract | 9:50–15:10; ACCESS@ | .01¢/gal. = $4.20 | None |
| Heating Oil | NYM | 1 NYM Heating Oil contract | 9:50–15:10; ACCESS@ | .01¢/gal. = $4.20 | None |
| H.O. Crack | NYM | 1 ea. NYM HO & Crude contr | 9:50–15:10 | $.01/bbl. = $10.00 | None |
| Natural Gas | KCBT | 1 KCBT Western Nat. Gas contr | 8:30–14:35 | .1¢/MMBtu = $10.00 | None |
| Natural Gas-Albta | NYM | 1 NYM Alberta Nat. Gas contract | 10:00–15:10 | .1¢/MMBtu = $10.00 | None |
| **Indexes:** | | | | | |
| All Ordinaries | SFE | 1 SFE All Ordinaries contract | 9:50–12:30; 14:00–16:10; SYCOM@@ | 1.0 = A$25.00 | None |
| Corn Yld. Ins. | CBT | 1 Corn Yld. Ins. contract | 10:30–12:45 | 1/10 bu./acre = $10.00 | 15 bu/acre=$1,500 |

+ Globex hrs. are Mon.–Thurs. & 17:30–normal close Suns. & holidays. @@SYCOM hrs.are 16:40–6:00. **DST evening hrs. are 20:00–23:00; 3:00–8:00 (9:00) trades on Dublin Floor.
@ACCESS hours are Sun. 19:00–8:00; Mon.–Thurs. 16:00–8:00. ++Trading on all series options stop when futures lock limit-up or -down.

**TABLE 11**

| OPTION | EXCH | CONTRACT SIZE | LOCAL TRADING HOURS | MIN. FLUCTUATION | DAILY LIMIT |
|---|---|---|---|---|---|
| **Indexes (cont.):** | | | | | |
| DAX | DTB | 1 DTB DAX contract | 9:00–17:00 | .1 = DM1.00 | None |
| Emergg Mkt Debt | CTN | 1 CTN EMDX contract | 8:20–15:00 | .025 = $25.00 | None |
| Eurotop 100 | CMX | 1 CMX Eurotop 100 contract | 5:30–11:30 | .05 = $5.00 | None |
| FT-SE 100 Index | CME | 1 CME FT-SE 100 contract | 8:30–15:15 | .5 = $25.00 | None |
| FT-SE 100 Index | LIFFE | 1 LIFFE FT-SE 100 contract | 8:35–16:10 | .5 = £5.00 | None |
| GSCI | CME | 1 CME GSCI contract | 8:15–14:15; Globex 14:45–8:00+ | .10 = $25.00 | None (Globex++) |
| Hang Seng Index | HKFE | 1 HKFE Hang Seng Index contr. | 10:00–12:30; 14:30–16:00 | 1 pt. = HK$50.00 | None |
| IPC Stock Index | CME | 1 CME IPC Stock Index contr. | 8:30–15:15; Globex 15:45–8:15+ | .01 = $25.00 | None++ |
| KR-CRB Index | NYFE | 1 NYFE KR-CRB Index contr. | 9:40–14:45 | .05 = $25.00 | None# |
| MMI | CME | 1 CME MMI contract | 8:30–15:15 | .05 = $25.00 | None# |
| Mini Value Line | KCBT | 1 KCBT Mini Value Ln contr. | 8:30–15:15 | .05 = $5.00 | Pls consult exchg |
| Muni-Bond Index | CBT | 1 CBT Muni-Bond contract | 7:20–14:00; Project A@ | $^{1}/_{64}$ = $15.625 | 3 pts = $3,000* |
| NASDAQ 100 Indx | CME | 1 CME NASDAQ 100 Indx cont. | 8:30–15:15; Globex 15:45–8:15+ | .05 = $5.00 | None# |
| Nikkei 225 | CME | 1 CME Nikkei 225 contract | 8:00–15:15 | 5 pts. = $25.00 | None |
| Nikkei 225 | SIMEX | 1 SIMEX Nikkei 225 contract | 7:55–10:15; 11:15–14:15## | 5 pts. = ¥2,500.00 | Pls consult exchg |
| NYSEC Index | NYFE | 1 NYFE NYSEC contract | 9:30–16:15 | .05 = $25.00 | None |
| PSE Tech Index | NYFE | 1 NYFE PSE Tech Index contract | 9:30–16:15 | .05 = $25.00 | None |
| Russell 2000 | CME | 1 CME Russell 2000 contract | 8:30–15:15; Globex 15:45–8:15+ | .05 = $25.00 | None# |
| S&P 500 Index | CME | 1 CME S&P 500 Index contr. | 8:30–15:15; Globex 15:45–8:15+ | .05 = $25.00 | None# |
| S&P MidCap 400 | CME | 1 CME S&P MidCap 400 contr. | 8:30–15:15; Globex 15:45–8:15+ | .05 = $25.00 | None# |
| US $ Index | CTN | 1 CTN U.S.$ Index contract | 19:00–22:00; 3:00–8:00; 8:05–15:00** | .01 = $10.00 | None |
| **Interest Rates:** | | | | | |
| Aus. Gov Bnd 10Yr | SFE | 1 SFE Austral Gov 10 Yr Bond cont | 8:30–12:30; 14:00–16:30; SYCOM@@ | .005%/Annum | None |
| Bank Bill 90-Day | SFE | 1 SFE 90-Day Bank Bill contract | 8:30–12:30; 14:00–16:30; SYCOM@@ | .01%/Annum | None |
| BOBL Bond | DTB | 1 DTB BOBL Bond contract | 8:00–17:30 | .01 = DM25.00 | None |

*Expanded limits sometimes. **DST evening hrs. 20:00–23:00; 3:00–8:00 on Dublin Floor. +Globex hrs. are Mon.–Thurs. & 17:30–normal close Suns. and holidays. ++Option ceases trading when underlying futures are limit bid offered. @Project A hours from 14:30–16:30 Mon.–Thurs. and 22:00–6:00 Sun.–Thurs. #Trading on all series options stops when futures lock limit-up or -down. ## Trades in other places at different times.

TABLE 12

| OPTION | EXCH | CONTRACT SIZE | LOCAL TRADING HOURS | MIN. FLUCTUATION | DAILY LIMIT |
|---|---|---|---|---|---|
| **Interest Rates (cont.):** | | | | | |
| Braz Avg Intrbnk Rt | BBF | 1 BBF Brazil Avg Interbank Rt contr. | 9:45–13:00; 15:00–16:30 | .01 = R$0.50 | None |
| Eurodollars | CME | 1 CME Eurodollar contract | 7:20–14:00; Globex 14:45–7:02+ | .01 = $25.00 | None |
| Eurodollars | SIMEX | 1 SIMEX Eurodollar contract | 7:45–19:00++ | .01 = US$25.00 | None |
| EuroMark (3 mo.) | CME | 1 CME EuroDM 3 mo. contract | 7:20–14:00 | .01 = DM25.00 | None |
| EuroMark (3 mo.) | LIFFE | 1 LIFFE EuroDM 3 mo. contract | 8:02–16:10 | .01 = DM25.00 | None |
| EuroLira (3 mo.) | LIFFE | 1 LIFFE EuroLira 3 mo. contract | 7:57–16:10 | .01 = ITL25,000.00 | None |
| Euro SF Int. Rate | LIFFE | 1 LIFFE EuroSF contract | 8:12–16:05 | .01 = SF25.00 | None |
| Euroyen (3 mo.) | SIMEX | 1 SIMEX Euroyen 3 mo. contr. | 7:58–20:05++ | .01 = ¥2500.00 | None |
| French Nat'l Bond | MATIF | 1 MATIF Fr. Nat'l Bond contract | 9:00–16:30; Globex 16:30–9:00 | .01 = FF50.00 | None |
| Ger. Govt. Bund | DTB | 1 DTB German Govt Bond contr. | 8:00–17:30 | .01 = DM25.00 | None |
| Ger. Govt. Bund | LIFFE | 1 LIFFE Bund contract | 7:32–16:15 | .01 = DM25.00 | None |
| Italian Govt. Bond | LIFFE | 1 LIFFE Italian Govt Bond contr | 8:02–16:10 | .01 = ITL20,000 | None |
| Japan. Govt Bond | SIMEX | 1 SIMEX Japan. Govt Bond contr | 7:45–19:10++ | .01 = ¥5,000.00 | None |
| LIBOR (1 mo.) | CME | 1 CME LIBOR contract | 7:20–14:00 | .01 = $25.00 | None |
| Long Gilt | LIFFE | 1 LIFFE Long Gilt contract | 8:02–16:15 | $1/64$ = £7.8125 | None |
| PIBOR (3 mo.) | MATIF | 1 MATIF 3 mo. PIBOR contract | 8:30–16:00; Globex 16:00–8:30 | .005 = FF62.50 | None |
| Short Sterling | LIFFE | 1 LIFFE Short Sterling contract | 8:07–16:05 | .01 = £12.50 | None |
| U.S. T-Bills | CME | 1 CME T-Bill contract | 7:20–14:00 | .01 = $25.00 | None |
| U.S. T-Bills (1 Yr.) | CME | 1 CME 1-Yr. T-Bill contract | 7:20–14:00 | .005 = $25.00 | None |
| U.S. T-Bonds | CBT | 1 CBT T-Bond contract | 7:20–14:00; 17:20–20:05** # | $1/64$ pt. = $15.625 | 3 pts. = $3,000* |
| U.S. T-Bonds | MACE | 1 MACE T-Bond contract | 7:20–15:15 | $1/64$ pt. = $7.81 | 3 pts. = $1,500* |
| U.S. T-Notes (2 Yr.) | CBT | 1 CBT 2 Yr. T-Note contract | 7:20–14:00; 17:20–20:05** # | ½ of $1/64$ pt. = $15.625 | 1 pt. = $2,000* |
| U.S. T-Notes (5 Yr.) | CBT | 1 CBT 5 Yr. T-Note contract | 7:20–14:00; 17:20–20:05** # | $1/64$ pt. = $15.625 | 3 pts. = $3,000* |
| U.S. T-Notes (10Yr) | CBT | 1 CBT 10 Yr T-Note contract | 7:20–14:00; 17:20–20:05*** # | $1/64$ pt. = $15.625 | 3 pts. = $3,000* |
| Yield Curve Spread | CBT | 1 CBT Yield Curve Spread contr. | 7:20–14:00 | ½ of $1/8$¢ = $15.625 | None |

*Expanded limits sometimes.  +Globex hrs. Mon.–Thurs. and 17:30–normal close Suns. and holidays.  ** Evening hrs. CST Sun.–Thurs.  #Project A hrs. 14:30–16:30 Mon.–Thurs. and 22:00–6:00 Sun.–Thurs.  ++Trades in other locations at different times.

## TABLE 13

| OPTION | EXCH | CONTRACT SIZE | LOCAL TRADING HOURS | MIN. FLUCTUATION | DAILY LIMIT |
|---|---|---|---|---|---|
| **Metals:** | | | | | |
| Copper | CMX | 1 CMX Copper Gr. 1 contract | 8:10–14:00 | .05¢/lb. = $12.50 | None |
| Copper, 5-day | CMX | 1 CMX Copper contract | 8:10–14:00 | .05¢/lb. = $12.50 | None |
| Gold | CMX | 1 CMX Gold contract | 8:20–14:30 | 10¢/oz. = $10.00 | None |
| Gold, 5-day | CMX | 1 CMX Gold contract | 8:20–14:30 | 10¢/oz. = $10.00 | None |
| Gold, New York | MACE | 1 MACE NY Gold contract | 7:20–13:40 | 10¢/oz. = $3.32 | None |
| Platinum | NYM | 1 NYM Platinum contract | 8:20–14:30; ACCESS+ | 10¢/oz. = $5.00 | None |
| Silver | CMX | 1 CMX Silver contract | 8:25–14:25 | .1¢/oz. = $5.00 | None |
| Silver, 5-day | CMX | 1 CMX Silver contract | 8:25–14:25 | .1¢/oz. = $5.00 | None |
| Silver | CBT | 1 CBT 1,000 oz. Silver contr | 7:25–13:25 | .1¢/oz. = $1.00 | $1/oz. = $1,000* |
| **Wood:** Lumber | CME | 1 CME Rndm Lngth Lmbr contr. | 9:00–13:05 | 10¢/1000 bdft = $8 | None |
| OSB Board | CME | 1 CME OSB Board contract | 9:00–13:05 | 10¢/1000 sqft = $10.00 | None |

*Expanded limits sometimes. +ACCESS hrs. Sun. 19:00–8:00 and Mon.–Thurs. 16:00–8:00.

example, Japan's Kobe Rubber Exchange grew 130.1% and Spain's MEFF RENTA VARIABLE grew by 139.7%, while Chicago's CBOT grew by only 22.8%. Of course, these figures must be looked at in perspective: the overall contract volume of the CBOT, at approximately 219 million, clearly had both the KRE's three million and MEFF-V's 34 million contract volume beat hands down.

This ends our look at the basic economics and mechanics of the industry. We've touched upon the who, what, where, when, how, and why of the exciting, high-finance world of futures trading. Now it's time to see how we can become one of its real-time players. Get ready! It's time to link-up and interface . . . .

Buy

# YOUR COMPUTER CONNECTION TO THE TRADING WORLD

## From the Floor to Your Screen— Like Magic (Almost)

When a trade is completed in a trading pit, two things happen immediately: the participants make written records of the transaction (contract traded, delivery month, price, and number of contracts), and an exchange pit observer reports the details of the trade and makes sure it is entered into the exchange's computerized price reporting system. From this point, the information is both displayed on the huge quotation boards above the floor and transmitted via satellite to brokers and investors—like you and me—worldwide, via data/quotation vendors. This happens fast—even before the information is reported via telephone to the customers whose trade we are talking about. And the time lapse between the board display of that price change at the exchange and the quote/chart display of that same price change on a home computer located thousands of miles from the exchange—and connected to it via a real-time quote service—might be a second or two. Real-time does mean real-time!

## Data Vendors: Real-Time Data

There are a wide variety of vendors to choose from, and some offer every type of financial data currently available. These top-of-the-line vendors provide the level of data service that is required by large FCMs and institutional fund managers, offering spot/cash commodity quotes plus other instruments like foreign currency forwards, in addition to the standard fare. Other vendors, also used by FCMs and the like, offer quotes for the financial products that are most commonly watched and invested in (stocks, options, commodity futures, and options on futures) and leave aside the fancy stuff for their higher-end competition.

Real-time quotes are not cheap from any vendor, but there is certainly no need to subscribe to a super-expensive service used by global financiers and banks who trade currencies via arbitrage and need to know instant spot prices of commodities. In other words, we should only pay for what we need. Therefore, it makes sense to go with the second type of vendor described above, and there are a number of these who can provide exactly what we need, and no more, at competitive rates. So how do we decide whom amongst these to go with?

Data vendors have their devotees who would rather fight than switch, especially when so much is riding on the data. It would be most disconcerting to have your feed go dead in the middle of a million dollar (or even hundred dollar) trade. This rarely happens with the currently available batch of vendors. Since this is a relatively small and highly communicative (at light speed) industry, a vendor with anything more than a rare transmission breakdown would tend to go out of business very quickly. However, there is always the fear that constant data blackouts *might* occur, and so vendor loyalty is strong. When deciding on a vendor, our main concern is to go with one that your chosen software supports, and one that can also grow with you. Their reputation for excellent service, reliable hardware/software, and ease of installation should make the finest real-time charting software packages want to support them.

Several vendors fit these requirements. The choice is yours and I give the contact info for some of them in the Appendix. I use BMI (Bonneville Market Information) offered by DBC (Data Broadcasting Corporation) for several reasons. It is one of the most popular of the lower cost services; it is one of the first choices of support by the best software vendors; it is easy to install both its proprietary software and its hardware; it has very helpful tech support with a toll-free number, and it is on the cutting edge of development into new areas. For example, it recently developed an upgrade to its data box which allows you to receive quotes from LIFFE, the main UK exchange, plus other international exchanges. BMI's data is very dependable and I have seen several instances where a fellow trader friend of mine using the same charting indicators as I—but another data feed— did not get some good buy/sell signals that I got. BMI is also one of the fastest data feeds, which means it captures more ticks in fast markets than many of its competitors, and tends to stay closer to "real-time," at least during those circumstances. BMI also gives you a choice of hardware, allowing you to receive the quotes via satellite dish, cable, or FM, so you can choose the best feed for your location and situation. Another wonderful feature is that you can obtain real-time trading news—both headlines and their backup stories—from them as well, on the same data feed (more on this later). BMI currently provides real-time services only to subscribers in North America and Europe, but they are growing fast. There are other vendors, such as Reuters and Bloomberg, who provide real-time data to just about anywhere on earth. (Please see the Appendix for addresses and phone numbers.) Signal, the other data feed offered by DBC, is also an excellent data choice.

The fees for any data vendor are usually broken down into two categories: the monthly service fee from the vendor itself, and the monthly fee from each exchange to which you subscribe. No matter which quotation vendor you use, the exchange fees remain the same. For example, the current exchange fee for real-time quotes from the Chicago Mercantile Exchange, where currency futures like the Swiss franc, Deutsche mark, and Japanese yen are traded, along with the popular S&P 500 Index futures, is $55/month. DBC's monthly fee is currently $210, so your monthly charge for receiving real-time quotes from the CME through Signal is $265/month. If you want the CBOT or the LIFFE, for example, you just add on their monthly exchange fees. DBC's monthly fee remains the same.

Connecting the BMI or Signal hardware/software to your computer is simple (see Figure 4) and their manuals are excellent. Basically, the data from either your FM antenna, satellite dish, or cable TV (the quotes ride on a side carrier on several cable channel frequencies) is fed by a coaxial cable into the BMI

44

Drawing by Kevin Allard

**Figure 4** From the exchange floor to your computer—in about a second! Here's how it's done (e.g. BMI/ Signal): The reported exchange floor prices are instantly received by the data vendor which continuously up-links that data to a geo-stationary satellite. From the satellite it is down-linked and ultimately made available to subscribers either through cable, FM, or satellite dish. A co-axial cable connects one of these receivers to the data feed box. The above inset shows the simple connections from that box to your computer. (Users of Omega TradeStation/SuperCharts software would insert the security/hardware key as shown.)

Signal receiver box where it is converted into digital data. A cable hooks the BMI/Signal box into a serial port on your computer. And that's it for the hardware connections (see Figure 4). Once you install your charting software, the data will automatically download into your computer and you are soon live, on-the-air(!), receiving real-time quotes and data from the exchanges you have subscribed to. You can see those quotes by either using the BMI/Signal software to construct pages of quotes for the stocks or commodities you want to see, or by using a charting package which converts those quote numbers into plots of the real-time price changes, along with plots of indicators and systems which can issue buy and sell signals. Charts are exactly what a real-time trader looks at, and in a moment we'll see what such a charting package should contain.

## A Note on Delayed Data

Delayed quote services are considerably less expensive than real-time quote services. They transmit quotes every 10, 15, or 30 minutes. Charting software is available for trading in these longer time frames and should serve you well, should you be a longer-term position trader (holding your trades overnight). There are many successful traders who use delayed information, and you might become one of them or be one of them now. Although the primary emphasis of this book is on intraday trading—closing all your trades by the end of the day—the basic methodologies and techniques can be utilized in any time frame. I stick with real-time data and real-time trading for a number of reasons. Real-time data affords the trader a level of market knowledge, risk management, and profit potential not possible with delayed quotes. You are right there as the market is moving: you see it changing live, are trading with the action, and can therefore catch much more of it. You are in tune with live pulse of the markets. Obviously, anything you can do with delayed quotes you can also do with real-time quotes—plus much more. Daytrading is not to be prudently attempted with anything but real-time data, and daytrading can be one of the most lucrative time frames in which to trade, because of all of the extra opportunities you are privileged to. Regarding the price difference between delayed and real-time data: one good trade during the day and you've paid your monthly fees!

## Charting Software Packages

A good general charting package must contain basic tools and indicators to allow the trader to effectively view the markets and analyze them in real-time. It is the trader's window on the trading world, and since it's the only view he has of the actual playing/battle field, it must afford him an *intelligent* view. Besides the basic tools and indicators (described in Chapter 6), a quality charting package should be judged by the extent to which it assists in the development and historical testing—quickly and effectively—of the hundreds of new strategies and ideas that will occur to the creative trader. It must be fully comprehensive, so that it will accommodate the trader's increasing knowledge of the business and of market action.

Excellent general packages are available. Most have free demos which show all of the capabilities of the software using sample charts of market data. I have listed some of the software vendors of these packages in the Appendix for your investigation. I use Omega Research's *TradeStation,* and there are a number of good reasons why it was voted the #1 trading software by the "Stocks and Commodities Reader's Choice Awards" for 1993, 1994, 1995 and 1996. I'll note a few that convinced me to purchase it as my primary charting package:

1) *Easy Language:* Omega created a relatively easy-to-learn programming language by which I can write my own indicators and trading systems and combine their code, if I wish, with the extensive library of supplied indicators. This is a distinct advantage over some other packages which only offer the standard library of indicators.

2) Some of the best traders have written profitable systems just for *TradeStation* using the *Easy Language* which you can purchase and add on to the basic package.

3) It offers unique *PaintBar* and *ShowMe* studies which add to the trader's ability to analyze market action quickly.

*TradeStation* is easy to install, has excellent manuals, and supports all major data vendors. It is also a Windows-based program; the charting graphics are excellent, the analysis tools extensive. They offer a free demo of the program. The latest version, 4.0, has many more helpful features as well.

Real-time programs are always considerably more expensive than EOD (end-of-day) programs that chart daily data only. Omega keeps *TradeStation* priced competitively for all that it offers.

For those needing to keep their start-up costs to a minimum, Omega Research also offers two other excellent charting packages: *SuperCharts Real-Time* is for real-time traders who can do without *TradeStation's* back-testing and power-editor/system-creation features. The other, simply called *SuperCharts,* is for end-of-day position traders. You will find Omega Research's contact information in the Appendix under "Sources/Resources."

The cost for charting software and the monthly data fees—whether delayed or real-time—must ultimately be viewed as simply the necessary cost of doing business. Fortunately, these costs soon become incidental as one becomes more knowledgeable in this business.

## Trading Systems/Black Box

There are scores of computerized trading systems available for purchase which issue buy and sell signals. They either stand alone or work in conjunction with all-purpose charting packages such as those mentioned above. Some cover specific markets, some cover all markets. Some scan specific time frames, some scan all time frames. Some cost several hundred dollars, some cost $10,000's.

Caveat emptor : some work pretty good; many don't. For a trading system to get on your purchase list, it becomes your task to first weed out the worthwhile systems from the worthless. If the software's methodology is not clearly explained (how to trade it and why it works) you may want to find out if a live demo disk is available. Although these don't really give a long-term time test, ideally you could paper trade the system in real-time and try to follow the signals and strategies of the system as closely as possible to help you see how it might perform in actual trading. When you are confident that it appears to work for you, you can begin actually trading it with the time remaining and, ideally, make enough money to buy the system (see "Trader Psychology" in Chapter 9, however, for a discussion of the very real difference between paper trading and actual trading). Critical factors in your decision to purchase a trading system should include knowing the maximum overall drawdown (loss) the system must experience over a historically backtested period in order to reach the overall claimed profit, and knowing the price stop-losses you are expected to set on each trade (see "Stop-loss," Chapter 9). The system may theoretically be very profitable, but the margins you require in your account to withstand the drawdowns in the "off" periods of the system may be too much to handle. The trading system must match the trader's style, market preference, time frame, and account balance. The research required to find that match can be worth the time, since a marriage between the right system and right trader can greatly simplify the trader's life, and dramatically improve his bottom line.

Black box charting software refers to closed-end programs which analyze markets in a certain way and issue buy and sell signals. The authors of these programs have often put in a great deal of time, research, money, and effort into developing and rigorously testing in real-time the computer code and algorithms that they've created. As is true for the science of topology and other advanced developments in mathematics, the formulas for the basics are usually considered public domain. In trading, there are basic formulas and concepts that are the distant starting points for virtually all complex computerized programs. Profitable trading algorithms usually take years to develop and bear very little resemblance, if any, to their distant conceptual and numerical ancestors. Short of resorting to copyrighting the developer's work, and legally enforcing the same, black box protection remains the author/trader's only choice should he desire (and feel he deserves) some profit from all of his efforts.

Naturally it is vitally important, no matter what type of software you finally acquire, that its author be able to explain to you how to use it and how to trade it. It does you no good to see trading signals appear on your screen if you don't know what to do with them. Ideally, there should be a clear synergy between the software's methodology and the larger pattern recognition discoveries that have proven themselves to be true and effective over the decades (e.g., The Elliot Wave Theory described more in Chapter 5).

Besides system software, there are other programs that can also increase the effectiveness of your all-purpose charting program. This includes the acquisition of new tools and indicators, plus increasing the memory and chip performance of your computer (which can make both your charting software and your data-feed perform better).

## Neural Nets

One of the main problems that every system designer must confront is the non-linear nature of markets described later in Chapter 5. The complex weather-like patterns of markets makes it imperative that a system be robust enough to deal with those patterns. A crude analogy would compare a trading system to a tree. If that tree is too stiff, it may break in a sudden market storm; too weak, and it will simply lay down flat or be uprooted. It needs to be just flexible enough, like a nice date palm tree, to allow it to bend with the weather patterns, with the market. A good trading system should keep functioning efficiently regardless of the market conditions.

This is not easy to find. In fact, it is so difficult for a system to be consistently profitable that many traders eschew them altogether and follow their own technical indicators, methodologies, and fundamental knowledge of underlying market forces. Traders like these are sometimes called discretionary traders, and there is an eternal debate as to who is ultimately the better trader—the system trader or the discretionary trader?

The latter trader insists that human intelligence and discrimination is ultimately the only real weapon the trader has on the market battleground. What mechanical system could possibly understand all the trading dynamics that go on simultaneously, and issue valid buy and sell signals?

Neural networks attempt to do just that: understand what is going on. Amongst the most sophisticated software ever developed, neural nets emulate the construction of the human brain itself. You may remember that *The Next Generation's* Mr. Data often discusses his own neural net—even those *Star Trek* writers can't think of anything more advanced to talk about. Elements of the technology include "neurons" which combine to "learn" a problem. This software has been available for several years and experts are often required to translate into computer code exactly what events the system needs to learn to recognize. Neural networks are used by the military to project complex missile trajectories and by industrial engineers to comprehend fluid mechanics. Wherever complex problems need to be solved, neural nets are being utilized more and more.

One way in which neural net technology is being used by traders is in complex pattern recognition systems. These attempt to spot chart patterns which have recurred historically and then to alert the trader by issuing buy and sell signals based on "fuzzy logic"—i.e., when the patterns come within a certain user-defined parameter of closeness to the ideal pattern—just as the trader might do using his own eyes. Other neural net software stresses the development of systems that recognize and act upon the many relationships and influences that markets have upon each other (see "Intermarket Relationships" in Chapter 7).

Neural networks are certainly on the very cutting edge of trading system technology, and it is wise for system-oriented traders to keep track of developments in this area; their competition in the marketplace is certainly doing so! (See the Appendix for sources).

## Hardware Requirements

To receive real-time data and chart it through a good charting package, your computer should have an absolute minimum of 4MB RAM and at least a 100MB hard disk. You should have at least a 486, if not a Pentium processor, in your computer, and the faster your chip is —75MHZ, 90MHZ, 120MHZ, and up— the better. Charting programs are graphics-based, which means they need a lot of memory. They simply work better and faster with more available memory and faster chips. Especially as you increase the number of charts on your screen for immediate reference and add more and more indicators, you will find that

4MB just doesn't make it, especially under Windows 95. Expect to eventually move up to 8MB RAM and higher.

I find that a color VGA monitor is essential, as it allows me to immediately distinguish the various indicator lines from one another and makes decision-making much easier. I wouldn't think of trading without one. If you have a Windows-based package, a mouse is required.

Since we need high-speed calculation, a math co-processor is recommended (Pentiums generally include them). Your charting software manual will inform you exactly what you need in your computer, but even before you make your purchase, you should find out this information from the sales/customer service department of the software vendor. While there's no need to go crazy with the latest and most expensive computer system (or system upgrade), it is best to make sure your computer has the speed and power it requires to enable your charting software to function correctly, and thus serve you effectively. Just as you wouldn't go into battle with a butter knife, you don't want to enter live trades with a questionable computer system. Your tools should be as transparent as possible; you want your concentration where it belongs—squarely on that trade.

Regarding the hardware requirements needed for receiving the live data/quotes, depending on whether your vendor transmits via satellite, FM, or cable, you will receive the appropriate box from them. You may also need to purchase a satellite dish, FM antenna, or make sure you are able to receive a specific TV cable channel. It is your data vendor's job to provide you with the best hardware solution according to your feed preferences, trading location, and budget.

# Summary

To wrap up, there are four software/hardware elements you will need to become a real-time, or delayed, computerized futures and/or stock trader from home (the data feeds also include—for the same cost—live data on virtually every stock issue existing in addition to the futures data):

(1) A high-performance personal computer

(2) A real-time or delayed data feed

(3) A high-quality general charting package

(4) A software system or methodology that will
load up into your general charting package—
sit "on top" of your charting platform—
and issue the actual buy and sell signals.

There are certainly software systems that attempt to combine (3) and (4), but most serious traders prefer the far greater creative latitude, broader trading options, and the natural market knowledge that develops when these four elements are made separate and distinct.

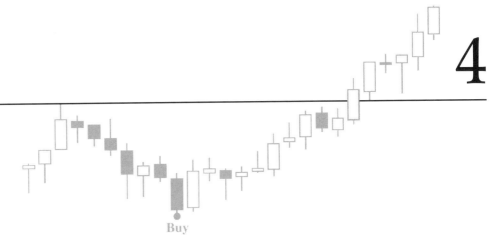

# TRADING PERSPECTIVES

## The Fundamentalist, the Technician, The Fundician, and the Technimentalist

In broad terms, traders can have several perspectives from which they view or approach markets. These views define the types of traders they are and the methods they follow. Traders can either be "fundamentalists," "technicians," or some combination of the two.

A fundamentalist trades the fundamentals. This means he attempts to interpret factors like global supply and demand statistics, interest rates, inflationary and deflationary trends in various global economies, seasonal price tendencies, weather conditions, government economic indicators, global geopolitics, and whatever else might influence the price of a given commodity over a specific time period. This trader must not only have access to vast resources of international news and economic data, but must know how to analyze it from a historical perspective, relate it all together, and ultimately funnel it down into answers to these apparently simple questions: Will the price of the commodity go up or down? Exactly when will that happen? For how long? True fundamentalists tend to be major fund managers and economic analysts who have the resources to get a handle (or think they can get a handle) on how to juggle the fundamentals and come up with price forecasts. Much of the fundamental data we hear about involves the stock market and the analysis of company assets, earnings, sales, and management. Again, this is very difficult to do successfully, and you may have heard where the performance of a "dartboard portfolio," obtained by throwing darts at names of publically-owned corporations, has beaten the fundamentalists time and time again. But to be fair, some fundamentalists are clearly better than others, and a few are enormously successful.

The technical trader, on the other hand, doesn't want to hear about seasonal influences or politics or inventory surplus. This trader understands that all of the fundamental influences on the marketplace certainly exist, but whatever they may be, the most dominant of them will ultimately find their way into the market price of the commodity at each moment. Therefore, by analyzing the dynamics of the price itself over time on price charts, along with technical indicators which measure things like average price movements over time, overbought and oversold conditions of price over time, momentum, and many other influences, the technical trader buys or sells on technical signals which have been historically proven to be statistically profitable.

The third trader tries to use a certain measure of each of the above perspectives in his trading due to their separate limitations. To come to clear trading decisions based on the fundamentalist point of view alone—considering all the myriad local and global factors which need to be analyzed—can indeed prove to be a difficult task for any trader. It is often considered too *wide* a view to see the details. And the technical view alone—considering how sudden events in the real world outside of the technician's computer can skew even the loveliest chart pattern—can become too *narrow* a view to see the overall picture. So how to deal with all this?

I believe the wise course for the futures trader is to be, what I call a "technimentalist"—about 80%–90% technical trader and 10%–20% fundamentalist (the "fundician" would theoretically reverse these percentages). A fundamentalist to this limited extent is aware of what basic "inside-the-market" or "outside-the-market" influences might influence the trade he's taken, or is about to take, *based on his primary technical signals.* It means being wary of trading stone-blind to certain fundamental influences. There is a way to find out this type of fundamental information instantly (see Chapter 11). Combining the strengths of both the fundamentalist and the technician to become an informed technical trader is one of the best trading perspectives we can possibly maintain as the private trader from home.

As our primary method of trading is technical, let us take a look at how traders use natural market forces to discover buy-and-sell opportunities in futures (and stock) markets.

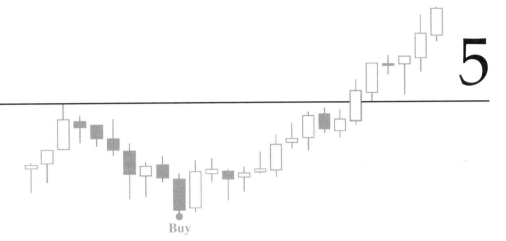

# MARKET DYNAMICS

## Markets As Natural Phenomena

A stone plunks into a placid lake. Wave upon concentric wave radiates outward in a most orderly fashion, each one a different height and volume from the preceding and succeeding one—all in exact mathematical ratios. We've all thrown that stone and enjoyed watching the orderly expanding patterns that follow. Winter follows autumn and spring precedes summer—each and every year. Billions of heliotropic sunflowers grace the planet, the number of upward bending petals of each and every flower existing in an unerring ratio to the number of their downward bending counterparts.

Like waves and wavelets, flower petals, the four seasons, and the orbits of the planets, natural phenomena tend to follow cyclical patterns—over and over again throughout time and space. Some patterns in nature are so evident that we can predict, with dependable accuracy, when that pattern will again occur. The sunrise is reliably forecast to the minute, each and every morning. The recurring patterns of the molecular structures of certain natural materials allow us to construct atomic clocks around them which are predictably accurate to the billionth of a second. Other natural phenomena display patterns that may not be as easy for us to predict or understand. Our inability to forecast the weather, for example, as accurately as we can the sunrise, lies not in some chance randomness inherent in weather, but rather in the *utter complexity of its orderly patterns.* The application of advanced supercomputers to the complex mathematics of these weather patterns is beginning to shed some light on this daily phenomenon, and perhaps we will someday be able to predict the weather as accurately as we can the timing of that first ray of morning sun.

It may at first seem strange to consider commodity futures or stock trading to be natural phenomena right alongside the seasons and diurnal cycles—until you take a look at trading charts, the graphs that plot commodity or stock market price action as a simple function of time. Viewing these, certain patterns become immediately apparent. Price bars, when seen over a long enough time period, start looking like rising and falling waves and wavelets repeatedly washing up onto some invisible electronic beach (see Chart 1). Other patterns described later may take a bit more effort to see, but are nonetheless very much there. Many of these patterns not only resemble some physical counterpart of nature, but in fact precisely follow an underlying mathematical order found to exist in nature.

An Italian mathematician by the name of Leonardo Fibonacci discovered in the 13th century a most unique number sequence that now bears his name. At first glance it doesn't look like much. It starts like this: you take the number 2 and add to it the previous number in the sequence, 1, to get 3. Then

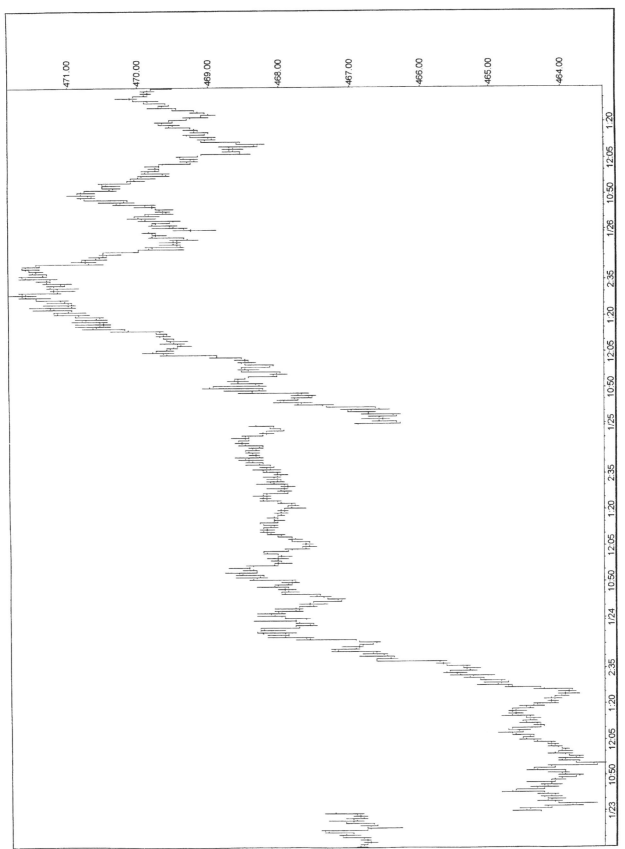

**CHART 1: Wavelike Motion of Market Prices Over Time**

Chart created with TradeStation™ by Omega Research, Inc.

63

you take that 3 and add to it the previous number and now you've got 5. The series continues on like this indefinitely and you wind up with the Fibonacci Series: 1, 2, 3, 5, 8, 13, 21, 34, 55, 89, and so on. Let's look at this: If you take any Fibonacci number and compare it to the next higher number in the sequence, you get the ratio 61.8% (actually it gets closer and closer to this ratio the higher up you go in the series). Fibonacci talks about other ratios but this is one of the most important.

Impressive, eh? OK, remember our billions of sunflowers? What would you say if I told you that every single one of them has 89 curves: 34 petals of which go in one direction, 55 in the other direction (all Fibonacci numbers), with the ratio between both types of petals equaling 61.8%? Now we're getting somewhere! Fibonacci claimed that his number sequence and its ratios occur throughout nature and help to explain many of nature's mysteries. Investigation over the centuries has proven this to be the case again and again.

What does this have to do with futures trading? If markets indeed display the underlying mathematical order found in nature, perhaps everything. And what we find is that after a market has made a strong move up or down, it tends to *retrace* a certain distance before again resuming the trend direction. That retrace distance can be measured, and is very often found to be precisely in a primary Fibonacci ratio to the  larger move. In fact, (1) an entire body of technical analysis exists called Fibonacci ratio analysis, (2) practically every charting package includes the "Fibonacci Fan" (which fans out lines in Fibonacci ratios that act like support or resistance lines—the price bars often bounce right off them), and (3) each morning special "Fib" (trader short-hand for Fibonacci) numbers are faxed to floor traders and to other savvy traders worldwide. These are considered critical price levels calculated from Fibonacci ratios that will tend to become important support and resistance levels throughout the trading day.

If Fibonacci ratio analysis is not evidence that markets are natural phenomena, I don't know what is.

How can this be? Most analysts agree that there is no explanation other than this: the global ebb and flow of supply and demand, and human fear and greed, as daily seen in any well-traded liquid market, is *itself* a vibrant part of nature. Not water nature, or planetary nature, or flower petal nature, but *human nature.* A chart of market action is nothing more than a graphic representation of human psychology, and as that psychology subtly shifts in one group, predictable psychological reactions occur in the other groups. For example, a commodity fund buying a significant volume of contracts may cause a large upward price movement in that market which will, in turn, produce a certain psychological reaction (!) in those investors who are short that market at that same time. That reaction will ultimately result in a price reaction to the initial price action. Isn't that natural? It is so natural in fact that these changes in global trader psychology throughout the day result in repetitive patterns on charts that can be recognized and analyzed in any number of ways. (Note: The comparison of market patterns to waves and wavelets has been fully explored in the writings of R. N. Elliot. The Elliot Wave theory provides one of the broadest perspectives on how seemingly random wavelike market movements fit into orderly larger patterns of five waves. These patterns repeat over and over again, and it was largely due to the early writings of Elliot that markets are now understood to display not irregular linear motion, but regular non-linear patterns. Elliot wave analysis is used by traders worldwide to help indicate future market activity. See the Appendix under Financial Publishers.)

This is all very good news for the trader whose success rides on how well he can predict the price rise and price decline of any market. With the learned ability to recognize and analyze repetitive patterns on charts, along with a sound approach to money and risk management, a trader can literally surf his way to profits on the natural psychological waves of market action.

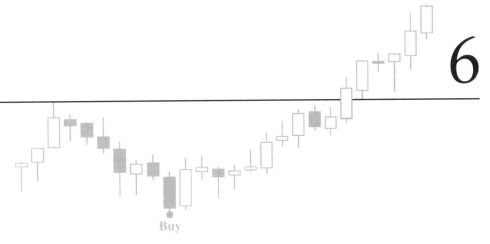

# TECHNICAL TOOLS OF THE TRADE(R)

## The Bar Chart

Chart 2 gives a close-up view of the standard bar chart, technically called the OHLC (Open, High, Low, Close) bar chart. Bars are the individual elements that comprise a price wave. An OHLC price bar graphically depicts the opening price, high price, low price, closing price, and all prices in between for the extent of time chosen for that bar. As Chart 2 was created to plot five-minute bars, each bar shows the above information for a five-minute period. The x-axis of the chart shows the time, advancing in five-minute segments as per each bar, and the y-axis shows the price of the commodity being plotted. As the time advances, basic market action and direction may be understood. Bar charts can be set up to show market price action over any time frame in a real-time charting package. Charts are generally assumed to be bar charts, and when traders talk shop with each other, they refer to their charts in terms of the time frame, commodity, and delivery month: As in "I've split the screen into five chart windows for the March S&P: 3-minute, 5-minute, 15-minute, hourly, and daily." By looking at different time frames of the same commodity, valuable information can be gathered (more on this later). The bar chart is the most common type of chart used by traders around the world.

# Japanese Candlesticks

In 1989, Steve Nison, a researcher on futures and options, wrote an article on a type of trading virtually unheard of in the West but used for centuries in the Far East. Within a year, Merrill Lynch, the publisher of Nison's follow-up booklet on the subject, received over 10,000 requests for further information. Nison had uncovered a new and exciting system of investment ideas and strategies—new to the West, that is. What made them so interesting to the Western financial world was that these were not new-fangled untested concepts, but were, instead, elements of an ancient investment system which views market activity from an entirely different and refreshing perspective, and which have proven themselves effective over centuries of trial and error. In 1991, after learning some of the techniques from a Japanese broker and from several key Japanese literatures (notably *The Japanese Chart of Charts* written by Seikos Shimizu, published by the Tokyo Futures Trading Publishing Co.), Nison published what is now considered the classic Western reference on Japanese candlesticks: *Japanese Candlestick Charting Techniques: A Contemporary Guide to the Ancient Investment Techniques of the Far East*. Charting software vendors immediately understood the significance of these methods and began to incorporate them into their

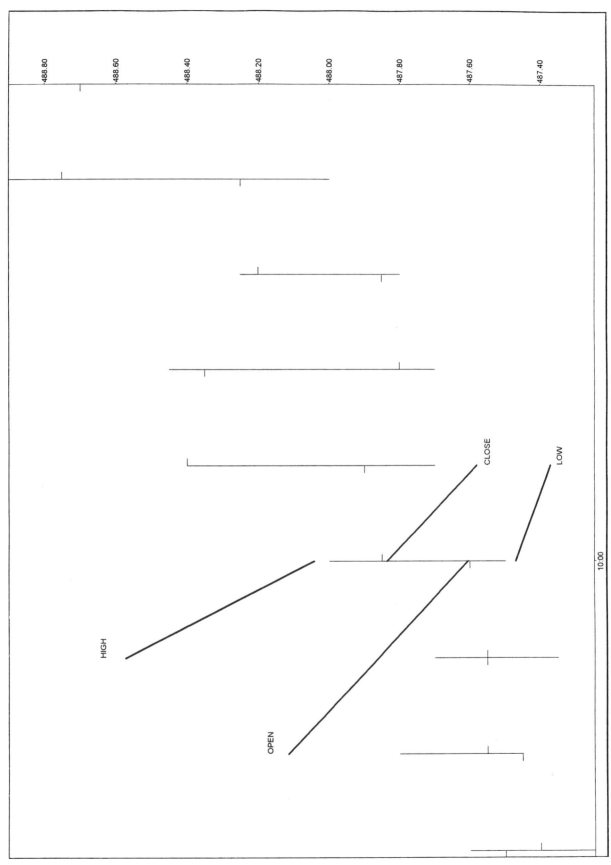

**CHART 2: OHLC Bar Chart**

Chart created with TradeStation™ by Omega Research, Inc.

69

packages. Today, barely five years after their introduction to the West, Japanese candlesticks are now very much a part of the Western financial lexicon. Many chartists use them in addition to standard bar charts.

So what are they? They are not bars exactly, although they do clearly provide the same information that a OHLC bar does, i.e., a market's open, high, low, and closing price, and all prices in between over a selected time span. Candlesticks tell us this, but also much more. Their unique shapes and forms, looking somewhat like candlesticks or outlines of candlesticks—some with long wicks and little bodies, some with long bodies and little or no wicks at all—can give clear market indications. Some of their leading indications include continuation of upward and downward trends, loss or gain in market momentum, and market reversals. Candlesticks have special significance, especially when they are found in groupings or patterns that have historically proven themselves to be highly predictive of market action.

Chart 3A shows a five-minute OHLC bar chart, and Chart 3B shows a five-minute Japanese candlestick chart for the same day and time period. I have circled the two-bar topping formation in both charts, just before the market made a major reversal in direction. Even without the benefit of any technical indicators to help us analyze what is happening, the *bearish engulfment* (a pattern known for centuries to be a sign of market reversal) on the candlestick chart has given us a strong indication of the most probable future direction of this market. As you can see, the downward market direction was successfully predicted by the pattern. The bar chart, on the other hand, is not at all as strikingly clear in its indication. (Note: There are certain pat-

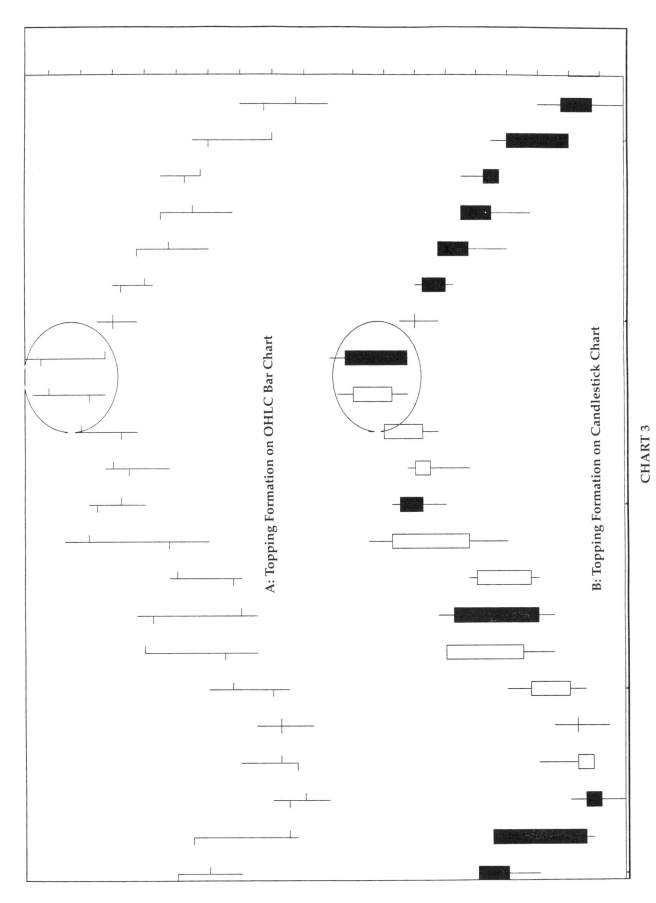

A: Topping Formation on OHLC Bar Chart

B: Topping Formation on Candlestick Chart

CHART 3

Chart created with TradeStation™ by Omega Research, Inc.

71

terns of OHLC bars, like breakouts from repeating identical lows and highs, that can be significant indicators of future market direction.)

Due to their development during, and just after, the warring feudal times of Japan described in Chapter 2, candlestick shapes, patterns, and investment techniques were given very colorful and often highly descriptive names borrowed from the battlefield. It is fitting, of course, that trading terminology reflect the battlefield, since that is exactly what trading is (to the victor go the spoils, to the loser . . . .) In the West we refer to the trader's tools as his *trading arsenal* and to "making a trade" as *pulling the trigger.* The Japanese nomenclature is especially expressive. There is the *morning attack* (the expression for large buy or sell orders on the open of the market, designed to significantly move it) and the *piercing pattern* (a major bottom reversal pattern). There's *dark cloud cover* (a bearish reversal signal) and the *hanging man* (an important top reversal sign). And these patterns tend to work, especially when confirmed by Western-style indicators.

It is for this very reason—that candlesticks can be freely used in conjunction with Western technical indicators—that they have become so popular with Western-trained traders and analysts. Combining the best attributes of both systems makes it possible to gain both Eastern and Western perspectives on market action—simultaneously. Many feel this gives a much clearer interpretation of market action than either method alone. Real-time software is now available which automatically generates buy and sell signals when specific candlestick patterns confirm Western technical indicators, and visa versa.

Steve Nison has written the definitive books on Japanese

candlesticks and candlestick patterns; they are listed in the Appendix, should you wish to research further on the subject.

## Chart Patterns

Bars and candlesticks often form repetitive chart patterns, and there are so many traders that base their chart trading on the most recognizable of these formations that the patterns are often self-fulfilling. (Note: Traders generally use other tools like technical indicators in addition to basic bar/candlestick pattern recognition to obtain trading confirmation). Some examples of chart patterns are *gaps* (*windows* in candlestick charts) and *head and shoulders*.

Chart 4 shows a gap down on the day's opening (i.e., a gap between the low of the last bar of the previous day and the high of the first bar of the current day). There is an important trading guideline which states "gaps are filled." And as we can see, the gap was filled by about 3:00 PM. These opening gaps are watched closely by many traders. The trading continued to form three major lows at 9:50 AM, 11:15 AM, and 1:40 PM. These formed a general pattern known as *reverse head and shoulders* (or upside-down head and shoulders)—a reversal pattern—and we can see how the market indeed reversed to an upward trend soon after the right shoulder appeared. The equal highs within the pattern can be joined together to form a line, the *neckline*, which forms the confirmed breakout point for the reversed trend. *Flags* form consolidation channels from which prices eventually tend to break out of and then trend strongly (Chart 5 [channel lines are mine]). *Double bottom* or *double top* patterns are similar to head

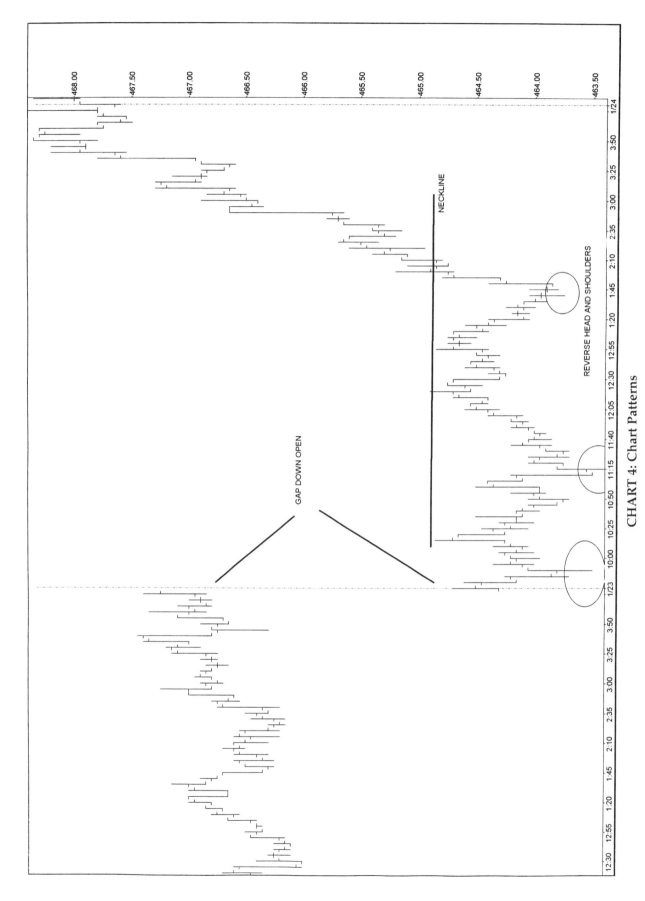

**CHART 4: Chart Patterns**

Chart created with TradeStation™ by Omega Research, Inc.

74

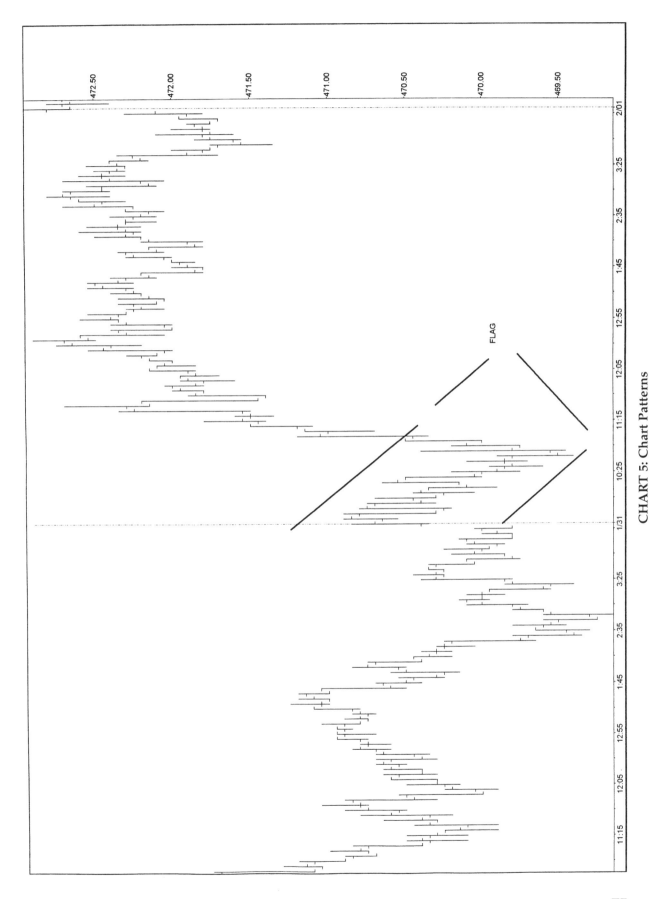

FLAG

472.50
472.00
471.50
471.00
470.50
470.00
469.50

11:15  12:05  12:55  1:45  2:35  3:25  1/31  10:25  11:15  12:05  12:55  1:45  2:35  3:25  2/01

**CHART 5: Chart Patterns**

Chart created with TradeStation™ by Omega Research, Inc.

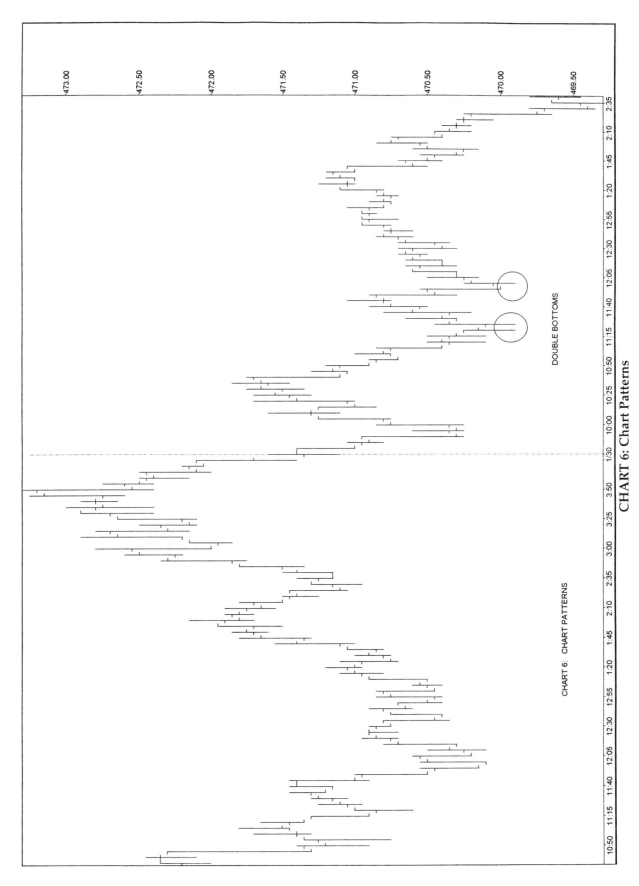

CHART 6: Chart Patterns

Chart created with TradeStation™ by Omega Research, Inc.

76

and shoulders reversal patterns. A double bottom is formed when a previous low is again tested and the market fails to penetrate that price level (Chart 6).

There are many other patterns which form recognizable pictures, and they are used by traders to good effect in conjunction with technical indicators.

## Technical Indicators

Charting indicators, the "guts" of technical analysis, are supplied in every good charting package inside of easily accessible indicator libraries. Indicators are created from mathematical functions that are programmed into the software. They can be plotted either as an overlay—laying on top of the price bars or candlesticks—or in a subgraph under the bars. They take the form of lines, histograms (vertical bars), points, crosses, or whatever styles you choose to plot it in, according to what your software provides. There are many kinds of indicators, some with very fancy names. All of them measure specific characteristics of price over time, with the goal of "indicating" future market activity (price momentum, direction, etc). Besides choosing the particular style for each indicator, the user can also set the *parameters* or *inputs* of each indicator. These are variables like the time lengths over which the indicator is active and the percentage levels for oscillator lines (see *stochastic* below). The charting software usually sets default values for every characteristic of each indicator, based on its most common use.

When the indication of an indicator or group of indicators shows market activity clearly enough at any point in time, good charting software can be programmed to visually or audibly (or both) signal the trader at that moment, who can then buy or sell the market by calling his broker and placing the order.

What a trader is always looking for is a *leading* indicator (or rather, the *ultimate* leading indicator) or group of indicators that will give a clear and correct prediction of future market activity. *Lagging* indicators are also widely used, however still with the intention of predicting future market activity (see *moving averages* below). Sometimes an indicator will act as an effective predictor, and sometimes the same indicator will fail to correctly indicate future price activity. Let's see how this can happen.

## Trends and Countertrends

Chart 7 shows a five-minute bar chart of the S&P 500 index futures with a stochastics indicator plotted in a subgraph. *Stochastics* indicate overbought and oversold conditions in the market. It is programmed here in such a way (using the single plot "Fast D" line) that when the indicator rises above the 80% line, the market price is considered to be overbought, based on the last fourteen bars, and may reverse and go down soon. And when it goes below 20%, the stochastic is indicating that the market is considered to be oversold and may reverse and go up soon. In other words, above 80% and below 20%, the stochastic is warning of a possible imminent reversal in market direction. For example, in Chart 7 we can see the two times the stochastic indicator went above 80%, which corresponded each time to one of the highest bars in the respective circles. When the indicator

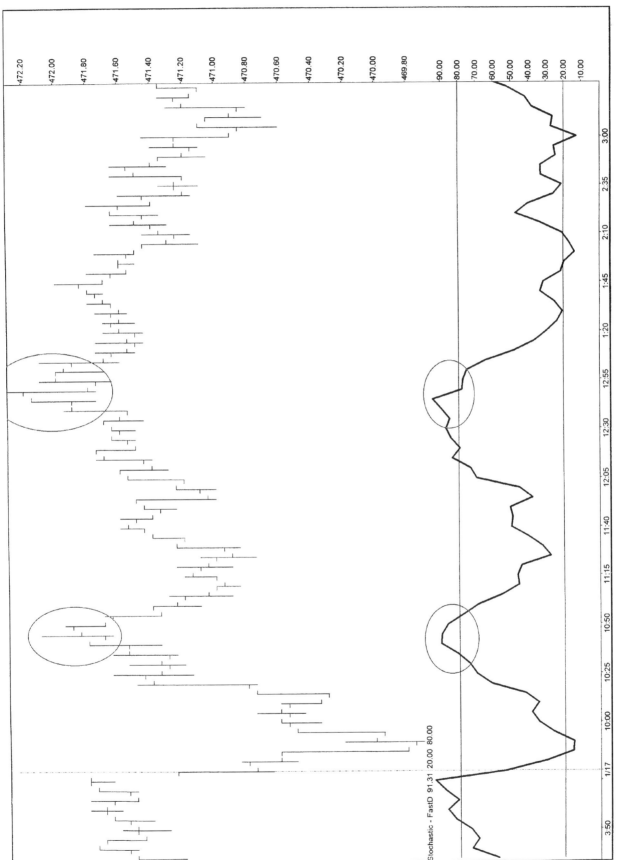

**CHART 7: Bar Chart with Stochastic Indicator Plotted in Subgraph**

Chart created with TradeStation™ by Omega Research, Inc.

79

again dipped below 80%, the price did reverse direction soon after, from its overbought condition—both times. In these cases, the stochastic acted as a true leading indicator of future price.

So does this mean that every time we see the stochastic peaking above 80% or dipping to a valley below 20% we should immediately sell or buy on this indication?

We all wish it was that simple. It worked well in Chart 7, but check out Chart 8. Here we see that although the stochastic went above 80% and dipped below, the price did not follow that stochastics indication, but instead kept rising and rising, remaining overbought. In this case, the stochastic failed as a leading indicator. Why?

The answer is that certain indicators tend to work better in trending markets and other indicators work better in countertrending markets. *Trending* markets refer to markets that are either rising or falling significantly in a clear direction over time (i.e., the price is on the rising or falling side of a major wave pattern); *countertrending* markets are markets trading up and down within a relatively narrow sideways range (or wavelet pattern). Chart 8 shows a major trending market: a major upward wave comprised of retracing wavelets. Chart 7 shows a sideways countertrending market.

Countertrending markets are also known as *oscillating* markets. Being an oscillating indicator, stochastics work well in this kind of seesaw market where there is no established up or down trending direction. In Chart 8, on the other hand, where the stochastic remained basically pinned above 80% in an overbought condition, the market was clearly trending. This made the stochastics apparently useless as a leading indicator of change in market direction.

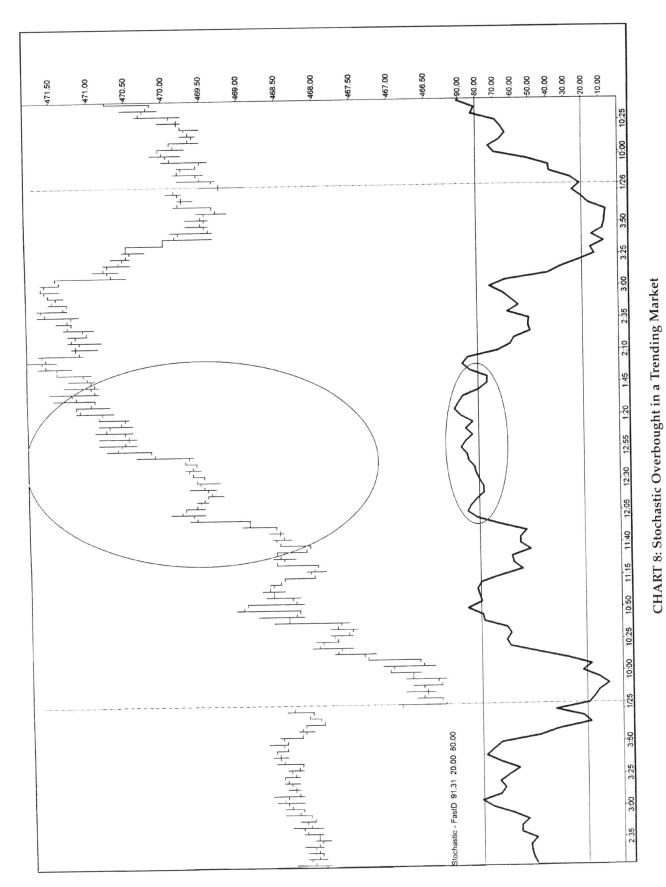

**CHART 8: Stochastic Overbought in a Trending Market**

Stochastic - FastD 91.31 20.00 80.00

Chart created with TradeStation™ by Omega Research, Inc.

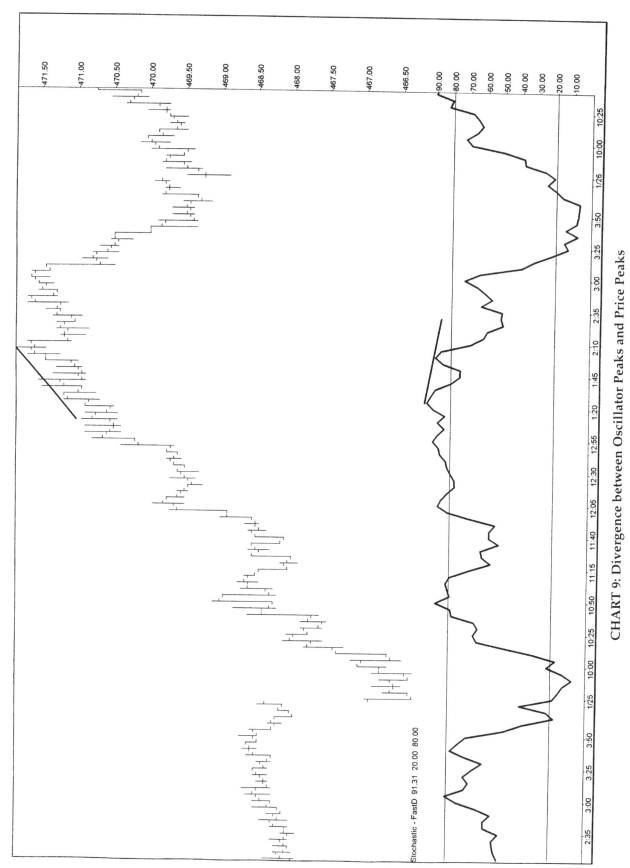

**CHART 9: Divergence between Oscillator Peaks and Price Peaks**

Chart created with TradeStation™ by Omega Research, Inc.

82

Does this mean that stochastics are useless in trending markets? No; but that definitely depends on how we analyze them. If we apply them to trending markets, but only look at them in their simplest aspect—as we would if we were in a clearly countertrending market—we'll get ourselves in trouble. To more effectively use this indicator, we need to take the analysis one step further.

A powerful way in which stochastic signals can be confirmed is by identifying their divergence from price extremes. *Divergence* is an important trading concept which can dramatically increase the statistical profitability of any oscillating indicator.

Double divergence occurs, for example, when two successive stochastic peaks above 80% indicate the opposite direction from their corresponding price peaks. In Chart 9 I have plotted lines joining price peaks—and their corresponding stochastic peaks above 80%—for the same trending market we analyzed in Chart 8. The two lines moving in opposite directions from one another is what we mean be divergence. In this case, the clear divergence of the stochastic line from the price line became an excellent leading indication of the end of the rally and the imminent reversal in the trend direction, i.e., toward the direction of the stochastic divergence line.

*Moving averages* (MAs) are traditionally used to help show a change in trend in a trending market. Although they actually lag the market, they work well in trending markets, especially when several are used in tandem. Traders often use crossovers of fast MAs over slower MAs to give buy and sell signals. A moving average is an average of prices over a specific number of time periods (time bars). MAs are generally based upon the closing price of each bar, although for some purposes they are

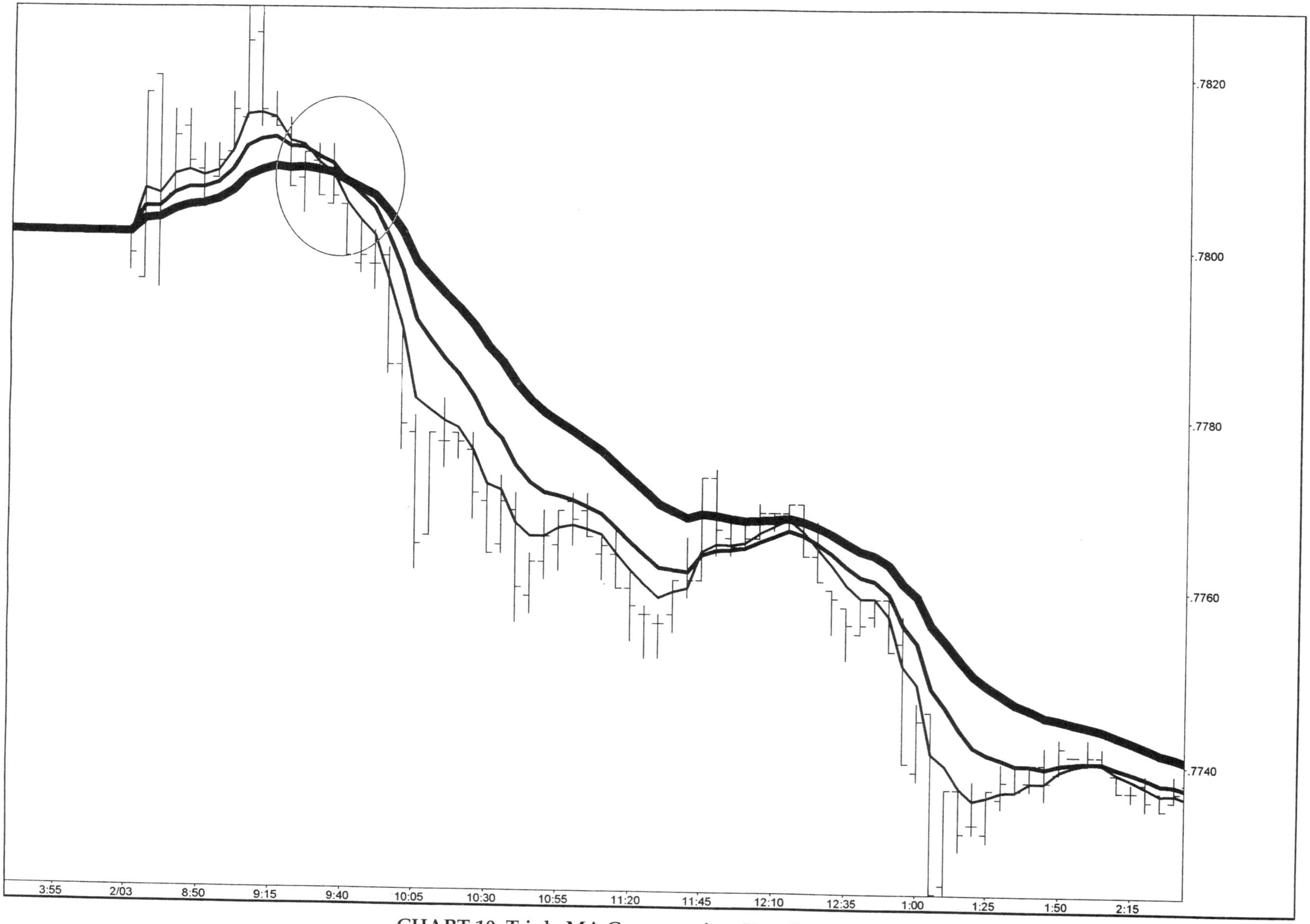

CHART 10: Triple MA Crossover in a Trending Market

Chart created with TradeStation™ by Omega Research, Inc.

84

based on the bar's high or low. They come in several forms: simple, weighted, and exponential are the most common. The various forms are plotted from calculations based upon how much emphasis is placed on recent bars relative to older bars. Chart 10 shows a five-minute bar chart of Swiss Franc futures onto which we have overlaid five-, ten-, and twenty-bar XMA (exponential moving averages) lines based on the bars' closing prices. The thickest line is the twenty-bar XMA, thinnest is the five-bar XMA. In the beginning of the day, we saw a rally which could have developed into a longer trend, but the triple MA crossover (circled) was a clear indication of a change in the major trend direction.

Moving averages do not work well in a sideways or counter-trending market. Since the MAs lag the market, the relatively rapid oscillations inherent in countertrending markets will result in *whipsawed* MA buy-sell signals: buying as the market is turning down, and selling as the market is moving up. The trader loses both ways in this case. However, in Chart 10 the triple MA crossover was clearly an effective signal, and the market developed into a powerful downward trending market.

So how do we determine when a market is trending or counter-trending, and how do we trade each market? Only through *confirmation*. Through a judicious combination of chart pattern recognition, technical indicators, and other tools and timing techniques described throughout this guide, we look for confirmation between as many indicators as possible before deciding (a) whether or not a market is trending and (b) whether or not to place our trades. More on this in upcoming chapters.

A good charting package's library of indicators should contain the above indicators plus the following (at least):

Accumulation Distribution

Bollinger Bands

Directional Movement Index

MACD: Moving Average Convergence Divergence

McClellan Oscillator

Momentum

Open Interest

Parabolic

Percent R

Price Channel

Rate of Change

RSI: Relative Strength Index

Up/Down Ticks

Volatility

Volume

# Things I Use[8]

You probably will not find the "Keltner" indicator in your package (it doesn't come standard in *TradeStation*), and in that case you may want to add it to your library as I did. Your tech-support people for your charting software should allow you to do this and have access to the default code for this indicator. Please see the Appendix for Omega *TradeStation's* default code for the Keltner channel.

I discovered the Keltner channel and other obscure formulas by investigating everything I could find in the way of technical indicators. Then I played with them, adjusted them, re-programmed them, added a number of algorithms, backtested them, and paper-traded them over thousands of hours until I found certain forms that worked best for me. For example, I always program center lines into price channels like the Keltner, since these central regions are important areas to focus on. Price channels are popular indicators which are designed to follow and adjust to the price movements. When the upper/lower channels are broken (a channel breakout), a new trend often begins in the direction of the breakout. The Keltner is a unique type of price channel in the way it is formulated: it uses moving averages and standard deviations from the price which makes it very responsive to price action. Of special interest is that with certain parameter values and algorithmic forms, market prices tend to move from top channel to bottom channel and back again throughout the day, or days, weeks, or months. This is useful for many reasons. For one, it gives us a price target: once the price has bounced off one channel, the target becomes the opposite side. Chart 11 shows price action inside of a Keltner channel. Note how the price tends to bounce from band to band. Another advantage of using the Keltner channel is the indication it gives not to necessarily buy a rally that is close to top band or to sell a bear market when it is near the bottom band. In other words, the Keltner cautions us that a price move may be nearly exhausted and that we should take a wait-and-see attitude. For example, in Chart 11 at 10:15 AM, we can see it would not have been a good idea to buy at that point; the price had just about reached a peak and was soon to reverse. The bar's position on the Keltner (near the top band) warned us of this possibility. Without using a price channel like this, we would have perhaps thought that we were entering a hot rally, just at the point the market was actually about to reverse. A third benefit

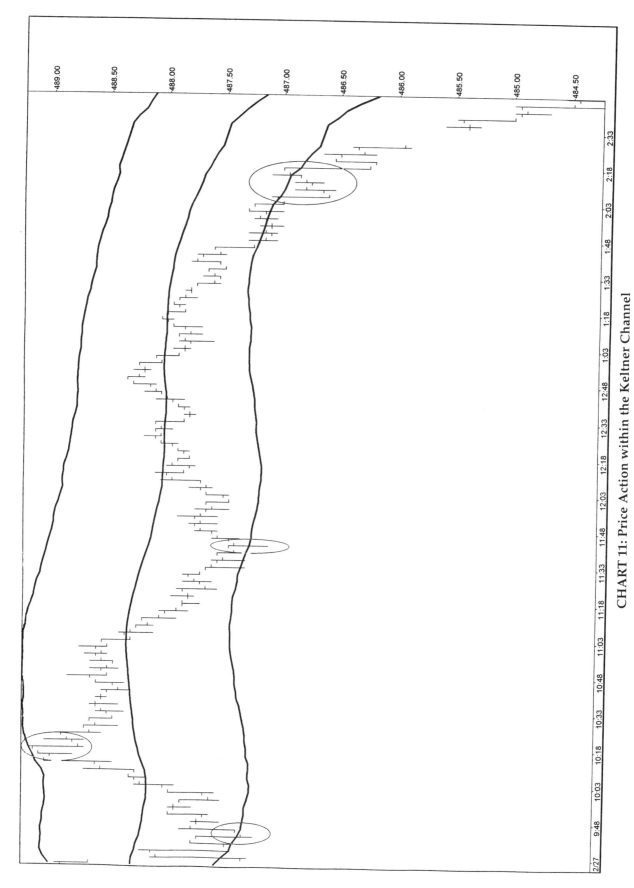

**CHART 11: Price Action within the Keltner Channel**

Chart created with TradeStation™ by Omega Research, Inc.

88

of the Keltner is that a breakout of its channel may indicate a strong move, stronger than for an ordinary price channel, and should be watched closely. Also important to note is the condition when prices are riding on top of or under outer bands. This can indicate a very strong market as well.

So should we simply sell off the top bounce and buy off the bottom? Let's analyze it. Although prices tend to travel from band to band, there is nothing stopping a strong market from blasting through either channel band. If we were to simply buy or sell off the band bounce, we could definitely get ourselves in trouble if the price broke through the band it just touched. How to deal with this?

We can take advantage of the fact that prices logically tend to spend most of their time near the central area of a price channel, *the average of the prices over time.* If we could devise a way to enter our trades from that central region, we would be able to (a) catch a price move in either north or south direction toward the outer bands, (b) be on the profitable, correct side of the trade (buying when the price is increasing and selling when it's decreasing—especially important when the market decides to break out of the top or bottom bands), and (c) still have time to exit the trade with a profit, should the market decide to bounce off the outer band and reverse direction.

So how can we know in which direction prices will tend to go from the central region? Well, the first step was to plot that center band for the Keltner that we saw in Chart 11. Then, to get an idea of the trend of the prices, it makes sense to use the most popular indicators of the trend as discussed earlier—moving averages. Chart 12 covers the same date and time as that of Chart

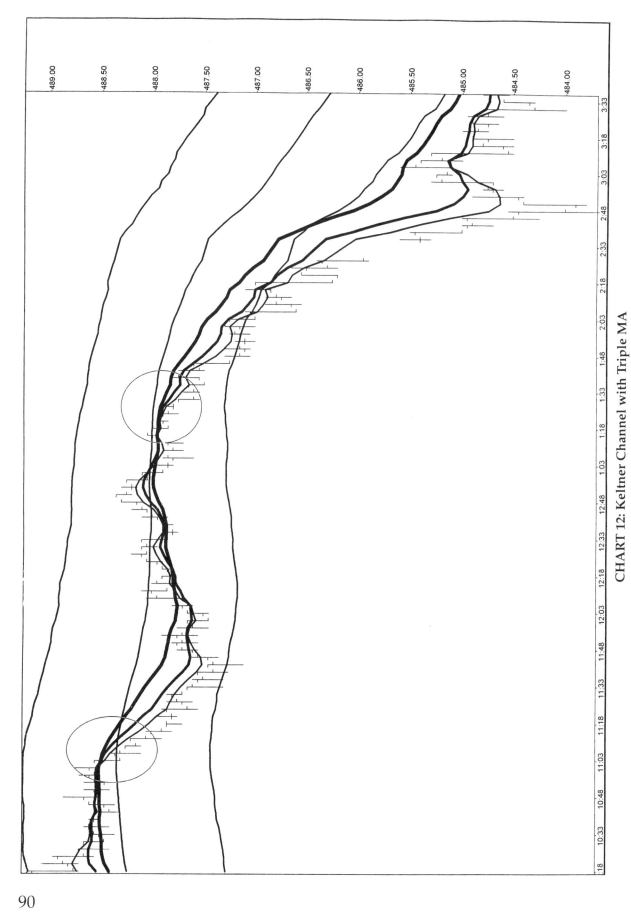

CHART 12: Keltner Channel with Triple MA

489.00
488.50
488.00
487.50
487.00
486.50
486.00
485.50
485.00
484.50
484.00

10:33 10:48 11:03 11:18 11:33 11:48 12:03 12:18 12:33 12:48 1:03 1:18 1:33 1:48 2:03 2:18 2:33 2:48 3:03 3:18 3:33

Chart created with TradeStation™ by Omega Research, Inc.

11, but now we have a 3-band Keltner plus a series of moving averages—a triple moving average—overlaying the price. And now what we get is a much clearer picture of the situation. Let's see what happens when the faster moving averages crossover each other and then move below the center Keltner band. If we entered our trade at this point and placed a market order (see Chapter 7 for order placement options) to go short at 11:10 AM, we would have been filled at about 488.10. When we saw the price hit the bottom Keltner band at about 11:35 AM, we could have exited the trade by buying back the contract "at-the-market" to get an approximate fill of 487.40. This would have given us a profit of $350 in 25 minutes (this is a chart of the S&P 500 index futures where each price tick equals $.05 x 500 or $25). Of course, we could have waited a bit longer to see if the price might have broken through the bottom band, but in this trade we decided to play it safe. Since the price reached its standard outer Keltner target, we exited immediately when the price touched the lower band. Another exit strategy is simply to sell before the price makes it to the outer Keltner band, since there is no guarantee that the price will make it to the top or bottom band; it simply tends to do so statistically over time. But rather than just exiting quickly the moment we see some profit, or even when the price bar touches a band, a more successful exit strategy over time will have us watching our indicators for a signal of an imminent change in price momentum and direction. In this way we will not exit trades prematurely and will therefore stay in profitable trades longer.

Exit strategies include a triple MAs crossover after an outer Keltner price bounce. This can signal the end of a move (e.g., in

Chart 12 at 12:15 PM we can see such a crossover happening). We can further increase the effectiveness of our exit strategy by adding other indicators to the picture. ADX and DMI are sometimes used to signal both the beginning and end of a trend move. We can also look at the oscillator divergences from successive price highs or price lows during the trend move to signal an imminent market reversal, as illustrated earlier. A simple trend line can work great with the Keltner (see next section). Whichever strategy or strategies we employ, we should be aware that most of the successful traders out there understand that a good exit strategy is at least as important than the entry strategy, even though so many traders place special emphasis on when to get in. While entry strategy is definitely important, a profitable trade can quickly turn into losing trade if we don't know when to get out. Profits once gained must be protected. In addition to exit strategies, risk management and stop-loss placement are also vital to the protection of our profits. These are discussed in Chapter 9.

Again, *confirmation* is what we always look for among our trading indicators. If one indicator says buy, but others say don't, then we should consider waiting. The old wisdom states: When in doubt, stay out. We shouldn't be in the market if our methods don't strongly indicate we should be. The more indicators that we have agreeing with each other, the greater probability there is that our trading will be profitable over time. We can't expect every trade to be a winner—that is impossible. There is not a trader alive that doesn't have losing trades. What we want is a trading methodology that is statistically profitable over time. And technical indicators take us a long way in that direction.

# Technical Tools

Besides indicators and bar patterns recognition, there are other technical tools that assist the trader in helping to make that all important decision: Do I take this trade or pass it by? Two of the most important and popular of these tools, and available in any good charting package, are *trend lines* and *support/resistance lines.*

Chart 13 shows the same market, date, and time span as Chart 12, but in addition I have applied trend lines to the picture. Although some traders place trend lines right up against the price lows or highs, I have found that trend lines are best placed *several ticks above the highs* in a descending trend, and *several ticks below the lows* in an ascending trend. What we are looking for is a clear breakout from the market trend and a reversal in market direction. This breakout will give us indication (and confirmation for our other indicators) to either exit the trade we are in, or enter a trade in the new trend direction. We place the trend lines a distance above and below the prices in order to give the market "breathing room." Market action is dynamic, and we want to know the general trend direction of that action. Keeping our trend lines too close to that action can result in false breakouts through the lines, giving us false indications of the general market direction and losing whipsawed trades.

The breakout of the trend line in Chart 13 at 11:50 AM was again confirmed at 12:00 PM, when the low of the bar bounced off the trend line, using the line now as a point of support rather than resistance. This was an excellent indication that the downward trend in this trade was probably over, and it would be a

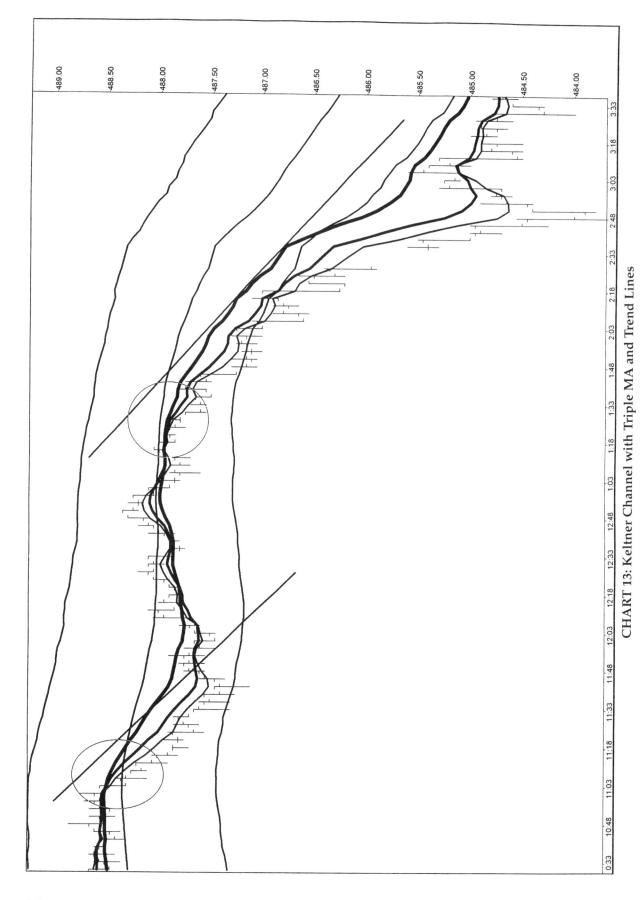

**CHART 13: Keltner Channel with Triple MA and Trend Lines**

Chart created with TradeStation™ by Omega Research, Inc.

good time to exit that first trade. The price had also just bounced off the bottom of the Keltner channel band—another statistically valid indication that the move was over. This is the type of indicator/indicator or indicator/tool confirmation we are always looking for in our trading.

The value of this confirmation strategy became even more profitably evident in the next circled trade. Let's say that we sold another contract at-the-market at about 1:25 PM and got filled at 487.75, after the triple moving averages crossed just below the center of the Keltner channel. We could have bought back the contract when the price again touched the bottom Keltner band—for a profit of about $500—and had we done that we would have made an excellent trade. No profit is too small!

But using our trend line confirmation strategy, since we don't want to exit our trade prematurely and do want to allow our profits to run—we decide to stay in the trade. Over the next few minutes we see the price bars straddling the bottom band, no doubt representing a fierce battle between the bulls and bears in the S&P pit. By sticking to our guns and holding on to the trade until it broke the trend line, we were ultimately and amply rewarded. The market didn't come close to our trend line; it finally blasted through the bottom Keltner band, plummeting down in a powerfully bearish trend. Had we bought back the contract when the market finally broke upwards through our trend line, our profit would have been approximately $1,500, or $1,000 more than we would have realized by simply exiting earlier when the bar first hit the bottom band.

Let's look at another example of the value of trading confirmation. On Chart 14, the day began with a strong upward move which penetrated the top Keltner band but failed to continue

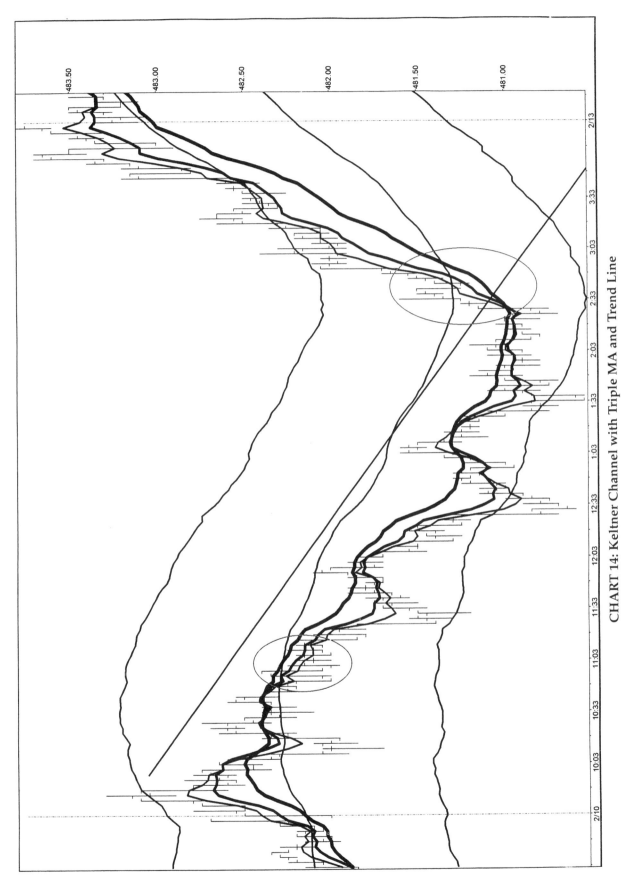

CHART 14: Keltner Channel with Triple MA and Trend Line

Chart created with TradeStation™ by Omega Research, Inc.

96

the move, falling as fast as it initially rose. This was the first sign of the impending market reversal.

We draw our trend line above the two highs of the day so far, at about 9:25 AM and 10:25 AM, and then extrapolate it forward. Good charting packages will allow you to activate the tool and enable it to keep extending itself automatically for you, keeping to its original trajectory. It is also helpful if your software can alert you audibly and visually when a bar breaks through the line. In this case, the bars continued downward after that first Keltner bounce and hovered near the center Keltner band. Selling one contract somewhere in the circled central Keltner region would have been a good idea since this market proceeded to move downward in perfect wavelets, coming close to the trend line but never breaking through until 2:30 PM. This became a perfect example of a downward trending market.

At 2:30 PM we had a very clear indication of when to exit our short trade, or *reverse* that short trade and go long. Not only did the price break through the trend line, but look where it happened: at the bottom region of our Keltner channel. In other words, the trend line breakout was confirmed by the price bounce off the bottom Keltner. We will see in Chapter 7 that there was a strong third confirmation to this breakout: the fact that it happened precisely at 2:30 PM, which is a Gann Time. In addition, very shortly thereafter we had a lagging indication of a trend change in the form of a clear triple MA crossover—a fourth confirmation.

The combination of all of these factors confirming each other would indicate that this trend breakout was leading not simply to a sideways countertrend, but to a strong market reversal and the creation of a new trend, this time "to the North." And this is

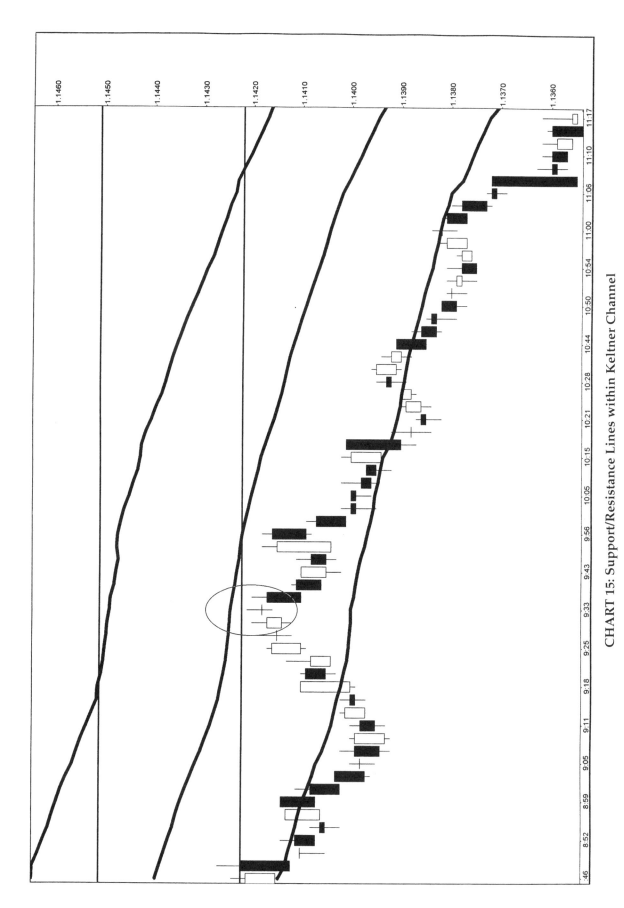

**CHART 15: Support/Resistance Lines within Keltner Channel**

Chart created with TradeStation™ by Omega Research, Inc.

98

exactly what happened. The new move after 2:30 PM shows a very strongly trending market (the slope of both trends gives an idea how much faster was the later day move: it traveled nearly the same distance as the "South" move, but did it more than twice as fast) right into the close of the day.

The clear confirmation of all these indicators and tools strongly predicted this move and was literally screaming for a buy order somewhere in the circled region following the trend line breakout. This day the S&P 500 index futures market traveled more than $2,000 per contract in these two major trend moves.

*Support/Resistance (S/R) lines* are another tool widely used by many traders. Based on Fibonacci ratios and market action over the previous day or days, trading tends to literally find support for further price increases on top of support lines, and to find resistance to the same under resistance lines. The market may test these levels throughout the day. If the market is strong enough to break through and close on the other side of a strong S/R line, it is a good indication that the prices will continue in that direction. In that case, a previous resistance line becomes a support line, and visa versa. The effect of these lines on the market tend to gradually decrease as they are repeatedly violated.

Chart 15 shows a market in which S/R lines were applied. The formulas for these S/R lines have proven themselves effective over time and comprise combinations of averages of the open, high, low, and close prices for the previous day's trading. Near the market's open (on the extreme left of the chart) we see the Japanese yen prices (depicted here in candlesticks) twice bouncing off the lower horizontal S/R line. This indicates that the line acted as resistance to further upward movement. Later, at 9:33 AM, a three-bar evening *doji* star formation occurred, which I have circled. This is a candlestick pattern that predicts a strong market reversal into a bear market. The central *doji* star part of the formation came within a single tick of the same S/R line and bounced off it. This third failure of a bar to close above that line confirmed again that this price level was a strong resistance point, which again indicates that this market may very soon reverse. As further confirmation of this, that downward bounce occurred just under the center Keltner band. The fourth confirmation of this turning point into a powerful downward trend would be a triple MA crossover, which certainly did occur a few bars later but was not plotted in this chart.

Again, the combination of all of these indicator and tool confirmations would have made the placement of a market order to go short near the circled area a very profitable one, especially if a trend line were added to improve our exit strategy.

Other essential tools your charting software should support are:

Alerts

Chart status

Cycle lines

Ellipse, rectangle

Erase

Fibonacci cycle lines

Gann Fan

Horizontal lines

Percent retracement

Speed/Resistance

Support/Resistance

Write

Zoom in/ out all/ out partial

Time has shown that the three most important rules that a trader should abide by are (a) Follow the Trend, (b) Let Your Profits Run, and (c) Cut Your Losses. This is easier said than done, but the closer our trading strategies and actions take us to these ideals, the more successful we will become. Indicators and tools (and well-designed systems) are the main technical weaponry of the chart-oriented trader. As we have seen, they enable us to read the market's intentions and to let us hear the market when it tells us where it wants to go. They allow us to trade *with* the market. This is the only way to trade successfully. Trading against the market has been likened to standing in front of a freight train. Except for certain types of options trading, discussed later, such a strategy can leave a trader rather bloody. We need to keep catching those sweet rides on that trending freight train, and we do that through consistent confirmational trading.

Also critical to the trader's success is knowing *when* to wield his trading weapons, and we have touched upon this issue. The next chapter deals further with that force of nature upon which rests the very destiny of our lives, be us traders or (wax) candlestick makers—time.

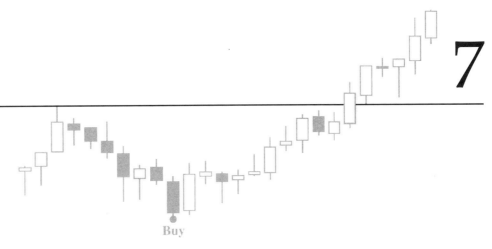

# TIMING
# IS EVERYTHING

For the trader, there is perhaps nothing so critical than how he deals with time. Time can be a tool or the end—the nemesis or the friend. Time directly determines the extent of our profits and losses through our own decision of when to pull the trigger to enter a trade, and when to pull the trigger to exit it. Let's look at some ways in which time enters the picture.

## Trading Time Frames:
## What Time of Trader are You?

The question of time and timing confronts the trader long before that first trade is made. Every trader must first consider the question: What kind of trader will I be? Or more specifically, how long do I intend to hold onto each trade? For weeks, months, years? For hours (or seconds)? For a day or two? The choices of timing in this sense boil down to three, and traders are known by these basic time lengths in which the vast majority of their trades last. We can be position (or long-term) traders, short-term traders, or daytraders, and there are some very compelling economic and psychological reasons why we tend to specialize in one time frame. Let's look at some of the advantages and disadvantages inherent in each:

(a) Position or long-term trading:  Traders who stay in a trade without liquidating or offsetting it for more than approximately three days are called position traders. I am broadening the category here to include what some call "intermediate traders," who may hold on to trades for six to ten days. There is no upper limit to how long a position trader can hold on to a trade, although you would find the majority of positions lasting from several weeks to several months. Some of the advantages of position trading are that there is comparatively more time to make the trading decision than in the other time frames, and since "at-the-market" orders are usually not necessary, better order fills may be experienced (see "Order Placement" below). There is also little chance of being whipsawed in a wild intraday price swing, since longer time frame charts are being used: daily, weekly, and monthly charts. Position traders also feel that chart patterns are easier to see and analyze in the long term than in the short term. Therefore, position traders say that they are able to stay in each trade longer and capitalize better on a major trend move. They also take less trades than short-term traders, which translates into less money spent on the required broker commissions. And because of the longer time frames, most position traders feel they have no need for real-time quotes, or even delayed quotes. Some don't use computers at all, but instead analyze the charts that are available from chart publishing companies. Therefore their monthly trading cost overhead is significantly less than it is for real-time traders.

Some disadvantages of this time frame are that wider stop-loss orders must be placed than in the shorter term. If you are using protective price stops and the market moves against you, the longer time frames involved mean that the price must travel further to reach your stop-loss point, and therefore your loss per stopped-out trade will tend to be greater than in the shorter term; i.e., a daily bar covers a lot more price distance than a five-minute bar. Another disadvantage is the overnight exposure that the trade is subject to. International trading and global events overnight often lead to a large price gap on the next day's opening, and that price move may not be in your favor. Another problem is that the margin requirements from the clearing houses, and by extension from your FCM, for keeping trades active overnight are considerably greater than for trades entered and exited on the same day; i.e., you need to keep a significantly larger account balance with your FCM.

(b) Short-term trading involves holding onto positions for one to approximately three days. These traders experience basically the same advantages and disadvantages that long-term traders experience—including those attributed to overnight exposure—although some advantages of intraday trading may surface here. Some short-term traders look at shorter time periods like fifteen- or thirty-minute bars to time their entries and exits. They want to see more action than their longer-term counterparts and tend to put on more trades.

(c) (Intra) Daytrading means that a trade is both entered and exited on the same day and not held overnight. This type of trading turns the trading experience into more of a full-time vocation than an investment avocation. There are some daytraders who use intraday systems that simply require them to phone in buy or sell stop orders at the market's open, or just before. If their price stop is hit, their broker will have been instructed to place a stop-loss order on the risk side to limit any loss and a stop order on the reward side to get out of the market with a profit. They may also exit the trade at the end of the day with an MOC order (Market on Close). After placing their daily orders in the morning, these daytraders then go off to work day jobs.

Most daytraders don't trade like this, however. As their experience grows and their trading becomes more and more lucrative, daytrading becomes their day job. They usually feel a need to be involved with every trade and to watch it develop in real-time on their own computer screens. They feel they can have a greater sense of control by watching the live market action. Experience shows that they will be better able to limit their losses and discover more profitable trading opportunities if they "stay on top" of the action themselves. I obviously agree with this, since I happen to be one of these folks.

Specifically, some of the advantages of daytrading include (a) the elimination of overnight exposure which eliminates the risk from the same. This translates into lower margin requirements and lower account balance requirements from your broker. For example, the margin requirements to daytrade the S&P 500 futures contract is currently $4,750 per contract from my broker. Keeping the same contract overnight requires a margin of over $14,000 per contract. A rough estimate is that overnight trading will increase the margin requirements of most futures contracts by three to four times that required for daytrading the same market; (b) the allowance for tight protective stops limiting the losses per stopped-out trade, since the time frames and bars are so short; and (c) the real-time vision of the market forces at play and ability to immediately take advantage of trading opportunities throughout the day. By trading liquid markets that display sufficient volatility and basic trending characteristics, the experienced daytrader can accumulate significant profits often on a daily basis. He can take advantage of the many smaller intraday trends (wavelets) comprising the larger and longer term uptrends or downtrends (waves).

The long-term trader is not able to take advantage of these intraday price swings. In fact, he can't even see them or be aware of them if he is looking at only daily and weekly bars. Therefore, the theoretical potential for overall profits can be greater in daytrading than for other trading time frames, simply due to the greater number of trading opportunities and buy/sell signals that are issued. I say "theoretical potential" because daytrading can be one of the most challenging trading time frames in which to trade. The potential is there without doubt—all that is required for the daytrader is to find those trading opportunities, pull the trigger, trade with the trend, cut his losses, and let his profits run. Simple. Surprisingly, what can make it difficult sometimes is not the markets, or the broker, or the trading methodology; it's that when the signal says "act," the daytrader must ACT, and act NOW! And there is not a daytrader alive that hasn't experienced a period of trading hesitation (we'll discuss that when we talk about trading psychology). It is said that trading is 80% mental and 20% everything else, and this fact is usually experienced more by the daytrader. However, if the essential mind-set is developed, then daytrading can definitely be considered the most profitable of all trading time frames.

Some disadvantages for serious daytraders are the higher overhead costs for real-time charting software and real-time data vendors and the need for real-time dedication. Real-time analysis means real time in front of the screen. Of course, a daytrader certainly doesn't have to trade every day, nor be glued to the screen from market open to market close. At the same time, you can't find those buy/sell intraday opportunities if you're not there, or at least in earshot distance of any audible alerts you may have set up. By virtue of the trading time frame itself, the need for a greater time commitment is a given.

And how does stress factor into all this? We'll talk more about this when we discuss trader psychology later, but a couple of things can be said about stress and the different kinds of traders just discussed. While there may be less stress for the position trader and perhaps the short-term trader in the ordering process, the stress induced from keeping overnight positions can more than compensate. Keeping an overnight position is known in the industry as "taking it home," and that's exactly what can happen. You can take that trade right into bed with you. That's one problem the daytrader doesn't have. He may have won or lost during the day, but after those results have been digested by dinnertime, the daytrader can at least get some peaceful rest at night. I am not saying that position traders and short-term traders can't sleep, but the risk of overnight exposure clearly exists, and it is the psychology of the trader that determines how that reality is handled. (Note: There are FCM services that will trade your daytrading methodology for you if your methods can be reduced to a series of easily followed rules. They charge for this service on top of their standard commission fees. For myself, I still prefer to be doing the trigger-pulling.)

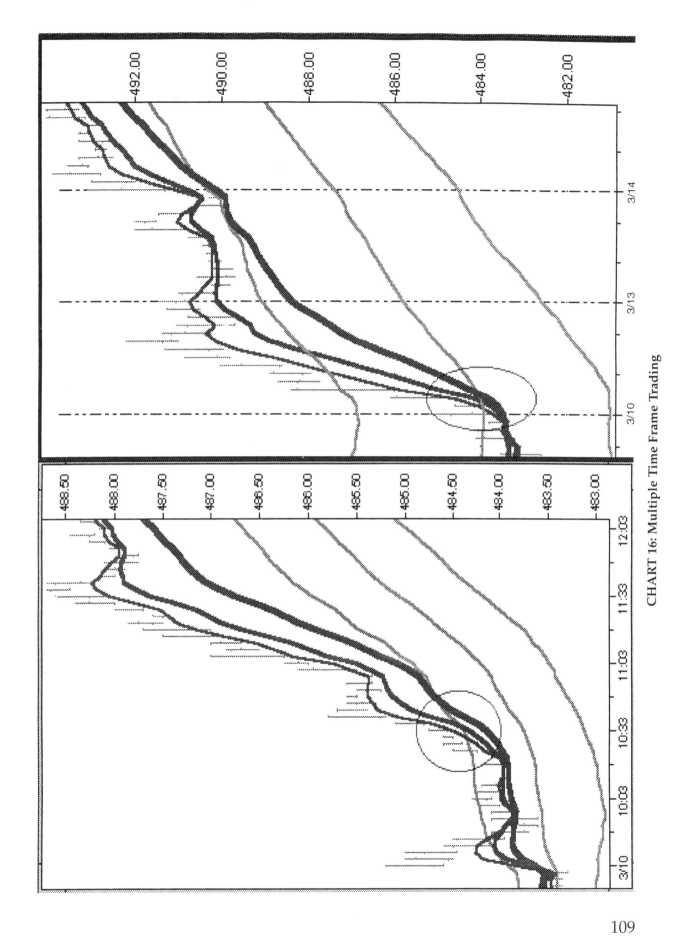

CHART 16: Multiple Time Frame Trading

Chart created with TradeStation™ by Omega Research, Inc.

109

# Charting Time Frames: Time As a Tool

We've seen earlier that a combination of technical and fundamental perspectives on trading can give us a broader view on trading than either method alone. In the same way, within the technical side itself, analyzing market activity in different time frames can give us a much clearer idea of future market action than viewing one time frame alone.

Chart 16 is actually a split chart: on the left is a three-minute chart of the S&P 500, on the right a thirty-minute chart of the same market. At about 10:20 AM, in the circled area on the left chart, we see a strong upward move of prices and triple MAs breaking through the top Keltner band. We could certainly put in a trade right here, but to feel even more confident about taking the trade, and to gain a broader perspective on what might become of it, it always pays to get further confirmation by viewing the intended trade in multiple time frames. Checking the same market in longer time frames—while using the same indicators that we are using in the shorter time frames—allows us to compare price bar/indicator positioning and indicator action, so as to better "see the forest for the trees." Both short and long time frames should ideally confirm each other and the trade. The idea is to *always try to take your short-term entry in the long-term trend direction.* We had strong multiple time frame confirmation in this case. Just as the price was blasting through the top Keltner band on the three-minute chart, it was simultaneously rocketing off from the center Keltner band on the thirty-minute chart (circled). The smooth arching formation of the moving averages and the perfect positioning of the prices on the top and central regions of the Keltner in both time frames was all the confirmation we could ask for that a powerful new trend was in evidence, and a market order to buy one or more contracts at this point might be a fine idea.

Experienced daytraders usually take a look at a number of these different time frames before pulling the trigger, such as three-, five-, fifteen-, thirty-minute, hourly, daily, and even weekly charts. Often they will see a promising formation shaping up in the longer time frame first and then examine shorter and shorter time frames for a precise entry point. Others do it the other way around. However it is approached, pulling back to get the big "time-picture" is a smart habit that you definitely want to cultivate. It is one of the most important ways by which you can confirm your trades, help you capture the best winners, filter out most of the losers, and statistically turn yourself into a much more profitable trader.

## Order Placement: Timing the Trigger

Tables 14 and 15 explain the more common types of orders that can be placed with your broker and some of the ways in which they are used. Some traders use a variety of orders, some focus on one type; the strategy used determines the type of order placed. For example, some trading methodologies exclusively utilize market orders and keep you in the market all the time, capitalizing on the up and down price swings throughout the day. In an uptrend breakout, a buy signal is issued instructing the trader to buy one contract "at-the-market" in order to get the fill as close to the trend breakout as possible. Then after the top of the move, at the downward trend breakout, the system will instruct an immediate reversal order. This means you

TABLE 14

# ORDER-PLACING GUIDE**

| Type of Order | Must Specify+ | What it Means | Duration | Best Use | Placement | Example |
|---|---|---|---|---|---|---|
| Market Order | 1. Buy or Sell<br>2. Number of contracts*<br>3. Commodity<br>4. Month/Yr. | Buy or sell now, regardless of price. | Good only for the current day. | Liquid Markets for quick entry or exit. | N/A | "I want to sell 5 Mar. T-Bonds at the market." |
| Stop Order | 1. Buy or Sell<br>2. Number of contracts*<br>3. Commodity<br>4. Month/Yr.<br>5. Stop price | Buy or sell at the market, but not until the bid or asked price reaches the stop price. | Good only for the current day unless specified otherwise.++ | To enter or exit when the market trend reverses. To enter or exit when the market establishes a trend beyond a support or resistance level. | Buy stop entered above the current market price. Sell stop entered below the current market price. | "I want to buy 3 June Eurodollars at 93.35 stop." (Current market price is 93.25.) |
| Market-if-touched (MIT) | 1. Buy or Sell<br>2. Number of contracts*<br>3. Commodity<br>4. Month/Yr.<br>5. MIT price | Buy or sell at the market, but not until the bid or asked price reaches the MIT price. | Good only for the current day unless specified otherwise.++ | To enter or exit the market in anticipation of a trend change. | Buy MIT entered below the current market price. Sell MIT entered above the current market price. | "I want to buy 2 June S&P at 464.25 MIT." (Current market price is 464.50.) |

# TABLE 15

## ORDER-PLACING GUIDE (cont.)

| | Order Components | Description | Duration | Usage | Market Placement | Example |
|---|---|---|---|---|---|---|
| Limit Order | 1. Buy or Sell<br>2. Number of contracts*<br>3. Commodity<br>4. Month/Yr.<br>5. Limit price | Buy or sell at the stated price or better. | Good only for the current day unless specified otherwise.++ | To enter or exit the market when price is more important than time. To enter or exit thinly traded markets. | Buy limit usually entered below current market price. Sell limit usually entered above current market price. | "I want to sell 4 Sept. DMarks at .6650." (Current market price is .6691.) |
| Stop Limit Order | 1. Buy or Sell<br>2. Number of contracts*<br>3. Commodity<br>4. Month/Yr.<br>5. Stop Price<br>6. Limit Price | Buy or sell at the limit price or better, but not until the bid or asked price reaches the stop price. | Good only for the current day unless specified otherwise.++ | To enter or exit a fast-moving market when awaiting a market signal, but unwilling to accept a price "worse" than your limit price. | Buy stop limit entered above current market price. Sell stop limit entered below current market price. | "I want to sell 5 Dec. T-Bills at 93.92 stop limit," or "I want to sell 5 Dec. T-Bills at 93.92 stop 93.87 limit." (Current market price is 94.44.) |

* For orders to buy or sell any grain, the order is stated in thousands of bushels, not in number of contracts. A CBT order to buy 5 Nov. Soybeans at the market is an order for 5,000 bu., or 1 contract. At the MACE, contracts are for 1,000 bushels.

**Not all types of orders are accepted at all exchanges—consult your broker for details. In an official exchange fast market condition, brokers are not held liable to fill any kind of order.

+ Always listen carefully to the broker taking your order when he repeats it back to you to make sure he has understood it correctly.

++Be sure to cancel GTC (open) orders when they no longer apply.

The information in this publication was compiled from sources considered reliable. There is no expressed or implied warranty as to the accuracy or completeness of the material. All information is subject to change without notice. Not all contracts traded have FN, LT, CS, or OE dates shown. ©1995, Center for Futures Education. Inc., Grove City, PA 16127. All rights reserved.

would sell two contracts at-the-market, offsetting your long with one of the sell orders (and locking in the profits from that trade), leaving the other sold contract free to accumulate profits in the down trending direction. Ideally, by repeatedly reversing positions like this, one can profit by staying in the market all day long.

Stop orders have many uses: they can get you into a market at a certain price, can act as protective orders (stop-loss) to define the extent of a loss when placed at a price point in the opposite to your profit direction, or they can be placed at a price point in your profit direction to get you out of the market at a profit. Using calculated stop-loss orders is the basis of good risk management described later. (Note: Don't forget to immediately tell your broker to "straight cancel" any and all stop orders that you don't want to keep active in the markets. Always keep a record of your orders! A sample of our "Daily Trading Log" is provided in the Appendix, which you can freely photocopy and use.)

Other methodologies use a judicious combination of different types of orders, depending on market conditions. It is important to become familiar with each of them and how they may best be used to your advantage.

## Gann Time

Like Elliot and Fibonacci before him, W. D. Gann was another market analyst who discovered unique repetitive patterns and cycles in markets. You may recall from the list of recommended technical indicators that the Gann Fan is one of them. Like Fibonacci Ratio Analysis, the Gann Fan spreads out into

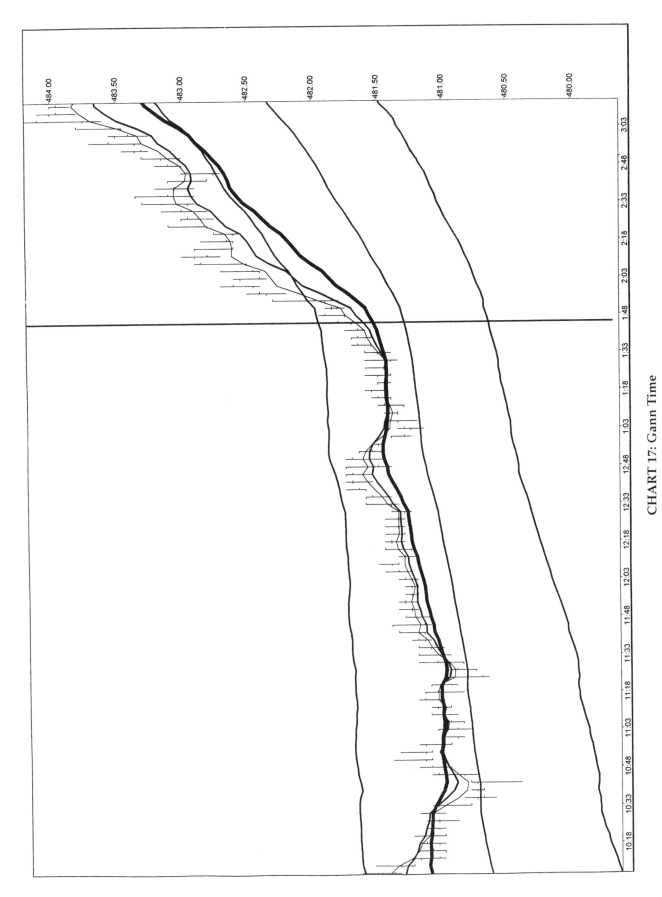

**CHART 17: Gann Time**

Chart created with TradeStation™ by Omega Research, Inc.

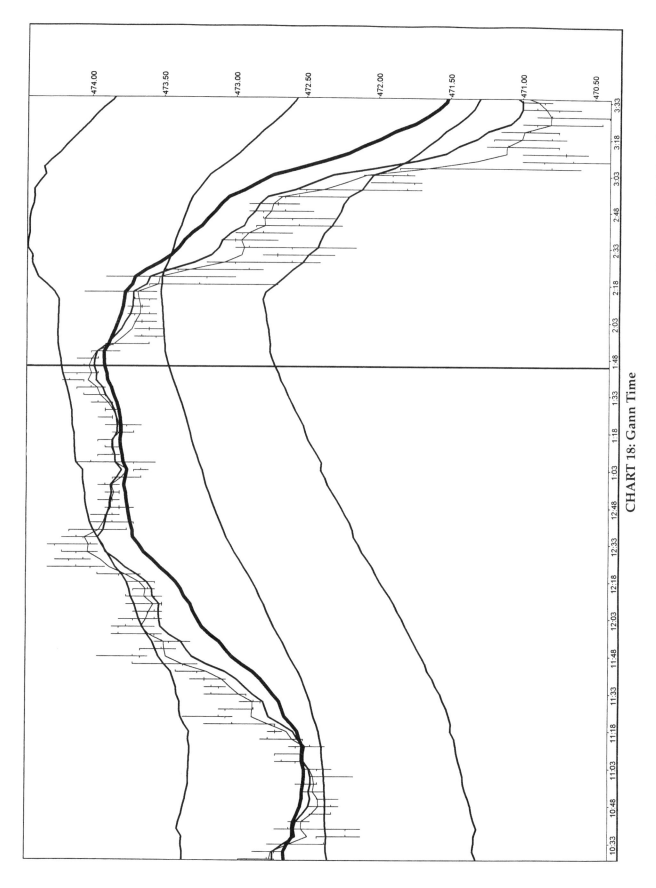

**CHART 18: Gann Time**

Chart created with TradeStation™ by Omega Research, Inc.

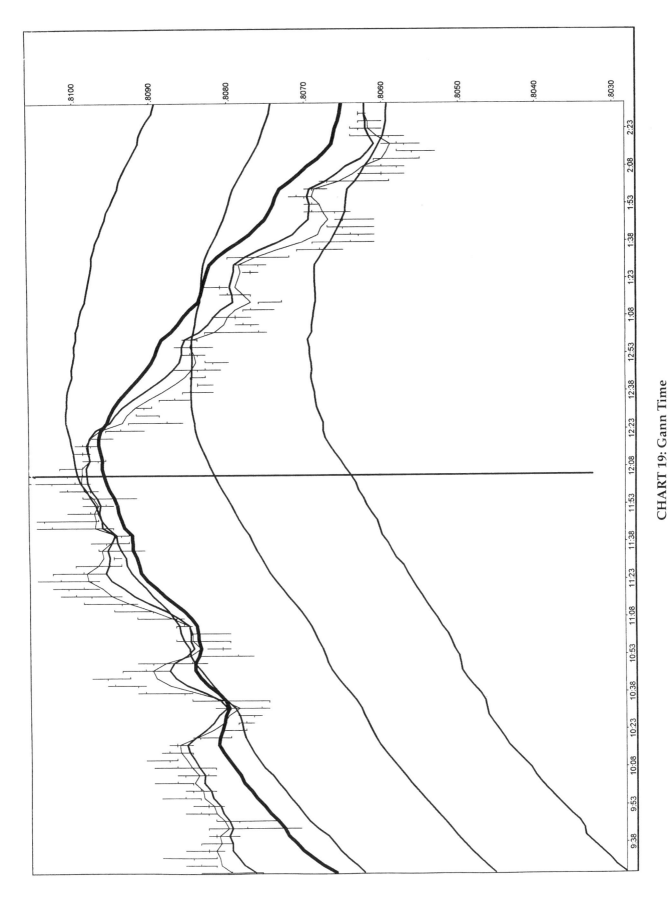

**CHART 19: Gann Time**

Chart created with TradeStation™ by Omega Research, Inc.

117

lines that act as support and resistance areas for the market.

One other way in which professional traders use Gann numbers is by splitting the market day into Gann intervals, a specific Gann number of time segments. Important Gann Times include 10:20 AM, 12:05 PM, 1:45 PM and 2:30 PM EST.

Let's go back to Chart 14. If you remember, at 2:30 PM we had many confirmations that the market trend was about to reverse. My experience is that one of the strongest Gann Times is during this 2:30 PM / 2:35 PM EST interval. Any market can be divided into Gann times like this.

Gann time represents a tendency for markets either to change direction or move with greater momentum in their current direction. It is just one more indicator to watch for confirmation of one's trading decision. Charts 17, 18, and 19 show market activity at Gann times (represented by a vertical line within the chart).

## Times to Trade—Times Not to Trade

**Gaps.** Although "Gaps are filled" is a valued maxim in futures trading, the manner in which gaps tend to skew the predictive qualities of indicators makes many traders wary of trading immediately after a market gaps on the opening bar. System traders usually wait about ten or fifteen minutes after a gap to trust any signals their methodology might give. After this period however, or if the market does not gap open in the morning, the time period from the open to approximately lunchtime (9:30 AM–11:30 AM EST) is one of the very best times to trade. (Note: Times in this section refer to the S&P 500 index futures, but can be extrapolated to any market.) Markets tend to be most liquid in the morning, as most traders are eager to find a predominant trend for the day and jump on board. If a trend is to develop it generally does happen in the morning. Signals issued from traders' systems tend to give purer and cleaner signals during this early trading period.

**Government Reports.** The time  just before, during, and immediately following a government report is considered by many to be a dangerous time to trade. There can often be wild and conflicting reactions at the moment these reports are broadcast to the monitors and boards on the exchange floors. Violent price movements may result—which can just as quickly reverse—when those same traders who caused the original price action study the numbers more closely, only to find out that their first reaction may have not only been exaggerated, but dead wrong! Chapter 11 discusses more about these closely-watched reports and their effects on the markets.

**Lunchtime.**  Traders, like most people, eat. Lunchtime is traditionally a slow trading time, and the period from approximately 11:30 AM to 1:30 PM EST has been termed "the death zone." This ghastly nomenclature derives from the same danger that arises in any lightly-traded market: illiquidity. Even though a system may issue a good-looking signal at this time, if the market has few participants there will be little momentum to carry the market in the direction of that signal. The result may be either a bad fill, or a market drifting in the wrong direction, or both. Again, this is certainly not always the case; we are talking about statistical tendencies. The market picks up again after lunchtime, and the Gann time following this slow period can become the spark that lights an afternoon trend formation. From approximately 1:45 PM to the market close at 4:15 PM is considered a good time to trade. One must take care when initiating trades during the last fifteen minutes of trading, since markets can get a bit wild during this time. Exiting trades is another issue: The last minutes of trading can be the most liquid period of the trading day, so traders often find that waiting to exit their trade until the market close, i.e., putting in an MOC (Market on Close) order, is more profitable than taking a slightly earlier exit.

**Holidays.** Holiday cycles have been studied by some traders who claim to have discovered certain statistically significant patterns of market activity just before and after holidays like Labor Day, Thanksgiving, and Christmas. I do not find these reliable enough to trade with, however. For the most part, trading activity leading up to these holidays tends to be listless, as most major players "close their books" prior to these days and cease market participation. Floor traders commenting on trading activity during these periods use phrases like "typical preholiday light trading activity." What we are left with, again, is illiquidity. It's a bad trading environment. Best to simply relax and enjoy the holidays and start trading again when they are over.

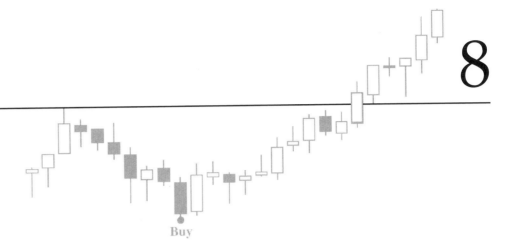

# THE MARKETS

## What to trade?

Winnipeg barley futures and Italian Government Bond futures. Sour crude oil futures and cheddar cheese futures. The Japanese Nikkei 225 Index, spring wheat, random length lumber, and pure platinum. Traders have a staggering variety of commodities markets to choose from. They are classified into general groups like the ags (agriculturals), financials, metals, equities, currencies, interest rates, energies and softs. All told, there are currently more than six hundred fifty different futures contracts that can be traded on seventy exchanges worldwide. Aside from the sheer numbers, it is equally staggering to realize that the choice of which futures contract to trade is one of the most important decisions a trader can make. So how to decide?

Here are some of the considerations:

The trader needs to determine the basic trading time frame he prefers, and that, in no small part, will depend on his financial resources. The overnight margin requirements for the contracts, his own temperament, how often he wants to trade, how closely he wants to track his investments—these and other personal considerations often combine to decide the trader's basic trading time frame for him. As a first step, especially in the case of short-term or long-term traders, market choices can often be narrowed considerably, simply by checking into their overnight margin requirements. Margin requirements are broken down into initial requirements and maintenance requirements (the amount required in your account to keep a position open). The minimum margins may be increased at any time by your broker if the price of the commodity has changed or if increased volatility of the market warrants it. This information is provided from your broker in its current listing of available contracts. Other financial considerations in choosing a market include the size of the contract in dollars, bushels, ounces, pounds, and so on; how prices are quoted; the minimum price fluctuation (tick size) and the corresponding dollar value; and its daily trading limits (the maximum amount the price can change from the previous day's close before it locks limit up or down). The trader must also know what are the delivery months for the contract and its expiration dates. Unless traders are trading spreads between the nearby (front) month and outer (back) month, most traders find that the best trading opportunities occur when they trade the front month, which is always the closest delivery month to the current date. The trader must keep himself aware of the expiry or delivery date of the front month and make sure he has closed all positions in the contract prior to that date. If somehow this is not done, he will be responsible for taking the delivery and paying the full amount due on the commodity, or providing delivery for same. Since we never want this to happen, it bears repeating that you must be aware of your delivery months and dates (your broker knows these dates). The trader must also know, of course, what are the daily trading hours of the contract and then make sure he keeps up on any changes to the same, including holiday schedules. Much of this market information is listed for you in the specification tables in Chapter 2; your broker can also get you the latest updates.

Aside from the fixed monetary specifications and requirements that are defined for each contract, one of the most important considerations in choosing a futures market to trade is—you've heard it before—its liquidity. How many contracts are being traded daily (What is the contract's daily volume and open interest)? Is there always going to be a ready buyer for my sell orders and a seller for my buy orders? How long will I have to wait for my order to be filled?

I have personal experience regarding liquidity, or rather, illiquidity. I was once trading on Globex (discussed later) which allows for overnight trading on overseas markets. I went long the Japanese yen at about 11:00 PM EST which was about lunch time in Tokyo — a slow trading period in any exchange. It also happened to be an extremely inactive day. I placed an "at-the-market" order, and the evening shift broker asked me to call back for the price fill (This warned me something was up—one normally stays on the phone for a market order and gets filled in less than sixty seconds, and more often twenty to thirty seconds). I called back in five minutes and the order was still not filled. I asked what was going on, since the Japanese yen is traditionally a well-traded, liquid market. He told me that my order was the only order being placed at that time! This means that amongst all the traders in the world, I, quite possibly, was the only trader alive interested in trading yen futures at that time—at least on Globex. Needless to say, I quickly lost interest and canceled the trade. It was definitely not the time to be trading yen futures.

Why didn't I just wait for someone in the world to sell me a contract? Because when trading conditions are so incredibly light, the difference between the bidding and asking price of traders can be very wide, and a trader can get a terrible fill for his order—putting him right where he does not want to be in the market. In other words, when there are not adequate players to assure ready order fills, a trader can get bad fills, both entering and exiting the trade, which can turn even a potentially profitable trade into a loser. Inordinately poor fills lead to too much *slippage,* and these losses can add up quickly. Therefore we definitely want our market to be liquid.

Next, we want a market that *trends.* Certain markets display sideways movements almost exclusively and then suddenly explode in one direction or another. Such a market is very difficult (and stressful) to trade. Other markets have developed reputations for being "trader's markets," which means they tend to trend for significant enough time periods to allow for statistically successful use of trading methods. These markets display, over time, the natural chart patterns we have talked about, and the indicators and tools of the trader can make sense out of them a profitable percentage of the time. In other words, these trending markets return to the trader a favorable "risk/reward" ratio over time and this is exactly what we want our market choices to do.

Next, the trader should clearly understand the *volatility* of the contract. This factor determines the average risk of trading the contract overall. If a market is historically a high-risk, high-reward market, it may not at all be a good place to begin trading (although it could provide significant returns when that same trader becomes experienced). Such markets can often be subject to locked limit up or locked limit down conditions. Without sufficient capital and knowledge of how to trade spreads of front-to-back months in such conditions, being in the wrong direction in a market that has locked limit—for several days at a stretch—can financially ruin an inexperienced futures trader. (It is a most unpleasant experience, no matter who you are.) Again, what we want are markets that tend to trend reliably over time, and this does not include the historically highly-volatile markets. Although this is always a controversial subject, some of the markets considered to be highly-volatile by many include the meats, lumber, certain energy futures and orange juice (Remember that Dan Aykroyd and Eddie Murphy movie? That was a pretty volatile day). Such levels of volatility are not what we are looking for, since such markets do not tend to trend reliably over time and the risk/reward ratio for a beginner can be skewed too unfavorably towards the risk end.

With *no* volatility, however, the market also does not display trending characteristics, since a listless market is just the other side of the trending coin. A market has to move in order to trend. Without some volatility, there will be a loss of liquidity, as few traders will be interested in participating in such a "blah" market, and again there is the danger of bad order fills.

What we want, therefore, is just enough, and not too much, volatility—enough to spark global interest in the contract and thus assure its liquidity, but not so much as to cause it to often react violently and even lock limit up or down in anything other

125

than extremely rare occurrences. Markets that historically display more or less balanced levels of volatility, liquidity, and trending characteristics are the ideal trader's markets. Fortunately for us traders there are a number of these. Understand that there are always periods where even these trader's markets get wild at times (when the fundamentals and global situations get wild), but we are talking here about the *historical tendencies* of markets—the way markets move over time. This historical "tradeability" of markets is what really comes into play in the statistical realities of the trader's bottom line. It is only what happens over time that matters and determines a trader's success, or lack of same.

So what do I use? As a daytrader, I am concerned and directly involved with those markets that exhibit the qualities of a good trader's market on an intraday basis—as far as possible, each and every trading day, statistically speaking. As you may have guessed from seeing the charted markets I have used to illustrate the technical points throughout this guide, I specialize in trading the currencies and the S&P 500 index futures markets. This is by no means all I trade; I also trade the T-Bonds sometimes and some of the agriculturals, like soybeans and soy oil, among others. Overall however, I have found that the currencies, specifically the Swiss franc, as well as the popular S&P 500 index futures, are excellent trader's markets. (Note: The Japanese yen can also be a very good market, but is generally not considered a classic trader's market, since the yen can trade erratically due to government controls and international government intervention. When the yen is rallying a bit too much for the US government's liking and our government suddenly decides to go short to the tune of a hundred or so billion yen, it is not very healthy to be long that currency. On any normal day, however, the yen is a fine market).

Due to its inherent nature as the primary futures index of the primary stock market (NYSE), related stock numbers can provide the S&P 500 index futures trader with valuable trading information not available in other futures contracts—things like the advancing and declining stock issues, the tick volume, and the Premium. These and other indicators can give the S&P trader an edge over traders in the same market who simply base their trading decisions on the futures price alone.

Along with a growing number of traders worldwide, environmental and ethical concerns also guide my choice of markets. For example, I stay away from the meat markets for a variety of reasons. Regarding profitability, I know I am not missing anything, since those markets are not known to be trader's markets—they're too volatile, don't trend well statistically, and are prone to go limit up or down anytime. Since there are so many other excellent markets from which to choose, an ethically- and environmentally-conscious trader can truly afford to be so.

## Intermarket Relationships

Like organs in the human body, markets do not exist in a vacuum but tend to affect each other. In the human body, of course, each part has more or less a direct relationship to the other parts—disease in one part of the body will eventually be transmitted to another, and the same is true for health. Markets, however, can have either direct, inverse, or neutral influences on each other, and in the complex world of finance, those influences can be more accurately termed as tendencies (more direct than inverse, more inverse than neutral, etc).

For example, the fact that some kind of relational tendency exists between the US 30-year Treasury Bond futures, the T-Bonds, and the S&P 500 Index futures, is widely known. Often a trading floor commentary will read that "the S&P is again tracking the Bonds." This means that as the Bonds go up in price, or *uptick*, the S&P is soon to follow, probably within seconds. However, at other times, the S&P price does not track the bonds, but instead diverges from the price of the Bonds. This means that as the Bonds are upticking, the S&P is now downticking. Since the S&P tends to have more of a direct relationship to the Bonds than an inverse relationship, traders may consider this divergence itself to be a significant indicator of strong market moves to come in reaction to the divergence. The S&P/US T-Bond relationship is a closely-watched non-linear tendency which is affected by fundamentals in the marketplace, such as interest rate changes and government national employment reports among many others. Other well-known intermarket relationships are the inverse relationships between the US dollar-denominated markets, like the S&P 500 index futures again, and the foreign currency futures markets. This is easier to understand—as the dollar value goes up, the value of the foreign currencies traded against the dollar goes down. If the markets are active, this relationship can be readily seen.

Chart 20 shows a market segment of S&P 500 index futures; Chart 21 shows the same date and time segment for Swiss franc futures; and Chart 22 shows the same for Japanese yen futures. It is clear to see that, starting at approximately 10:30 AM, as the

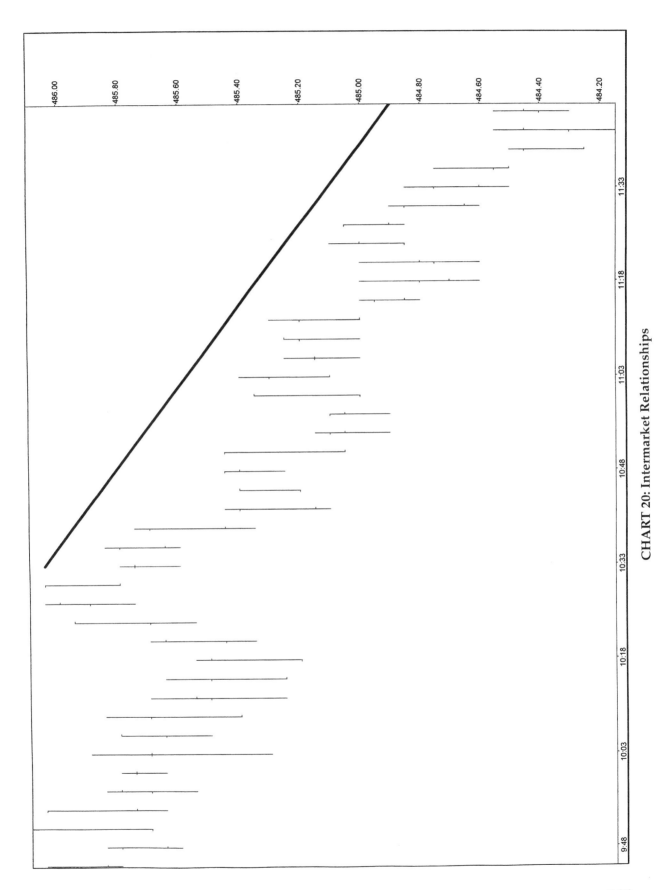

**CHART 20: Intermarket Relationships**

Chart created with TradeStation™ by Omega Research, Inc.

129

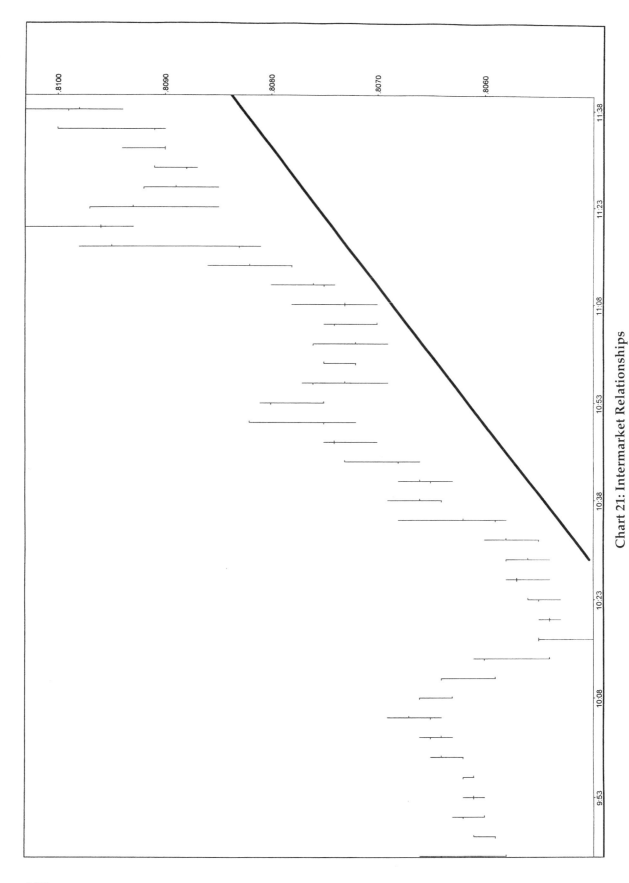

**Chart 21: Intermarket Relationships**

Chart created with TradeStation™ by Omega Research, Inc.

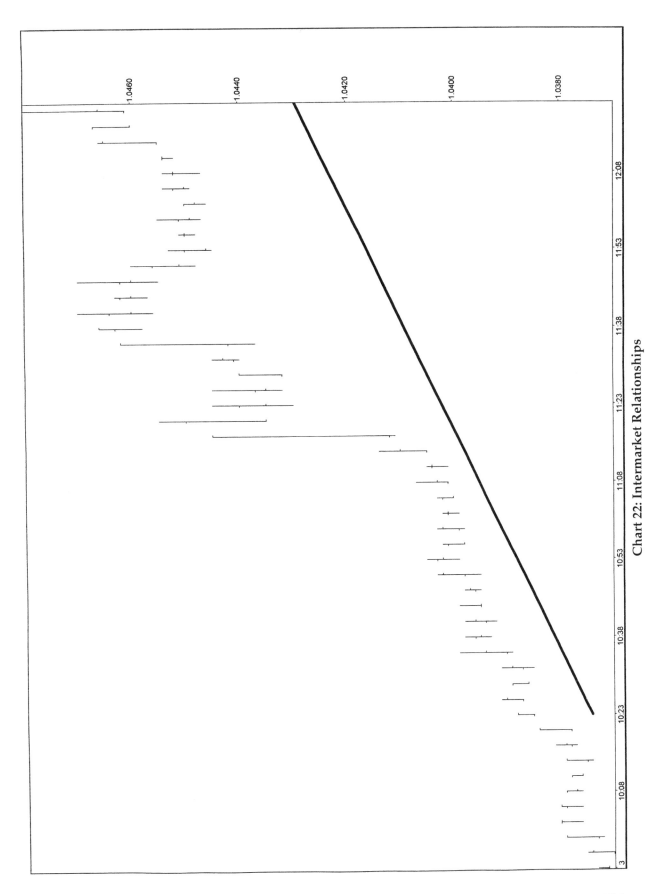

**Chart 22: Intermarket Relationships**

Chart created with TradeStation™ by Omega Research, Inc.

S&P futures market was falling, both the Swiss franc and the Japanese yen were doing exactly the opposite and rallying. This makes sense, since a strongly negative move in the S&P 500 index futures (a dollar-denominated commodity) often indicates weakness in the dollar, which has an inverse relationship to the foreign currencies. Similarly, a strong move in foreign currencies usually causes a bear market in the S&P 500 index futures. Whether, in this case, the S&P was the cause of the foreign currencies reaction, or visa versa, the result of the strong move in these basically inversely-related intermarket commodities was evident. A trader who understands these intermarket relationships knows to check related markets during strong moves in the market he is currently watching. In this case, there was an excellent chance of having profitable trades in all of these markets—going both short the index futures and long the foreign currencies futures at the same time. By *diversifying* in this way, further profit potential and equity protection can be realized.

There are many other intermarket relationships, not only between the financial and currency markets, but also between physical commodities like the agricultural and metal markets. It is not difficult to imagine that there would probably be a relationship between crude oil and unleaded gasoline futures, or between soybeans and soy oil futures.

In fact, there is an entire category of trading, mentioned earlier, in which traders attempt to take direct, rather than indirect, advantage of the differences between prices in related futures markets. This is called *spread trading,* where that difference becomes the profit or loss (a long spread-trader profits when that difference increases, and a short spread-trader profits when that difference decreases). The most common type of spread-trading is *intra*market, rather than *inter*market. The former is where the trader is trading the spread between the front delivery month (closest delivery month) and a further delivery month of the same commodity. The latter trader is spread-trading different but related commodities.

Just as a holistic physician strives to understand the bigger picture when diagnosing his patients, the "holistic trader" will often keep real-time charts of several different interrelated markets on his screens and use his diagnostic knowledge of intermarket relationships to help him confirm his trading decisions. See the Appendix under "Intermarket Analysis" and "Financial Publishers" for resources.

# THE BUSINESS OF FUTURES TRADING

W e mentioned in the introduction that it is critical to approach futures trading as a business, not a casino game. This is not to say that no one ever makes money at the casino. You can always get lucky. Look at Hillary! Many people in the futures industry were very pleased that Hillary Clinton made such a splash in futures trading, as she brought positive world attention to commodity trading. So how did she do it?

Mrs. Clinton's trading began on October 11, 1978 with $1,000 and ended on May 13, 1980 with $99,876.45. That has been calculated to be a 1,716% annual compound return. This was possible for her in exactly the same way it is possible for any futures trader—through the power of *leverage*. Just as the dealer in real estate can, with a small deposit, trade the "paper" on a house—leveraging the entire value of the house with a small deposit—so can the futures trader control and trade huge amounts of commodities with a small margin. By accepting the liability (for a brief time) to purchase or deliver the total value of the futures contract, the earnest money margin guarantees performance and acts as leverage. If prices move favorably, as in Hillary's case, such a large return on the margin can be earned from the leverage. Conversely, unfavorable price moves can result in equally large losses from the leverage (especially if there is poor money management).

So was it luck for Hillary? Could she have done it again? You make the call. As reported in the March 29, 1994 edition of *The New York Times*, the First Lady was guided in her trading by James Blair, a knowledgeable trader and top lawyer for Tyson Foods, one of the nation's largest meat producers (and he was helping her trade meat futures). In addition, as corroborated at that time by Jack F. Sandner, chairperson of the Chicago Mercantile Exchange, Mrs. Clinton's trading period just happened to coincide with the one-time biggest bull market in the history of her futures contract. Mr. Sandner's exact words were: "When you are *lucky* enough to catch a dramatic market, you can take $1,000 and scale up. . . ."

Although we may never know if Hillary Clinton missed her true calling, the above information plus the fact that, according to a senior White House aide, she closed down her commodities account because "she did not have the stomach for it any more and found it to be too nerve-wracking" makes me think otherwise. I agree with Mr. Sandner. When that rare bull market ended, both her luck and her winnings could have disappeared very quickly along with it. What is most admirable was her honesty and intelligence in recognizing her trading limitations, and perhaps *that*, more than anything, enabled the Clinton's to hang on to those profits with which they bought a house, invested in securities, and provided a nest egg for their daughter. The story of Hillary Clinton's short career in commodities would have been much less impressive had she won it all just to give it all right back.

Traders know that chance spectacular results for most beginners is, however, one of the worst things that can happen. Sooner or later the markets take away with a vengeance all the profits and existing equity from the trader who doesn't really know what he is doing, and that means over time, and no matter what the market is doing. Early chance success can readily bring on a dangerous and unjustified "I-can't-lose" confidence that can quickly lead to over-leveraged financial disaster. If the trading bug ever bites the First Lady again, one thing is for certain: her continued trading success would fully depend on her consistent application of time-tested trading principals; principals that would keep her profits increasing through the management of her own emotions, as well as that downside potential inherent in every trade — the risk.

## Risk (The Big "R")

The daily taking of risk is an essential part of any healthy life. Crossing any city street at anytime or driving your car anywhere involves major risks that we generally take for granted. By undertaking such actions we are clearly risking our very lives everyday. Of course we could reduce our risks greatly by never leaving home, but then most of us would soon risk getting evicted from that "safe" situation of taking no risks to support ourselves and our families. In fact, as I am sure you would agree, the greater risk in life is to *not* take action, for then we will lose the blessings of opportunity.

Risk cannot be avoided in any normal life. By developing the habit of taking greater and greater *calculated* risks, we can turn a normal life into an extraordinary life. The application of one's God-given intelligence to risk-taking, in business or in life, tends to make those risks both more fruitful and less dangerous. We can choose to cross a Manhattan street with our eyes open or closed. With eyes shut we are gambling on the results of our action. With eyes open we are taking the exact same risk, but are adding the use of our intelligence and knowledge gained through experience. In this way we have dramatically increased the likelihood of success — getting to the other side alive and unharmed.

It's the same in business. What separates the gambling business person from the calculated-risk-taking business person is that the former bases the outcome primarily on hope or some other uncalculated method or lack of same, while the latter bases the outcome on a well-thought-out and carefully conceived business plan. "Nothing ventured, nothing gained" is a cliché as true in business as anywhere, and I know of no similar cliches that state that risk-taking has to be foolhardy! Intelligent risks should not only be accepted, but embraced, for it is only through such an intelligent approach to risk-taking that our lives can become richly rewarded.

In the business of futures trading, the methods that deliver us from the unprofitable casino mentality to the profitable business mentality are 1) *risk management* and 2) *money management.* The following sections include important points of each.

# Risk Management

Some of the important factors of risk management have already been discussed in previous chapters. Based upon the particular trading methodology and account equity, the market's liquidity and volatility, and the trading time frame, the trader establishes an acceptable level of risk-per-trade which he is willing to assume. The trader began to establish risk control by locating a basic trading system or methodology that he backtested and paper-traded and which returned a good number of favorable trades. He also made sure that the methodology returned a favorable ratio of profits/losses for those favorable trades (the net profitability skewed strongly in his favor with the level of profits being statistically considerably greater than the level of losses). One way that this is accomplished is by adding to the trading *entry* methodology a trading *exit* methodology that involves a way to strictly limit the losses, while keeping the profit side free to develop. This is the mechanics behind the "cut-your-losses-and-let-your-profits-run" trader's credo, and it means establishing the risk/reward parameters of your system. It is done through the placement of mechanical and trade-based stop-loss orders.

It might at first seem too restrictive in the real-time, liquid world of futures trading to place stop-loss orders at all—especially when they can often get hit (and get you stopped-out of the trade with a loss, albeit defined) just before the market turns once again in the originally profitable direction. That can indeed be frustrating. Why not just place a mental stop-loss order in your own head, and then if the market goes against you, you can get out at that same price but still have the opportunity to see if the market is going to turn around near your stop-loss point? Thus, you could turn what would have been a mechanical stopped-out loss into a live human-engineered profit. After all, we are watching the markets in real-time, aren't we? We should be able to react fast enough, right?

Not so, according to most successful traders and market psychologists. It sounds good on paper, but it usually doesn't work that way in practice. Human nature may prevent us from admitting to ourselves that a trade may be a loss (and we may have been wrong!). And so we may stay in that losing trade hoping it will turn around. Of course it usually doesn't, and then what could have been a manageable loss becomes an unmanageable nightmare (and we're back in the casino again). The market may also simply move too quickly for us to catch it. Both points are factors that can lead to major losses. The placement of defined stop-loss orders helps to keep our methodology mechanical and our trading a business, free from hope and other stressful emotional reactions (the enemy!).

## Stop-Loss Orders

There are basically three methods for calculating these well-named stop-loss orders. Each controls loss for you by automatically liquidating trades in a market that has moved against you—with a loss that you have defined. They can be defined through trade-based methods, mechanical money management methods, or a combination of both. (Note: As mentioned earlier, stop-loss orders are used by nearly all traders because they work, statistically, in the trader's favor. In any single trade, there is always the possibility of slippage from a bad stop order fill, but that does not make the use of stops any less valuable. Fortunately, a good broker can help you sometimes with any seriously bad fills. See Chapter 10.)

A straight, mechanical stop-loss uses the risk/reward ratio the trader has established in that market based on all the parameters of his trading methodology, account equity, and comfort level. For example, the ratio may be 3:1 (this ratio is often used), and this means that for every, say, $300 of price objective indicated by his methodology, he is willing to risk a total of $100. A trade-based stop-loss, while still being mechanical in nature, keys into the specific nature of the trade itself. It takes advantage of the support and resistance levels developing throughout the day and is placed on the far side of one of these levels, using either the support or resistance as a protective barrier against the price (the trade-based method depends on the statistical tendency for the price to bounce off these levels). The third stop-loss method uses a combination of both trade-based and mechanical-money-management stops.

Chart 23 shows a three-minute bar chart of the S&P 500 index futures. The indicator set-up should look familiar to you. We are looking at the Keltner Channel and three moving averages. At approximately 10:00 AM in the circled area, we can see that a favorable indicator formation has lined up in a pattern that has statistically predicted a market rally. I have found that by placing a stop-loss order just below the middle Keltner band in such a formation, the band itself, plus the other three moving averages, all become strong support lines which can shield and help prevent my stop-loss point from being hit. As we can see in this example, the trade did develop profitably as predicted, and

141

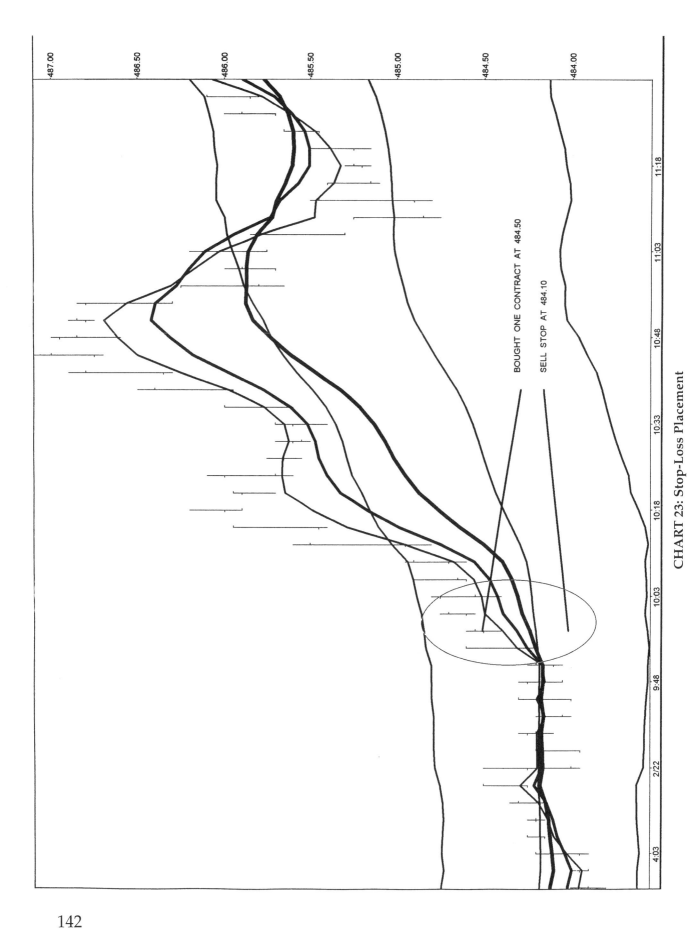

BOUGHT ONE CONTRACT AT 484.50

SELL STOP AT 484.10

**CHART 23: Stop-Loss Placement**

Chart created with TradeStation™ by Omega Research, Inc.

it could have been exited—with the use of a trend line breakout strategy—when the prices had rallied well above the top Keltner band. My stop-loss point was protected, and the middle Keltner band with the triple MA lines became an integral part of a trade-based, stop-loss methodology.

Ideally, we are looking for trades that can take advantage of *both* types of stop-loss methodology. It is best to fix the limit of our financial loss on any trade by using a mechanical stop-loss amount, while simultaneously getting further protection from specific trade-based support or resistance indicators. If we look again at the point where the market order entry was made, the amount risked at the stop-loss point was $.40 in the S&P 500, or $200. I have found that in these types of trades in this market, I can stay within a fixed mechanical stop-loss risk of approximately $200–$300 with a profitable risk/reward ratio. I have also found that the indicator lines tend to protect that stop-loss point. In this way, I use both methodologies to increase the probability that my stop-loss will not get hit (the fixed dollar stop-loss itself tends to give the market exhibiting this indicator pattern enough breathing room not to get hit, and this protection is reinforced through the support/resistance nature of the indicator). It is important to note that during periods of significantly increased market volatility, you may need to increase the stop-loss dollar value in order to simultaneously take advantage of indicator protection.

## Moving Your Stops

An important part of stop-loss methodology involves moving the stops upward or downward with the market as the trade develops in our direction. As far as possible, we want to avoid the unpleasant experience of seeing a profitable trade turn into a losing one in front of our eyes. The timely movement of our stop orders helps to prevent this by first preserving our existing capital and then locking in our profits.

The first priority is to *move the stop to break-even.* As soon as our methodology and market knowledge tells us we can do so safely, we should move our stop-loss to the price point which, should the market suddenly reverse on us, lets the market stop us out of the trade with a net loss or gain of zero. This means that when we move the stop-loss point, we should move it above our original fill (if we are going long the market) to cover for the commissions to our broker, plus a bit for fill slippage. The idea is to do so as soon as we see the market giving us enough room. For example, say we have experience that it is statistically to our advantage to move our stop-loss to break-even in Swiss franc futures when we have picked up  eight ticks profit in that market. This means that eight ticks distance from our stop-loss price to the current market price generally gives this market sufficient breathing room to move further without stopping us out, as long as our indicators are still confirming the profitable direction. It is important that we don't keep moving our stop to break-even too soon, since that will just get us stopped out constantly with no positive results (while little money is lost, much time and effort is). Nor do we want to wait too long to move our stop to break-even and thus risk a market reversal and loss of both profits and existing capital—i.e., time, effort, and money lost. When to move the stop-loss to break-even can be as much an art as a science, but we should do it, since it is good money management. As far as the timing is concerned, market experi-

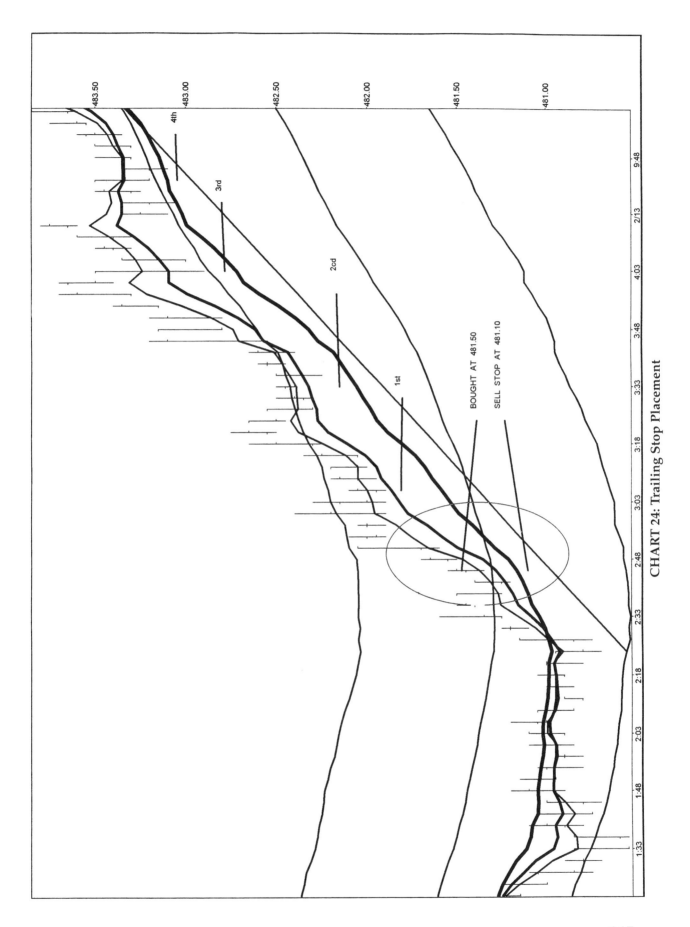

**CHART 24: Trailing Stop Placement**

Chart created with TradeStation™ by Omega Research, Inc.

145

ence brings clarity.

Moving our stop-loss to break-even helps to accomplish our first money management goal: protecting the money we started out with, our existing capital. The use of *trailing stops* allows us to accomplish the next: preserving the gains we have made in the current trade. Trailing stops take advantage of the progressive wavelike patterns of trending markets and enable us to let our profits run.

In Chart 24, at 2:45 PM, we see the beginning of what was to become a nicely trending market in the S&P 500 index futures. As the market develops, we see natural wavelike retracements bottoming out four times: at 3:06 PM, 3:36 PM, 4:06 PM, and then as this powerful trend continued on, at 9:45 AM the next morning. Let's say that we decided to enter this trade somewhere in the circled area and got filled at 481.50. Using our mechanical/trade-based, stop-loss methodology, we place our stop-loss under our technical support lines.

As the market develops in our direction we use what we know about the market's tendency to trend in wavelike retracements, which then develop into higher waves, which again retrace, and so on. We use a trend line as our tool to confirm either trading support and trend continuation, or a price breakout and end of the upward trend. As soon as we see the upward trend continuing from the first retracement, we move up our stop-loss point to just under that retracement's support area, noted as "1st" (Note: This simultaneously covered our stop-loss's "move to break-even." This market didn't give us a clear enough earlier indication to move our stop to break-even until this point). It was not too difficult to find a support area here: no less than five bars had identical lows at about 481.95, which meant that the market kept testing the strength of this price level, but found it too supportive.

In a similar fashion, we move up our trailing stop-loss to the second and third support levels, locking in our profits and letting our profits run to higher and higher levels. Near the end of the day, we could have exited the trade by placing a "Market on Close" (MOC) order, which would have given us a profit of more than $1,000 per contract as the market rallied right into the close. The next morning, the fourth support point plus the bar's position in relation to the indicators and tools would have given us the "go" signal to enter the market again in this strong and clearly continuing-upward trend.

By moving our stop-loss up or down in concert with the trend, we are letting the market tell us when the trend is over (when it finally takes out one of our trailing stops). Trading with the market and flowing along with the price waves is the only way to assure ourselves consistent equity protection and maximum trading profitability.

## Money Management

First survive, then thrive. These apparently obvious words are never taken for granted by successful traders, as they are the very foundation for any good money management philosophy. Some say that about fifteen percent of futures traders are actually successful at trading. If that be the case, then in this zero-sum industry, it would be even more accurate to say that fifteen percent of futures traders consistently take the money from the remaining eighty-five percent. That is indeed a sobering statistic. In its wake, survival becomes the first critical issue. Learning some ground rules will protect us from being swamped in that wicked wake and from becoming just another part of the larger statistic.

The basic aim is to protect the money we have started out with and preserve what we have gained. This goal can be approached in many ways, and good planning involves most or all of them. We have discussed previously some important methods by which we can control, define, and limit our losses through the application of well-placed stop-loss orders. Doing this allows us to define the level of risk we are willing to accept, based on our unique trading methodology and trading temperament. This is a major step toward establishing control of the risk and protecting the assets we started with. By the careful movement of those stops in concert with the market, i.e., letting the market show us what to do, we took the next step: preserving what we have gained. These steps take us a long way toward our goal of survival and success.

Another critical part of survival and success in the markets is *capitalization*. If we start with insufficient equity in our account, we will generally not be able to withstand the losses which can occur to even the best of trading systems. Every trading methodology has a statistical string of losses sooner or later, and our account equity must be sufficient to provide adequate margin even at these times. If not, our ability to trade will cease. In other words, our brokers, no matter how hard they may strive to work with us, will be forced to shut us down and will refuse to take our orders if we cannot meet the minimum margin requirements for our chosen markets. They have no choice in the matter: as FCMs, they are guaranteeing performance to the clearing house through issuance of margin to the latter. If we do not have sufficient capital in our account, our FCM will have to make up any losses should we default on a margin call, and brokers do NOT like that to happen. Undercapitalization tends to *increase*, rather than decrease, risk, as it often leads to risky trading practices forced upon the trader by the limited capital at his disposal. The minimum amount of risk capital considered today to be survival-prone is $10,000 (although many traders do start with less).

One of the most important means of survival in the futures markets is the conscious link, if any, that the trader makes between the amount of current equity in his account and the amount he risks per trade. Money management analysts say that a trader's survival/success rate increases exponentially if he simply limits the amount risked per trade to no more than two percent to four percent of total equity (even at five percent, the trader's chance of survival can move up to ninety-eight percent). Using the more conservative two percent figure, this means that if one's trading methodology calls for stop-loss orders of $200/trade, the total equity available in the account should be maintained at a minimum of $10,000 ($200 is 2% of $10,000).

The next concept of money management to look at is the power of *leverage:* the trading of multiple contracts. Leverage is what makes futures trading so incomparably lucrative on one side and so utterly devastating on the other. A $1,000-gain on one contract becomes a gain of $10,000 on ten contracts, just as a loss of $1,000 becomes a loss of $10,000, using the same formula.

Leverage can certainly result in financial ruin as quickly as it can make us a fortune. If managed intelligently, however, leverage can be used as a powerful trading tool to protect what we have, preserve what we have gained, and greatly increase our profit potential.

Let's look again at Chart 24: At around 2:53 PM we see that the market reached that first peak at the top Keltner band. Let's say that we are trading one contract. We know that we might get a Keltner bounce at this point. Do we exit here or wait for the trend line to be broken? Well, we have seen that it certainly pays to wait for the latter to happen. But what if the market bounces too quickly and plunges through our stop-loss point? How can we lock in our profits here and not lose out on further profits? In other words, how can we be at two or more places at the same time? Only through the power of leverage.

Trading only one contract strictly limits your trading choices and especially your exit methodology. In the above case you had to decide to either sell at that bounce or stay in; you had no other choice. But let's say that in this same trade you had decided to buy three contracts instead of just one. Using the added leverage to your advantage, you are now actually able to have your cake and eat it too. You can simultaneously get out of the market and stay in the market. You can liquidate two of the three contracts at the bounce area, locking in the profits thus far gained, and still keep that third remaining contract alive to enable the opportunity to let your profits run, should the market continue to trend—which, in this case, it most certainly did.

The additional leverage accomplishes much: (a) we can protect our existing equity from a possible market reversal; (b) we can preserve and lock in our gains from an initial market move (in this case we profited twice as much as we would have by liquidating that single contract); and (c) we are free to remain in the market and profit from any continued market rally. Trading with multiple contracts clearly increases the latitude and effectiveness of trading. It widens our trading choices and thus our profit potential. Using leverage wisely is smart trading and smart money management. If your trading methodology works good for one contract, it should work just as well (or even better, as we've just seen) with more than one contract.

At the same time, we must be even more vigilant to maintain our good trading habits and risk/money management when we start trading multiple contracts, because along with the profit potential our downside risk is on that multiplier as well. Traders, for their own protection, should keep all those conservative ratios sacrosanct, as far as possible, e.g., the conservative two percent survival trade for three contracts traded at a $200 stop-loss/contract/trade dictates that we should have $30,000 of total equity in our account to be conservatively safe ($200 x 3 contracts = $600, which is 2% of $30,000). A more aggressive five percent survival rule would keep us at a total equity of $12,000. It is up to each trader to decide how conservative he can afford to be (or afford not to be).

The most important rule of money management is to trade with *risk capital.* The simplest definition of risk capital is: money you don't need and won't miss. Do you have any of this stuff? Only you are in the position to decide whether futures trading is suitable for you, in light of your financial condition.

High rewards are the upside of futures trading, high risks the downside. The former are more than worth the effort to carefully learn and consistently apply the rules of this fascinating business — rules that can definitely help tame the latter!

## Trader Psychology—The Critical Business Of Controlling Emotion

*bandhur atmatmanas tasya*

*yenatmaivatmana jitah*

*anatmanas tu satrutve*

*vartetatmaiva satru-vat*

"For him who has conquered the mind, the mind is the best of friends;  but for one who has failed to do so, his very mind will be the greatest enemy."

This is the Roman transliteration and English translation of a five thousand-year-old Sanskrit *sutra* found in the *Bhagavad-gita*[9], a seven hundred-verse-long song from the ancient *Vedas* of India. The *Gita* has been studied and revered for thousands of years for its timeless wisdom. I include it to illustrate that as far as the human mind is concerned, not much has changed since this *sutra* was first written down, and it has us traders pegged cold . . . .

It is astounding to see, and even more debilitating to experience. Some traders say it is one of the strangest and most remarkable feelings they've ever had (they usually express this *after* they've learned to deal with it). And there are few, if any, parallels to it outside of trading. What is "it"?

Just this: You've put it all together. A real, working trading methodology. You've back-tested it; you've paper-traded it. You've seen it work—time and time again. You know it works, because you've seen it work. Your methodology is theoretically making thousands of dollars in profits. In fact, you've even traded it a little in real-time and made some money with it. You've also lost some money with it. Recently you may have had a short string of losses, which is statistically the norm for any trading system. And then it happens.

The perfect trade has just formed on your screen. Everything has lined up — every indicator you have is confirming each other and your charting software is beeping at you and popping up visual alerts all over the place. Everything is screaming at you: Buy, Buy, Buy—NOW!

But you don't. You can't. Something, somehow, is preventing you from picking up the phone and placing the order. Here you are with the perfect trade, a trade you know has the highest possible probability of not only going your way, but going your way with a *vengeance* and a *huge* profit potential — but you can't pick up the phone. Instead, you just watch your screen as that trade inevitably does go your way, picking up hundreds and, perhaps, thousands of dollars of profit from the very point your system told you to get in. And then it happens *again:* you get another signal, again telling you to get in, since now the market has developed a major trend in your direction. And again you don't pick up the phone, but just watch the market action from the sidelines. And so you sit there, watching the market rally right into the close, making the market participants — the ones who acted on their similar signals — a literal fortune.

The next day it happens again.

"Why all of a sudden can't I pull the trigger?" you ask your-self. "What is going on here!?"

What you are experiencing is known as "trader hesitation," and it is safe to say that it happens to all traders, to some extent, sooner or later. The causes are many, and the phenomenon can either be a brief visitation or a long-term, most unwanted guest. One of the first realizations to strike a trader experiencing it is that paper trading for profits and real trading for profits are two very different things. At times, they can be as different as playing in a flight simulator is to being buffeted in "light turbulence" at three thousand feet in sun-brilliant skies, your hands on the vibrating controls of a trainer aircraft, the pilot-teacher ordering you to go — "Right Now!" — into a forced stall. Although paper trading is an essential preparation for any trader and trading system, there is really nothing like the actual physical and emotional experience of trading where you are risking real money in real-time. It is natural, initially, to have some wild emotional swings while trading — from euphoria to fright to panic — as the market follows its natural patterns, taking you with it. Once the trader understands his statistically successful methodology and the markets better, however, and let's his own stops worry about the possibility of loss, while he instead concentrates on the trading process, he experiences a gradual decrease in emotional attachment to each trade—with a con- comitant rise in profits.

Why? Because trading is about twenty percent trading methodology and about eighty percent trading psychology. Of course the trader must first do his homework; he must have researched and learned the basics of trading. He must have either devised or bought (or both) a good trading methodology which has proven itself to be profitable over time. But after this has been accomplished, there is NO methodology, no matter how remarkable, that is worth a dime unless the trader can trade it, physically and emotionally. The first thing the trader did to trade in his own emotional comfort zone was to choose a trading time frame: long-term, short-term, or daytrading, as described earlier. But then, when the trade actually appears in that time frame, his emotions have to be under sufficient control to (a) take the trade, (b) manage the trade, and (c) positively deal with the winning or losing results of that trade.

It really comes down to how well we deal with loss. One trader may become hesitant to pick up the phone and pull the trigger. Another trader may get angry after experiencing a few losses, pick up the phone with a vengeance, and try to "get even" with the market. This has been termed "Kamikaze trading," an apt description of this mentality. The market always wins ultimately, and if you try to beat it or go against it, the result is that you will simply crash and burn. Needless to say, a bout of Kamikaze trading can certainly lead to a period of trader hesitation. The particular ways in which we deal with loss may be specific to our childhood experiences. What is remarkable is that traders may have to confront these issues while trading, and what is wonderful about that is that learning to deal with these issues in the context of one's trading can help one to deal with them in one's life.

There is an entire field of trader psychology that deals with these and other emotional trading issues. Excellent books have been written on the subject, and successful traders with expertise in psychology offer courses, seminars, and practice sessions ultimately designed to help traders develop the mental discipline needed to succeed in this business. (See the Appendix under "Financial Publishers".)

# Qualities of CSTs (Consistently Successful Traders)

Being a CST, or consistent winner, does *not* mean never having losses. Every trader existing has losses, but the successful trader (1) uses a methodology that profits significantly more than it loses and (2) knows how to deal psychologically with both the losses and the profits.

What separates the CSTs from the CUSTs? Here are some of the qualities:

1) They develop the "loner" mentality: This refers not to cave dwelling, but to the careful guarding of one's own mental hermitage. There are as many trading opinions as there are grains of sand, and the successful trader views them as such. When he has taken all of the trouble to learn the business and then develop all the intricacies and interlocking aspects of a successful trading methodology, his confidence in that methodology and in himself gives him the strength to ignore the endless predictions, dire warnings, and "hot tips" issuing forth from innumerable market "gurus," brokers, and other well or ill-intentioned souls. He knows that the market has its own inherent order and that his profitable system hears that order. So he finds it relatively easy to avoid the ocean of confusion around him and is more than happy to keep himself deaf to it, except perhaps for entertainment purposes.

2) Successful traders do not try to pick tops or bottoms of markets, but are interested in turning points, because they rep-

resent the possible development of a trend. And getting a piece of that trend is what it is all about.

3) They maintain a winning psychology and try to emulate the winning mindsets of the finest traders. They do NOT take losses personally, but understand them to be exactly what they are: the unavoidable statistical downside of their trading methodology. In fact, in a properly back-tested and well-designed system, those very losses can be an indication of significantly profitable trades soon to come. Emotions are kept at bay, and when their methodology says act, they act. When they are in a trade, they think less about the money and more about the trading process. Whether any particular trade is a winner or a loser, they are simply concerned whether or not they have strictly followed their own trading methodology. They realize that *it is only what happens over time — statistically — that is important.*

4) They manage their money very carefully, use only real risk capital, and do not over-commit to any single trade, but instead build up the leverage gradually and only if profitability is reached and further profitability is confirmed (they are not looking for the "retirement trade"). They also don't over-diversify into too many markets, but stay with markets they have studied closely. They are quick to act, whether moving stops to break-even, moving trailing stops, or taking profits—no matter how small—if their methodology indicates they should do so. They unerringly follow their plan. They are very protective of both existing equity and profits gained. They trust their methodology and take every signal it issues (and don't second guess it), since they know that their methodology is profitable when traded steadily, over time.

5) When the money is pouring in, they have a clear plan for

steadily taking profits out of their account. This keeps them from getting too cocky and losing it all.

6) They keep their knowledge current and keep learning. They know that to remain on the profitable side of this zero-sum game, they need to keep learning the markets and the most effective way to follow them since their best competition is doing just that.

7) They never try to fight the market, but always strive to flow with it. Although their indicators may be leading indicators, they want to see the market confirming any predictions. The market is always in complete control, and their object is to figure out what it is doing and simply follow it.

8) They understand that markets move in complex, yet orderly, patterns that represent nothing more than the moment-to-moment distillation of the global trading psychology. And they use those predictable emotional patterns to their advantage.

9) They do everything necessary to consistently cut their losses, trade with the trend, and let their profits run.

## Other Ways to Trade

Like many traders, I trade straight, standardized futures. This means I either simply buy or sell the contract and then liquidate it by the opposing trade. There are other ways to trade futures. As you will recall, spread traders trade both sides of the transaction at once, buying one delivery month and selling another in order to profit from the difference — the price spread — between the front and back contract months. Spread traders often feel that their method is less risky than others: since contract prices of front and back delivery months tend to rise and fall together, opposing trades move toward neutrality in the same way that opposing cash and futures trades move toward neutrality for hedgers. Profits are limited in this way and so are the losses. However, it does not always work like this, and certain market conditions can put a spread trader, with his two positions, in double the jeopardy of the straight futures trader who simply enters and exits his "naked," one-sided trade (every Risk Disclosure Statement warns that spread trading may not be less risky than a simple long or short position).

Another popular method is the trading of options or options on futures. If an option on a future is exercised, the result is a straight long or short futures position. In the simplest terms, a *call option* is the right to buy futures, or exercise the option, at a specified price prior to expiration of the option. A *put option* is the right to sell futures, or exercise the option, at a specified price prior to the expiration of the option. The price paid for the option is called the *premium*, which is dependent at any point in time upon what the actual futures price is in relation to the specified price — the strike price — of that option. (Options terminology and strategies are defined in Appendix F.) Options trading is certainly worth further study, simply because options trading increases your trading options. It positions you to take certain trades that you might not otherwise take in an outright futures position. For example, if you feel that the market may reverse soon, you could purchase an option going in the opposite direction of the current market (e.g., a call option in a falling market), effectively putting yourself right in front of a market freight train. This is basically the opposite of what traders want to do, which is to hop aboard that train and trade with the trend.

However, in the options trade, you can purchase the call option in the falling market and decide whether or not to exercise it. You have nothing to worry about, since you are not in the market until you exercise your option to be so. If the market keeps falling and moving against your option, you can simply let the option expire without exercising it. But if the market does reverse and go your way before its expiry date, you can exercise your call option when the futures price is profitable for you in relation to your option's strike price. At that point, you would simply be long the futures contract at a profitable position, and then you'd follow your straight futures methodology of trailing stops, etc. In either case, all you have risked to attempt this "against the trend" trade is the premium originally paid.

I plan to employ options more and more in my overall trading strategy. So much to learn, so little time!

## Advisory Services

Although it flies straight in the face of "loner mentality," many traders who have not yet developed their own strategy, or who wish to depend on the advice of others, subscribe to advisory services. As you can well imagine, with market opinions never in short supply, there are a plethora of these services— some good, some not so good—which you can receive via mail, e-mail, fax, hotline, modem, satellite, you name it. They are widely advertised in every market/investment-oriented magazine. There is even a 900 hotline, called the All-Star Traders Hotline, with twelve famous traders on different extensions offering their recorded advice.

It is highly recommended when working with advisory services that you examine their real-time track record and stay away from those that cannot provide you with the same. An advisory service may consist of actual trading experts who are following their own advice (the best kind), or may consist of predictions based on some fundamental or technical analysis and possibly a lot of guesswork. One of the finest sources, which analyzes the best of the former newsletters for you by following their recommendations and rating their performance, is Bruce Babcock's *Commodity Traders Consumer Report*. Mr. Babcock is a well-known expert in the industry, and his report looks at the top advisory services using a variety of measurements. One of the most important things to remember is that the profitable numbers issuing from any trading methodology are always based upon statistical performance, so in order to match the results of a successful advisory service, you must take every trade they recommend. Trying to find only the best trades can be disastrous: you may see a string of large winners and decide to begin trading just as the statistically correct number of small losers begins. If you use them at all, these advisory services and market letters must be followed—to the letter!

# OUR COMMISSION HOUSE (FCM)

## The Broker: What We Want, What We Don't Want

What we want first of all is a discount futures broker, as opposed to a full service broker. We want the lowest possible total commissions per round turn per contract. Commissions do add up — especially for daytraders and/or multiple contract traders. Approximately five dollars will be added to any rate you see; this covers clearing fees, NFA/SEC fees, and other brokerage charges. So an advertised rate of $17 per round turn actually becomes about $22 when the trade is made. A basic advertised rate of $15–$20 per round turn is a good standard range to be in.

We also want a discount broker because we neither want them to decide our trades for us, nor do we want their advice or opinions. (Note: If you want to surrender your money to a full-service broker and have them trade for you, you will find them most willing to accommodate. The commissions will be about $50–$100 per round turn, and since your money will be traded by them, at their discretion, you will have no need for computers, charting software, data vendors, or this book. And best of luck!) Remember that we need to isolate ourselves from the opinions of others, and brokers are the most highly opinionated of all, since that is their business. What we don't want is a discount broker that keeps hounding us and trying to "sell us up" to full service. This can be a warning sign that we are working with the wrong firm. We want our discount brokers to remain discount brokers and to efficiently execute our orders. And there is a lot that goes into that word "efficiently."

Since most of the markets we trade are traded on the Chicago exchanges, it is essential that our discount brokers be located in Chicago. Not only should they be in Chicago, but they should have trading desks located near to the pits inside the very exchanges where our chosen markets are being traded. The best situation is to arrange with your account executive to let you call in your orders right to that desk. If your account is large enough to easily cover the margin with some room to spare (and if you've shown them that you definitely know how to place orders), the FCM should allow you to do that. You will be assigned a particular desk, like the "K Desk," which should be in eye shot of the brokerage's trader in the pit. As you increase the volume and frequency of your trading, you can negotiate even lower commissions, possibly into the single digits. Brokers consider a steady trader "golden," and they will definitely not want you jumping ship to another firm. When your trading warrants it, you will have the power you need to negotiate your commission rate downward.

Why you want a hot line to the desk on the exchange floor is for one reason: flash fills. When you get your buy or sell signal, naturally the market is not going to wait around in your ideal position forever. The window of opportunity can be very small, especially in real-time daytrading, and what you want is for your order to literally be filled "in a flash." Every second can mean slippage and loss of profits; a bad fill can also turn a once profitable trade into a loser. Your market orders especially should be filled in seconds, and the close eye contact between your desk and the pit allows your desk broker to hand signal your order for flash fill order placement. If you have to first call your account executive, who then has to make another call down to the floor, you are clearly wasting precious time that could have been saved by your calling the floor in the first place. As for your stop orders, even though they will only get executed when the market reaches your stop price, you still want the order known to the pit immediately, since your stop price may be hit at any time.

Whoever you place your order with, you must make sure that the conversation is being recorded (almost every futures broker does this) and that the broker repeats your order back to you. You should also have him tell you the ticket number for easy reference if later required. If there is any discrepancy—bad fill, wrong order, clerical error on the P&S statement—you should have them check the time stamp of the order and the recording as soon as you've discovered the error. This is how everything can be reconciled and how all parties to the trade are protected.

You want to do whatever you can to develop a rapport with your account executive and your desk traders. It can mean money saved and increased profits. A good broker will fight for you if you have gotten an unjustifiably bad fill and will still fight for you even if it is justifiable. He can also work with you a bit on the margin requirements, should that become necessary, i.e. he may let you trade your account for a while under the current minimum margin, but that is not recommended from a money management standpoint. Of course, your account executive may not be thrilled to get you connected directly to the desk, since his percentage of your commission can drop when he is not directly involved in calling in the order. He also may not be in a position to fight for you when you get bad fills. But a good desk trader can help you with that, and you should be able to get the best of both worlds if you keep everyone happy. This means being friendly, speaking your orders clearly and correctly (you can't expect much help if you said "Buy" when you meant "Sell," or gave the wrong delivery month or number of contracts), and trading! Nothing will make your people happier than a steadily increasing volume of orders. That's how they make their money and how you make yours.

It is also an advantage if your FCM is an official clearing member of the exchanges you are working with. Clearing members are the big shots of the business. In other words, they have clout. There are innumerable ways in which this can help you — from getting better order fills, to getting better records of your trading transactions (Purchase and Sale statements) with less clerical errors.

When you open your account you will fill out a Risk Disclosure Statement, a very detailed statement of the risks involved in futures and options trading. This is sent to you along with the standard account information forms, as required by the Commodity Futures Trading Commission. By law, a firm's prospective clients must sign these statements declaring that they understand the risks involved. These must be returned with the other paperwork along with a deposit check to open your margin account.

Please see the Appendix for a source of further information to help you with the important decision of which discount broker to select.

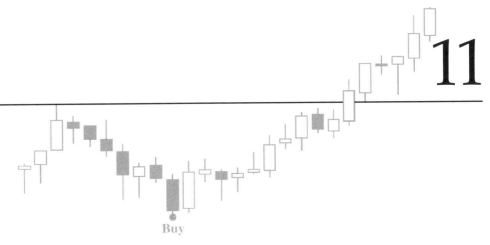

# ALL THE NEWS THAT'S FIT TO TRANSMIT

Here we take a look at the "mentalist" end of the technimentalist trader described earlier in Chapter 4. As you will recall, the technimentalist is primarily a technical trader who keeps an eye on that fundamental news likely to have either a catalytic or catastrophic effect on his trading.

Certain major scheduled reports by government and related agencies can do either or both. What is good about these reports is that they can often "jump-start" listless markets that are drifting in search for fresh news to trade on. While markets can trend very well after major fundamental news, it is wise not to trade during such news as the markets may react in too volatile a fashion (known as the knee-jerk reaction).

## Scheduled Reports

Here are some of the major scheduled government reports affecting the financial and foreign currency markets, which are the fastest growing of all futures markets:

**FOMC**—The "mother" of all government reports. Undoubtedly the most watched, feared, and influential of the scheduled fundamental news to rock the markets, especially the financial and currency markets, is the reporting of the results of the Federal Open Market Committee meeting. This is the meeting of the powerful Federal Reserve Board, the group of seven appointed by the President of the United States and confirmed by the Senate. The "Fed" directs the federal banking system and both formulates and executes monetary policy for the nation. By manipulating the discount rate — the interest rate at which banks borrow from the Federal Reserve — millions of homeowners, car owners, and bank account/credit card holders are directly affected as the banking community immediately passes along these changes in interest and loan rates to their customers.

As these decisions ultimately have a direct affect on the value of the US dollar, here and abroad, there is an immediate impact felt in any market related to the cash dollar (and most are). The T-Bonds, the DJIA (Dow Jones Industrial Average), the S&P 500 index futures, and all the major foreign currency markets can undergo a very major instant reaction to one of these reports. An upcoming FOMC meeting can even affect the markets a week or two before and after the event.

As the meeting day approaches, trading can be very jittery and markets illiquid, as nervous major players stand aside, not wanting to hold open trading positions in the uncertain economic climate preceding the meeting. On the day of the meeting things can get really crazy, since no one knows exactly when the announcement will be made. And at the moment the report is announced, charts of some of these commodities can look not unlike a seismograph of a (+10?) Richter scale earthquake — i.e., huge price moves up and down, and fast. In short, the markets go wild.

Chart 25 shows such a market. Throughout the day, as every market participant not sleeping under a rock was aware, the FOMC was meeting to decide whether or not to once again raise interest rates. The wild choppy price action throughout the day is a perfect representation of the nervousness pervading the market. With market participants so jittery, rumors preceding the announcement can have violent repercussions. The announcement was finally made at (you can probably guess the tim): 2:20 PM. The market went right off the Richter scale, moving over forty ticks up and down in three minutes and then did the same thing again for the next three minutes. (Note: We are not looking at cash T-Bonds or the cash dollar here — this is a chart of Swiss franc futures!).

What can happen to a trader holding an open position of a contract—or worse, several contracts—at that moment isn't pretty. When trading gets extremely heavy in a trading pit, the exchange officially reports that contract is trading under *fast market conditions.* This means that it might be some time before an order can be executed. Even with a wide protective stop-loss order in place, such a market can blast right through it. Although stops orders are filled at the best possible price, closest to the stop price, in such a wild market that best price can translate into a disastrous fill. Of course one could also make a fortune in such a market, but that brings us back to casino rolls again. Since we want to avoid that stuff, it makes sense to also avoid those

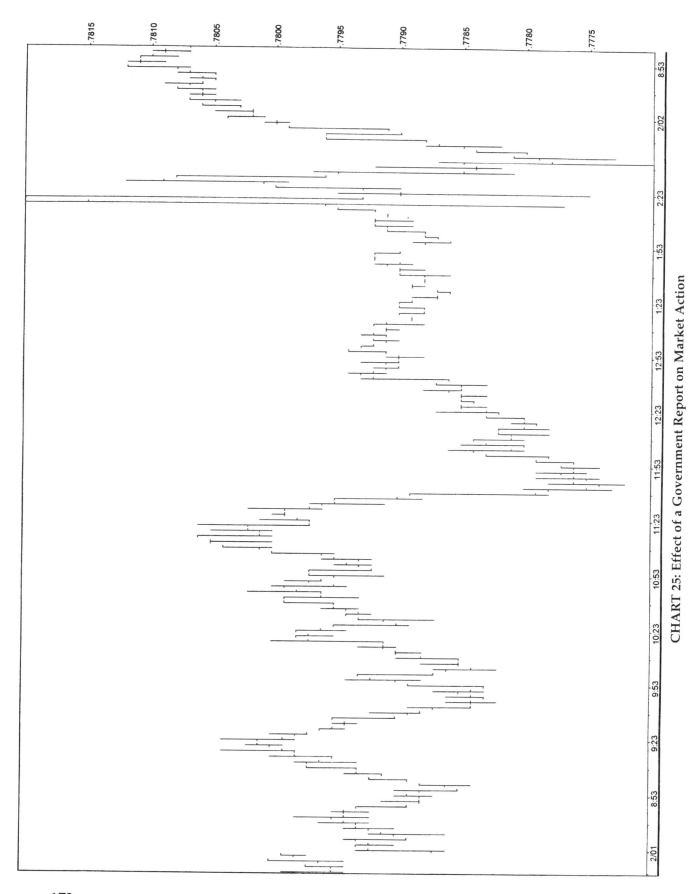

CHART 25: Effect of a Government Report on Market Action

Chart created with TradeStation™ by Omega Research, Inc.

172

casino-like market conditions and time periods in which traders cannot reliably (statistically) predict price direction. Trading during an FOMC meeting report is one of those times. (Note: There are options traders who use strategies to attempt to profit from major report-instigated price moves, in a single direction, but even most of them stay away from a FOMC report, since price movements in both directions can occur within minutes of each other.) As mentioned in Chapter 7, it just statistically pays to wait at least fifteen minutes after a major report like this before considering a trade. Before that, let the major institutional players and fund managers surf this pipeline.

The FOMC is headed by what some call the most powerful man in Washington, and perhaps the world: the Chairman of the Federal Reserve Board, currently Mr. Alan Greenspan. Even when the FOMC meeting is nowhere in sight, the Chairman is the Chairman, and his every word is hung onto by the markets. His often vague statements have to be so, simply because he wields so much power. Therefore, when I know that Mr. Greenspan is testifying before the Senate Finance Committee or simply talking to anyone, anywhere, all I can do is lean back and wait. Most market participants are going to do the same, and the nervous, light trading conditions during these times reflects that fact.

Bottom line: watch out for the Fed and its illustrious Chairman. (The Oliphant cartoon on the next page was penned soon after Mr. Greenspan expressed his concern that market players were perhaps displaying too much "irrational exuberance", resulting in technically overbought markets. He made these brief comments at a recent evening banquet. The next morning, most of the world's stock and futures markets — from Chicago to

OLIPHANT©UNIVERSAL PRESS SYNDICATE. Reprinted with permission. All rights reserved.

Zurich to Tokyo — plummeted on fears of an imminent tightening of monetary policy by the Federal Reserve. With a few well-placed words, Mr. Greenspan tamed the markets — and surely "fried crisp" many of its participants).

**LEI**—A closely watched report is the government's own set of leading indicators of the overall economic state of the nation. These indicator numbers are issued in the Leading Economic Indicators report. This comes out monthly and tends to immediately move markets when announced.

**Unemployment**—The non-farm payroll unemployment numbers are also important indicators of the nation's economic health. Unexpected numbers in either direction can significantly affect markets.

The following are also key government reports that can have an immediate effect on markets when announced:

Consumer Price Index
Producer Price Index
US Housing Starts/Permits
US Home Sales
Gross Domestic Product
US Business Inventories
Factory Orders
Retail Sales
Durable Goods
Industrial Production
Personal Income

Table 16

# INDEX OF SELECTED GOVERNMENT REPORTS

| | |
|---|---|
| **Agricultural Prices** | 1/31, 2/28, 3/27, 4/30, 5/30, 6/27, 7/23,* 7/31, 8/29, 9/29, 10/31, 11/26, 12/30 |
| **Cold Storage** | 1/21, 2/21,* 2/21, 3/21, 4/18, 5/20, 6/30, 7/18, 8/20, 9/19, 10/20, 11/21, 12/19 |
| **Consumer Price Index & Real Earnings** | 1/14, 2/19, 3/19, 4/15, 5/15, 6/17, 7/16, 8/14, 9/16, 10/16, 11/18, 12/16 |
| **Corporate Profits** | 3/28, 5/30, 6/27, 8/28, 9/26, 11/26, 12/23 |
| **Crop Production** | 1/9, 1/10,* 2/12, 3/11, 4/11, 5/12, 6/12, 7/11, 8/12, 9/12, 10/10, 11/10, 12/11 |
| **Employment Situation** | 1/10, 2/7, 3/7, 4/4, 5/2, 6/6, 7/3, 8/1, 9/5, 10/3, 11/7, 12/5 |
| **FOMC Report** | 2/7, 3/28, 5/23, 7/7, 8/22, 10/3, 11/14, 12/19 |
| **Gross Domestic Product** | 1/31, 2/28, 3/28, 4/30, 5/30, 6/27, 7/31, 8/28, 9/26, 10/31, 11/26, 12/23 |
| **Industrial Production & U.S. Capacity Utilization** | 1/17, 2/14, 3/14, 4/16, 5/15, 6/17, 7/16, 8/15, 9/16, 10/17, 11/17, 12/15 |
| **Personal Income** | 2/3, 3/3, 3/31, 5/1, 6/2, 6/30, 8/1, 8/29, 9/29, 11/3, 11/28, 12/24 |
| **Producer Price Index** | 1/9, 2/14, 3/14, 4/11, 5/14, 6/13, 7/11, 8/13, 9/12, 10/10, 11/14, 12/12 |
| **U.S. Productivity & Costs** | 2/11, 3/11, 5/7, 6/18, 8/12, 9/9, 11/13, 12/4 |
| **WASDE (Wld. Ag. Supply/Demand Est.)** | 1/10, 2/12, 3/11, 4/11, 5/12, 6/12, 7/11, 8/12, 9/12, 10/10, 11/10, 12/11 |

* Denotes Annual Report

Table 16 lists the major government reports for 1997.

## Unscheduled News

You can always find lists of important scheduled reports in investment magazines and from your brokers. What you obviously can't find in print is the unscheduled fundamental news happening right now as you are reading these words. Events like global catastrophes, political upheavals, and trade wars can have direct and major influences on markets worldwide. For example, the bombing of the Russian Parliament by Boris Yeltsin caught many foreign currency traders by surprise. When the news hit the exchange floors, a panic ensued, and a knee-jerk reaction to "sell-sell-sell!" all European currencies caused many markets to plunge. No one knew what short- or long-term implications Boris's action would have on the global economy. The Swiss franc and Deutsche marc plummeted all day. Without knowing why this was happening, a purely technical trader could have found himself in trouble. Many did. On the other hand, those who knew what was happening also knew that their normal trading signals were being skewed and overpowered by the fundamentals putting the markets into a tailspin panic. And so they reacted much better to the crisis.

Several real-time news feeds exist. *Futures World News* is a good example:

FWN covers all market-impacting news, twenty-four hours a day. It reports on the United States markets, European markets, and Far East markets. For many commodities it gives opening, midsession, and closing comments, both technical and fundamental. It also transmits all the government reports from around the world with progressive backup stories explaining the reports' effects, if any, on trading.

After the US markets close, the news again begins when the Far Eastern markets open and then again with the European markets. When you wake up in the morning, scores of headlines can be scrolled through which cover all the salient news and information concerning the overnight trading that took place in the major overseas markets. By hitting the return key on a highlighted headline, the backup story appears. There are over 500 market-related items reported on each day.

Not only is the world's trading news covered, but, in concert with UPI, all of the major general world news is reported on as well (like Boris's activities on that fateful day). All of the news is transmitted as it happens and time-stamped to the hundredth-of-a-second. Actually the news and reports are sent as fast as the FWN typists can type and transmit it. To save time, critical news and reports are sent first as a flashed headline to be followed later by the backup story; other news is transmitted with both the headline and backup story available at the same time.

As an added incentive for longer-term traders, for whom it is primarily designed, FWN also transmits ten-minute delayed quotes on futures and options traded on the major exchanges, along with tabulated indicator numbers and longer-term price charts.

FWN sells a satellite dish and control box along with the service and sometimes comes up with deals where the equipment is thrown in if a commitment is made on the length of the service contract.

Although news wires like this are used more for "fundicians" and longer-term traders, as a technimentalist daytrader I feel they can still be very cost-effective. A special bit of breaking news that can either make me more confident to stay longer in a profitable trade or get me out of a losing trade faster can also wind up paying for itself — even a year's charge for the service — in one trade. Quite simply, there is no need to trade "blind," and I feel that subscribing to a news service like this can turn a technical trader into a super-informed technical trader, i.e. a true technimentalist. And now that there are data vendors who are starting to provide news services like FWN as part of their own data feed, keeping an eye on the global fundamental picture is becoming much more convenient and cost-effective as well.

# SPECIAL TRADING— UNIQUE, FASCINATING, FUN!

## Are You a Night Person? Trading the International Markets in Real-Time

If you can get by on a few hours sleep at night and just can't get enough trading during the day, then global trading is for you. You can trade Belgian bonds on the BELFOX exchange at 3 AM EST or Japanese Raw sugar at 10 PM EST on the TIFFE or just continue trading the international CME and CBOT contracts most of the night on GLOBEX, the fastest-growing electronic global trading exchange.

What you require in order to trade overnight depends on how extensively you wish to be a global trader. Some real-time quote feeds, like Signal, transmit GLOBEX quotes, and if you have a broker that has an evening desk with a GLOBEX electronic terminal you are on your way. You can trade the overnight CME, CBOT and MATIF contracts — first when they are traded in Asia and then in Europe. (Note: Some of the Europe trading hours in those contracts overlap the Chicago hours of the same markets.) For most of the other global markets, however, you may have to subscribe to a more expensive data vendor like Bloomberg or Reuters. These high-end vendors, mentioned earlier, offer just about everything a trader could possibly want in market data, including electronic trading to all of the accessible global exchanges. (Note: While not all of the world's exchanges are hooked up to an electronic trading system, most of the larger exchanges are.)

Again, as with any market, illiquidity is the enemy, and markets must be found which attract sufficient volume to allow for valid computer technical analysis. The contracts traded on GLOBEX are growing in popularity. Other important and popular markets are:

(a) the Hang Seng Index on Hong Kong's HKFE exchange, (b) the Brent/West Texas Intermediate spread (crude oil spread) on London's IPE exchange, (c) the French Notional Bonds — the world's second most liquid bond contract after the US 30 Year Treasuries — on the MATIF in Paris and, (d) the German Bund on the both the LIFFE and DTB exchanges. Some global traders say that it is easier to profit from certain international markets, since there is not such a vast number of sophisticated traders in those markets with which to compete compared to, say, the most liquid of the Chicago markets. That is debatable. What is for sure is that you certainly don't have to fly to Malaysia, Japan, Finland, Australia, or Singapore to trade there, and with the right equipment and broker, global electronic trading opens up the world to the overnight trader (and the insomniac).

# Tetherless Trading—Trading from the Yacht

You saw him as the arch rival to the famous "Greed is Good" character in the blockbuster film, *Wall Street*. He was that suave, ultra-rich and knighted British investor, Sir Lawrence "Larry" Wildman, who ultimately helped to bring down the ruthless Gordon Gecco (played by Michael Douglas) with a little help from the overly ambitious Bud Fox (Charlie Sheen).

In one later scene, Sir Larry is giving Bud some critical trading advice during the highly frenzied market activity in which they were all intimately involved. In that scene, Sir Larry is doing this from aboard his yacht while talking over his cellular phone to Bud, who is in New York. The British multi-millionaire is watching the markets in real-time on the computer that is in front of him on a deck table, as the waves softly lap his yacht in some warm sunny clime. Sounds luscious, doesn't it?

Here's one relatively inexpensive way to do it (the hookup — not the yacht, although trading can make that happen too):

Get DBC's Signal as your real-time data vendor. When they ask you what kind of data receiver you want, ask them for their PCMCIA SignalCard. This allows you to receive the data over the FM airwaves, wireless to your laptop. (Note: Desktop computers can now be fitted with PCMCIA adaptors, so your computer could also be plugged in to your vehicle's power outlets. Your computer doesn't have to be a laptop.) The monthly real-time fees are the same as for the standard real-time FM quote service; you are simply picking up the feed through the SignalCard's FM antenna rather than through your roof-mounted or other fixed FM antenna connected to Signal's FM

Receiver box. If you are using a laptop it will have to come with a PCMCIA port, but most good models now have this standard.

DBC transmits the data feed as a side carrier on dozens of FM radio frequencies. For best reception, plan to keep your vessel within continental US or Hawaiian waters and no more than forty miles from shore.

You can also receive real-time quotes to your laptop off your yacht as well, and in fact when I last checked, yacht ownership wasn't even required.

## Cybertrading—Trading and the Internet

This section assumes you already know how to "surf in cyberspace," or, in other words, navigate online through the fascinating and often stormy electronic currents of the world-wide Internet. Excellent cybersurfing lessons can be had by purchasing any number of Internet guides; in the opinion of many, the *Internet for Dummies* series is a fine choice.

As of this writing, real-time futures trading in cyberspace does not yet exist. Neither do real-time futures "cyberquote" services that could theoretically provide real-time price charting and indicator plotting software online or else link into your own software. There are, however, delayed quote services that offer price quotes plus a whole lot of online talk about every aspect of the subject. Since the Internet is currently growing at an uncontrollable rate of about 300,000 new international surfers per month, including financially-related business services and products, there is no telling what may have appeared (or disappeared) by the time you read this. As of this writing, here are some of the current places you can go:

On the WWW (World Wide Web) point your favorite web browser at:

### http://www.investorama.com

Considered by some to be the most comprehensive financial source on the Internet, Invest-o-Rama has received dozens of awards and accolades from both print media and online reviewers. It acts as a financial hub and currently categorizes over 4,000 online financial links that you can instantly connect to. As they say, anyone who is anyone in investing or finance is listed at this site (Yes, even we're there).

### http://www.quote.com

This is the home page of the first quote vendor to appear on the Internet. Long-term traders may find this useful, since the service currently provides daily quotes for the futures and stock markets. An extra charge gets you the forecasts of the Freese-Notis Weather service which long-term ag future traders would find useful.

### http://www.wsdinc.com/

Home page of "Wall Street Directory," an online financial mall of sorts. It has many hypertext links to companies offering a wide variety of products and services currently including the Elliot Wave and Time Cycle Update, the Trader's and Investor's Calendar, Technical Market comment, a slide show from DBC's Signal, press releases, software demos, trader psychology gurus, and much more.

### http://www.jpmorgan.com

Home page of JP Morgan, Inc. The 150-year-old company

describes its financial services, including its "RiskMetrics" investment strategies.

### http://www.cme.com

For a look into one of the world's largest futures exchanges, you will find it here at the home page of the Chicago Mercantile Exchange. You can tour their newly refurbished trading floor complex from color photos or view the trading action via a MPEG movie clip. You can see how much it will cost you for a seat on the exchange (currently $925,000 for a full membership seat on the CME or just $850,000 if you want a membership seat in the IMM division), find out what are the latest contracts being offered (the Mexican peso is new), learn which contract is currently the world's most actively traded futures contract, plus all kinds of other interesting trading information. They currently have the largest trading floor in the world and bill themselves as the world's largest marketplace. (Note: The Chicago Board of Trade handles more contracts but in a smaller space. So which exchange is larger depends on what you are looking at; but no matter what you are looking at, the CME and the CBOT are the world's #1 and #2 heavyweight champion exchanges.)

### http://infomatch.com/~adas/adv.html

This is the end-of-day quote service Commodity Traders Advice company. The cost is currently $29.95/month and they also give "buy, sell, stay away from" trading recommendations for their futures and options quotes. According to their home page, they are soon to offer delayed intraday quotes as well.

### http://baervan.nmt.edu/prices/current.htm

You can find the Daily Petroleum Report here: the daily futures prices for crude oil, fuel oil, unleaded gas, and natural gas.

**ftp://ftp.netcom.com/pub/pi/pierre/invest/data/**

This page is a source of historical futures prices showing several years of futures back data for a number of different contracts.

**gopher://wuecon.wustl.edu:671/11/holt/weekfut**

Huang's Weekly Futures reports are located here. They show the net price change in the markets, plus a relatively thorough fundamental analysis for most of the major futures markets.

**http://www.timely.com/**

This service shows daily and long-term charts for a variety of domestic and international stock index futures markets.

**http:/centrex.com**

Home page of Investor's Galleria, an online financial link source for a number of companies such as Dow Jones Telerate, Barron's, and Trader's Press. It has a helpful "Info Center" with comprehensive updated lists of commodity and stock symbols, glossaries, current margin requirements and so on, plus links to other financial servers.

There is a growing presence of stock and futures brokerages on the net. A source page for futures market professionals will be online shortly, where a new client will be able to get Risk Disclosure Statements and fill in the account paperwork from his choice of online FCMs.

Besides the World Wide Web, which is the most exciting place to be in cyberspace, there are also "Usenet Newsgroups." Some of these are news-based locations, but most are places where net users discuss (in every imaginable nuance of that term) an unlimited variety of subject matters, including, of course, stocks, investments, and futures trading. For up-to-date news, interesting and highly-opinionated comments, price reports, or dire requests for help from clueless traders, you can check out: **misc.invest.stocks, misc.invest.futures, misc.invest.technical, clari.apbl.reports.commodity, clari.biz.commodity, and clari.biz.market.commodities.** (The "clari" group of newsgroups are news-based; you cannot post comments to these). A listing of the 10,000+ newsgroups now active can be found in many Internet guides. You can easily access them through the newest versions of the popular web browsers, which can be downloaded for free from the Internet.

As the Internet continues to grow at an exponential rate, it is important to know where to go on this electronic superhighway to find out what is currently available on the net in your field. You need electronic roadmaps to get around — nothing is worse than taking an off-ramp to nowhere! "Yahoo" was one of the first of the "search engines" on the Internet, and some still consider it the best Internet Web directory in existence. It has well organized subject listings and hypertext links. The Yahoo World Wide Web address is **http://www.yahoo.com.**

A search engine is a remarkable device which allows you to enter a few key words relating to your field and then it initiates a worldwide search for you, scanning millions of pages, documents and links relating to those words — in seconds — to ultimately provide you with a prioritized title and web address listing. Online directories and search engines are important ways to keep yourself from getting "lost in cyberspace."

Your Internet guide and Internet provider will give you further details on how to best utilize the Internet for your purposes and help get you happily zooming down that ever-expanding information superhighway . . . .

# THE CLOSING BELL

And it's another winning day!

I do hope that this study has given you experienced traders some profitable ideas, and you beginners a gentle yet firm shove forward on that "CST" path. The consistently successful trader is, above all, a synergist. With his own style, personality and intelligence, he has learned to creatively put the whole works together: tools, indicators, pattern recognition, timing techniques, trading confirmations, a technical/fundamental mix, market experience, intuition based on that experience, emotional discipline and excellent risk and money management techniques— all into a comprehensive personal trading methodology[10].

And if this look into the world of futures trading has helped some of you decide that futures trading is not for you at this present moment, for whatever reason(s), then that is an equally important and wise decision. Successful trading of futures contracts in real-time involves substantial investments of real time, real money and real knowledge. Until you are ready to commit all three, it is best to keep building up your reserves of each before making that first trade. As your knowledge grows, you will know when you are ready to step up to the plate and become a real player in this fascinating game and lucrative business!

For further specifics on getting setup to trade from home,

plus information concerning the latest trading software products offered by The Futures Group, please check our Internet web site at:

**http://www.futures-trader.com**

I would welcome and appreciate any comments/suggestions you may have about this publication for future editions. Please send these to:

e-mail: guidebook@futures-trader.com

"snail" mail: The Futures Group

P. O. Box 131

Leeds, MA 01053

USA

May you always cut your losses, trade with the trend, and let those profits run. God bless you and happy trading!

# FOOTNOTES

1. Hybrid swaps, inverse floaters, exotic options and other complex derivatives and synthetics are varieties of highly sophisticated financial products used primarily by large institutional traders, banking executives and CFO's. They are certainly more "exotic" than standardized futures but not necessarily more lucrative (their inherent complexity can, in fact, make them more risky). Certain financial publishers I have referenced for you in the Appendix also publish, in addition to literature on straight futures trading, the very latest in financial "exotica" should you be interested.

2. Throughout this book I am using the grammatical convention of referring to the trader as "he" solely for lack of a graceful unisexual pronoun in the English language ("He or She" or "S/He" just doesn't work for me). A number of women also suggested the I use "he" along with an explanation. I hope it is by now needless to say, but women can make fine traders, just like men can.

3. Glamann, K., *European Trade 1500-1750*, in C.M. Cipolla, *The Fontana Economic History of Europe, Vol.2*, London: Collins/Fontana Books, 1974.

4. Haccou, J.F., *Termijnhandel in Goederen*, Leiden: Stenfert Kroese, 1947.

5. Hauser, W.B., *Economic Institutional Change in Tokugawa Japan*, London: Cambridge University Press, 1974.

6. One of the latest developments in trading technology is the

emergence of automatic execution of trades through electronic terminals. These are currently becoming available to individuals and companies through private leasing agreements with the exchanges. Here are some reasons I am not interested in using them: (a) their high monthly fees and installation rates (b) the need to qualify for and obtain a special electronic trading permit (c) the fact that I'd have to keep my current setup anyway since the terminals don't have any of the charting capabilities I require and (d) no one to fight for me on the floor should I get a computer-glitched bad fill.

7. Accurate as of November 1996. These specs can change from time to time. Check with your broker for current information.

8. For further information about custom-programmed software for trading indicators and systems, please contact one of the addresses in "The Closing Bell".

9. The ultimate "de-stresser" for thousands of years, it's the perfect trading companion. Puts it all into a clear and most serene perspective. Recommended edition: *Bhagavada-Gita As It Is* by A.C. Bhaktivedanta Swami Prabhupada.

10. Recommended further reading to help piece together the technical end of your own trading system: *How to Build a Trading System*, the special October 1994 issue of *Futures Magazine*. See Sources/Resources below for contact information.

---

**Note:** Opposite is a facsimile of our Daily Trading Log. Please feel free to photocopy it and use it to record the important details of your trades.

# DAILY TRADING LOG

| Date | Time | Tkt | B/S | # | Market | Entry Price | OK | Exit Price | OK | Results |
|------|------|-----|-----|---|--------|-------------|-----|-----------|-----|---------|
| | | | | | | | | | | |
| | | | | | | | | | | |
| | | | | | | | | | | |
| | | | | | | | | | | |
| | | | | | | | | | | |
| | | | | | | | | | | |
| | | | | | | | | | | |
| | | | | | | | | | | |
| | | | | | | | | | | |
| | | | | | | | | | | |
| | | | | | | | | | | |
| | | | | | | | | | | |
| | | | | | | | | | | |
| | | | | | | | | | | |
| | | | | | | | | | | |
| | | | | | | | | | | |
| | | | | | | | | | | |
| | | | | | | | | | | |
| | | | | | | | | | | |
| | | | | | | | | | | |
| | | | | | | | | | | |
| | | | | | | | | | | |
| | | | | | | | | | | |
| | | | | | | | | | | |
| | | | | | | | | | | |
| | | | | | | | | | | |
| | | | | | | | | | | |
| | | | | | | | | | | |
| | | | | | | | | | | |
| | | | | | | | | | | |

# APPENDIX A

## The Keltner Channel

For traders using either *TradeStation* or *SuperCharts* charting software by Omega Research, the following is the *Easy Language* software code for the Keltner Channel. This is the default version which also includes the code for plotting the central band:

```
Inputs: Price(Close),MALen(10),Const(.8);
Vars: CentLine(0), AvgRange(0), Upper(0), Lower(0);

CentLine=Average(Price,MALen);
AvgRange=Average(TrueRange,MALen);
Upper=CentLine+(AvgRange*Const);
Lower=CentLine-(AvgRange*Const);

Plot1(CentLine,"CentLine");
Plot2(Upper,"Upper");
Plot3(Lower,"Lower");
```

*Printed with permission, Omega Research, Inc.*

# Appendix B

Further Examples of
Multiple Time Frame
Trading Confirmation

# Buy Formations

The following charts illustrate the "profit fan" combination of moving averages (e.g. 5 bar MA over 9 bar MA over 20 bar MA) spread just above the middle Keltner band. The simultaneous formation of this type of pattern in both short and longer intraday time frames (as occurred at the same date and time on these charts) is a powerful "go" signal to trade.

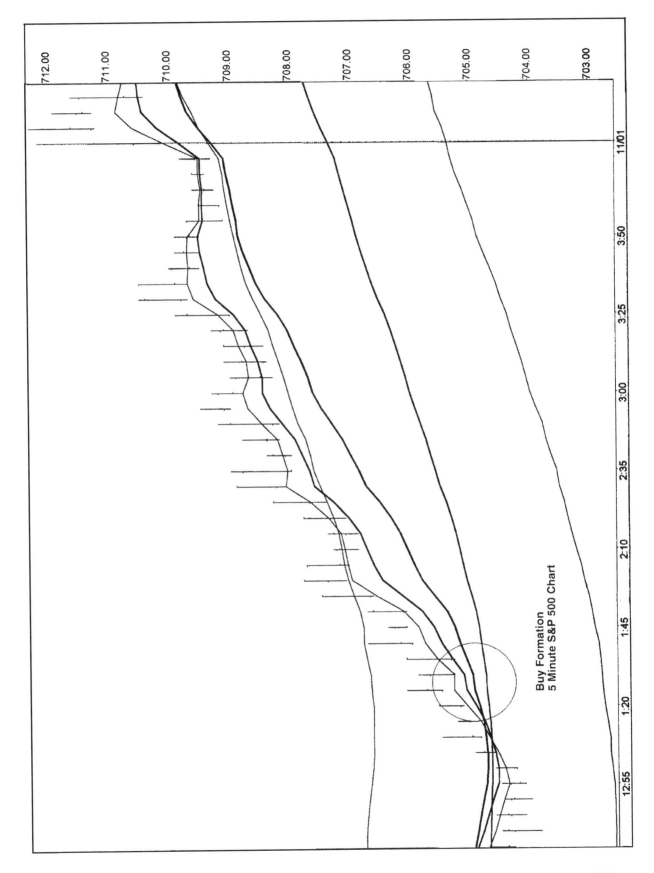

Buy Formation
5 Minute S&P 500 Chart

Chart created with TradeStation™ by Omega Research, Inc.

201

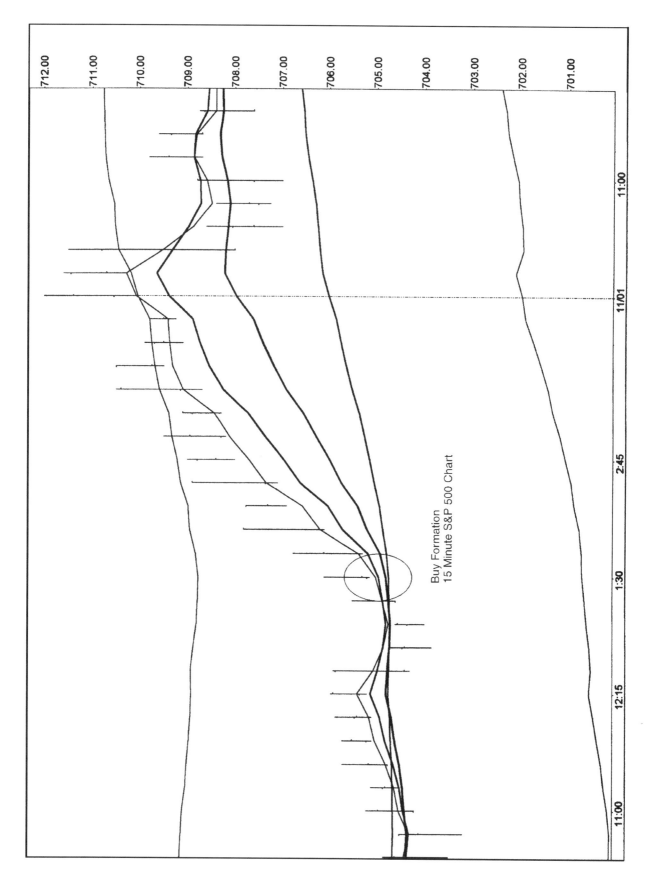

Buy Formation
15 Minute S&P 500 Chart

Chart created with TradeStation™ by Omega Research, Inc.

202

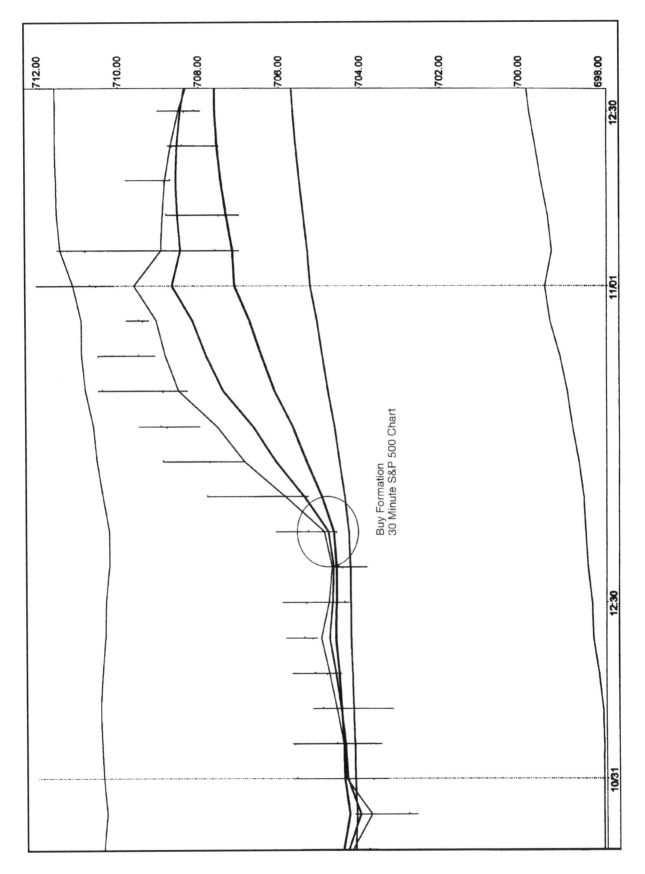

Buy Formation
30 Minute S&P 500 Chart

Chart created with TradeStation™ by Omega Research, Inc.

203

# Sell Formations

Although many traders compare multiple time frame charts first in the shorter time frames and then progressively to longer and longer time frames, the following charts illustrate how it can also be done in reverse: long-term to short. The first bar to close beneath (or above) a Keltner band can be particularly significant, and we pay close attention when this first occurs on the thirty minute chart. The circled areas show where that event happened in all three time frames.

The same thing occurs the next day when a bar closes beneath the thirty minute middle Keltner band (of course, we are also noticing that the moving average/Keltner patterns are confirming the downward trend). A day later, the market will not give us a clear closing bar under the bottom Keltner band, and this indicates an imminent market reversal. A powerful trend line breakout occurred "to the North" soon after.

Comparing both the fifteen- and thirty-minute charts to the five-minute chart has many benefits. One of the most important is that the broader perspective can definitely help us to stay in this profitable trade much longer — and let our profits run. If we were viewing the five minute chart alone, we would get a good entry on the trade, but might exit it prematurely when the bars repeatedly tested the bottom Keltner band throughout the entire period. The longer time frames, however, give us a clear picture of the real nature and extent of the move, as well as the best exit (profit target) areas for this downward trend.

Combining the information from all the time frames can enable us to secure both the best entry and exit points, and the largest profits for each trade. (This goes for buy formations as well).

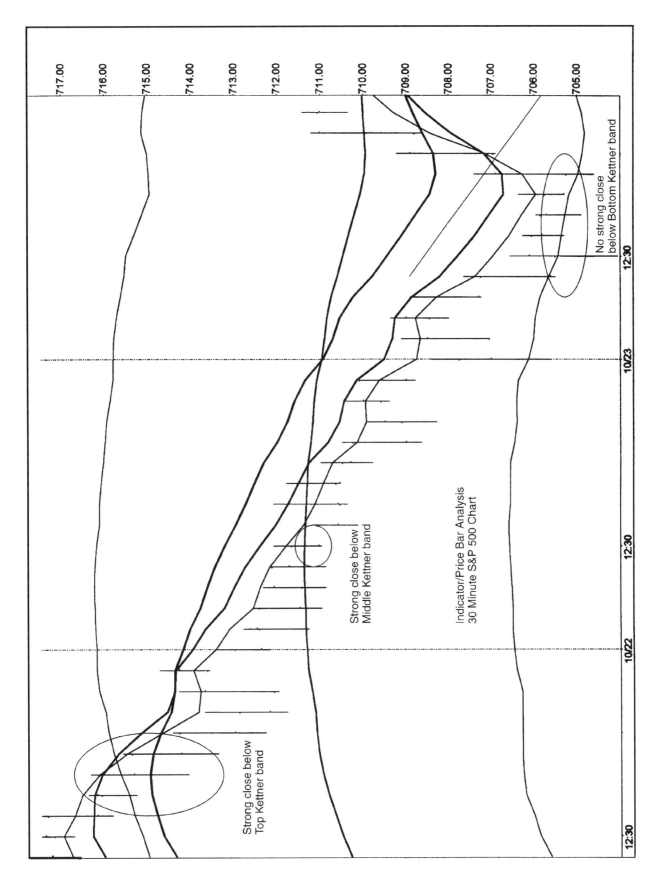

Strong close below
Top Kettner band

Strong close below
Middle Kettner band

Indicator/Price Bar Analysis
30 Minute S&P 500 Chart

No strong close
below Bottom Kettner band

717.00
716.00
715.00
714.00
713.00
712.00
711.00
710.00
709.00
708.00
707.00
706.00
705.00

12:30
10/22
12:30
10/23
12:30

Chart created with TradeStation™ by Omega Research, Inc.

205

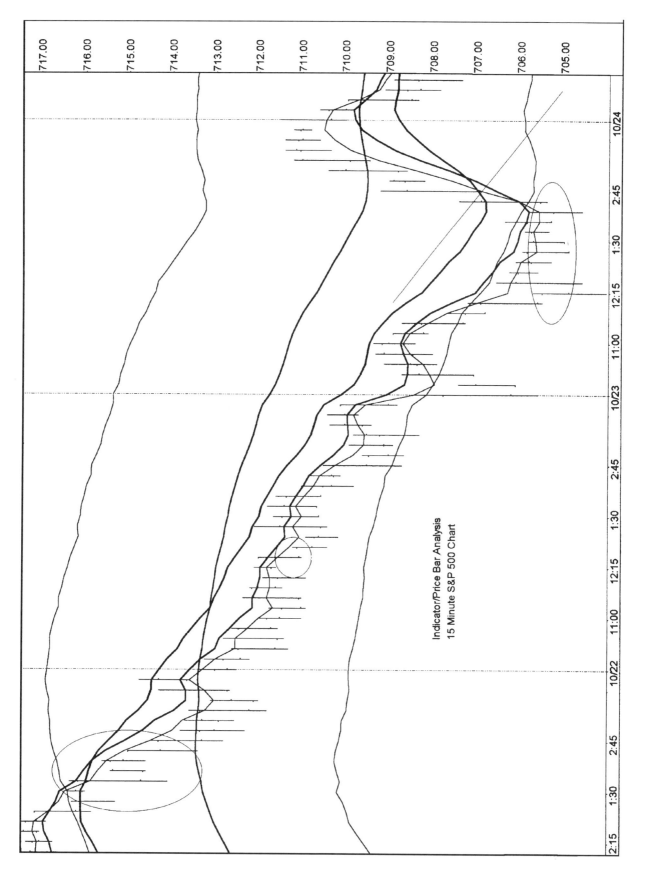

Indicator/Price Bar Analysis
15 Minute S&P 500 Chart

Chart created with TradeStation™ by Omega Research, Inc.

206

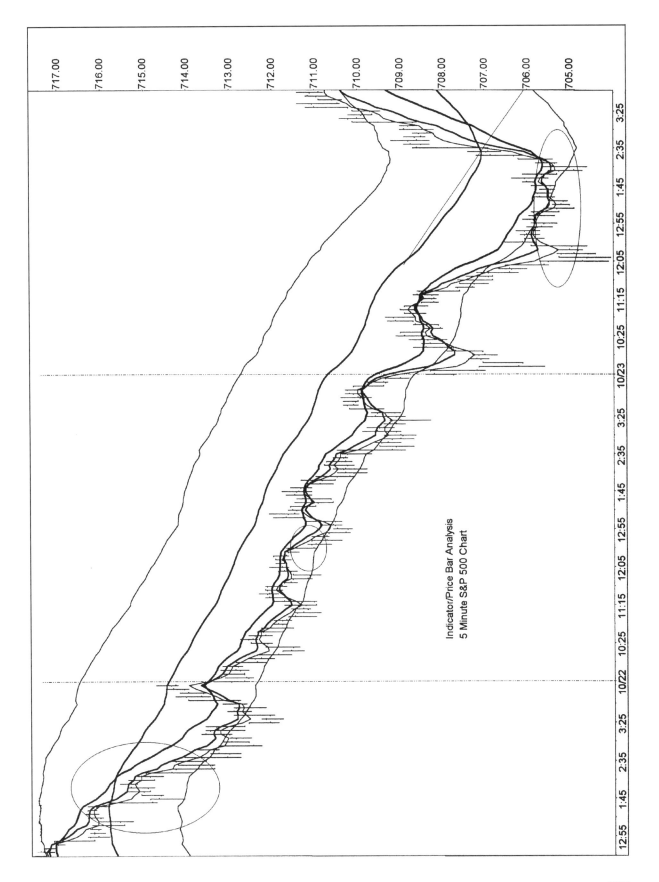

Indicator/Price Bar Analysis
5 Minute S&P 500 Chart

Chart created with TradeStation™ by Omega Research, Inc.

207

## Position Trades

The previous three charts illustrate the multiple time frame analysis of a short-term position trade. Entering and exiting according to the indications would bring a profit of approximately $4,000 per contract over that three day period.

The following charts show what can happen when even further confirmation is obtained. Here the "profit fan" formed on the 5, 15, 30 and hourly charts, an exceptionally strong trend-forming indication. By taking a short-term entry in the 5 minute time frame, this trade could be managed very profitably over the next four days. Entry on day 1 to exit (MOC) on day 4 would bring profits of approximately $11,000 per contract.

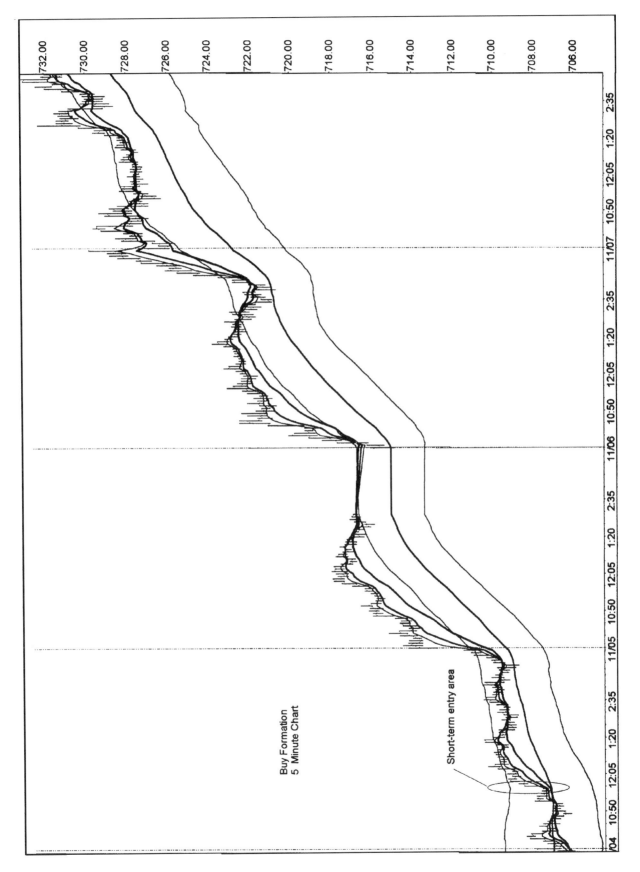

Buy Formation
5 Minute Chart

Short-term entry area

732.00
730.00
728.00
726.00
724.00
722.00
720.00
718.00
716.00
714.00
712.00
710.00
708.00
706.00

10:50  12:05  1:20  2:35  11/05  10:50  12:05  1:20  2:35  11/06  10:50  12:05  1:20  2:35  11/07  10:50  12:05  1:20  2:35

Chart created with TradeStation™ by Omega Research, Inc.

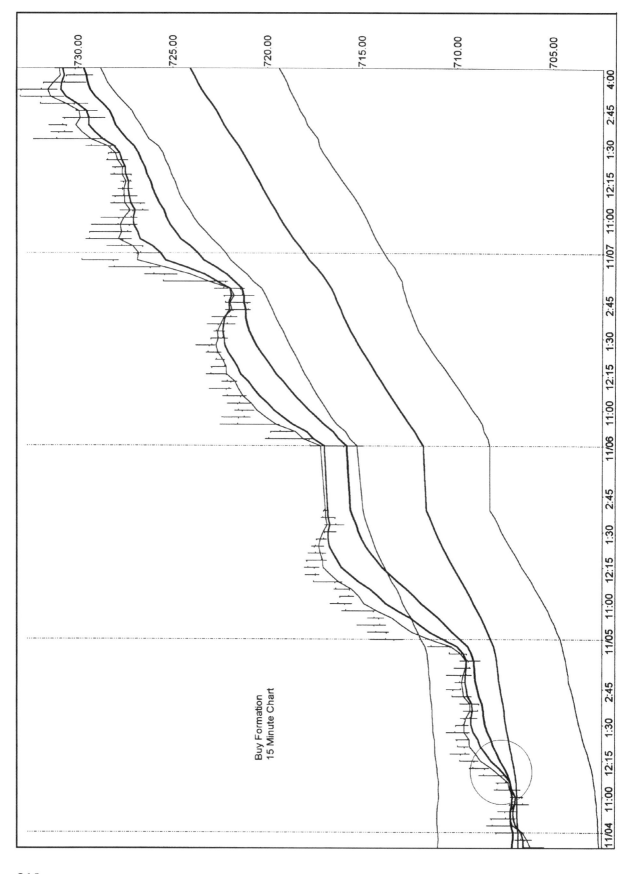

Buy Formation
15 Minute Chart

Chart created with TradeStation™ by Omega Research, Inc.

210

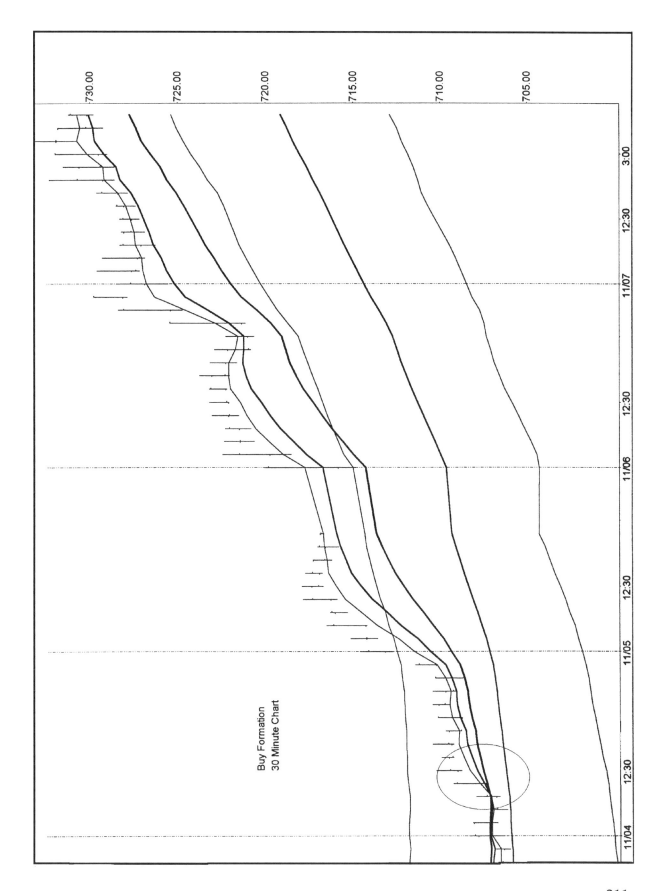

Buy Formation
30 Minute Chart

Chart created with TradeStation™ by Omega Research, Inc.

211

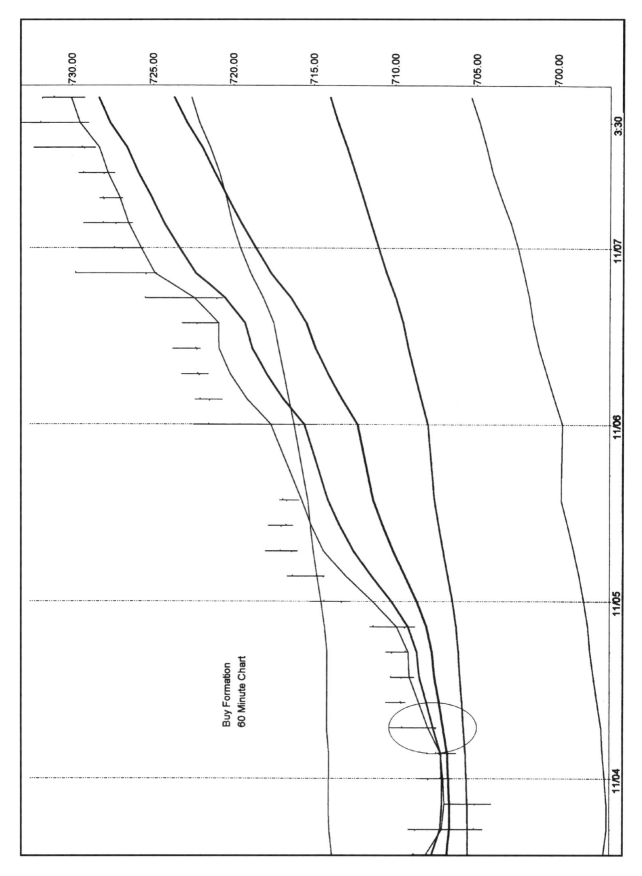

Buy Formation
60 Minute Chart

Chart created with TradeStation™ by Omega Research, Inc.

# APPENDIX C

## The Keltner Confirmation (KC) Method

# The Keltner Confirmation (KC) Method

The KC Method, elements of which have been described and illustrated throughout this book, is a highly-effective and profitable trading methodology.

Using our re-programmed version of the Keltner Channel as the template, we have developed 10 more confirming/filtering indicators, studies and functions that all work to synergize powerfully with our Keltner (see Appendix E and its discussion of trading "synergy"). This software package is designed to alert you, visibly and audibly, exactly when the optimal timing and pattern characteristics have developed to produce *confirmed* winning trades (see Appendix D and its discussion of how to examine performance summaries).

We call it the *KC Collection* and are now offering it to users of *Omega TradeStation* or *SuperCharts*. The charts on the following pages illustrate a sampling of actual signals generated in different time frames for a variety of commodities. Profits are calculated from the KC entry signal to the breakout exit through the diagonal trend line or MOC order.

For further information, including examples of actual trading signals on full-color charts, plus descriptions of the different software elements of the *KC Collection*, please visit our World Wide Web (WWW) trading site on the Internet:

**http://www.futures-trader.com**

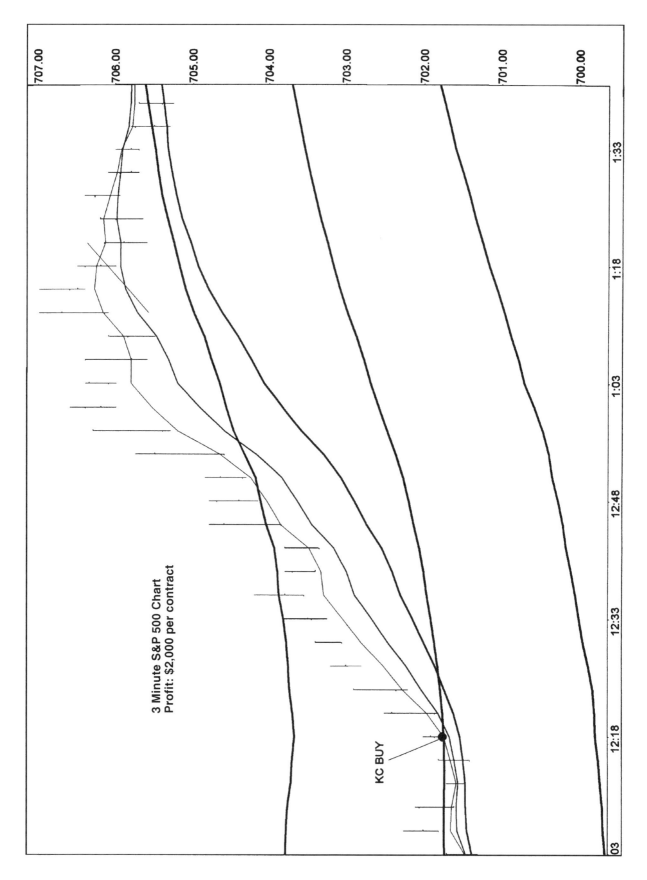

3 Minute S&P 500 Chart
Profit: $2,000 per contract

KC BUY

Chart created with TradeStation™ by Omega Research, Inc.

216

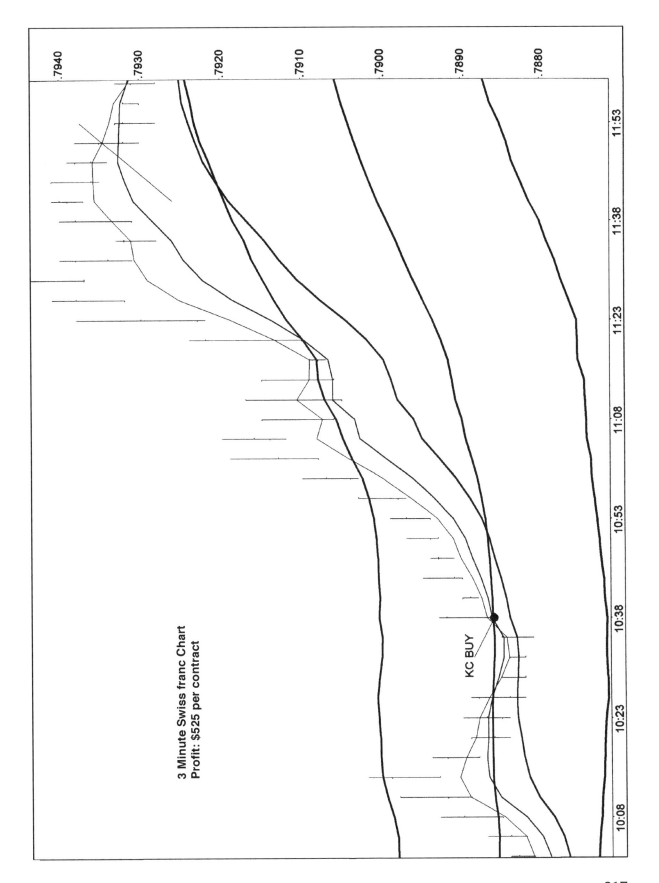

3 Minute Swiss franc Chart
Profit: $525 per contract

KC BUY

Chart created with TradeStation™ by Omega Research, Inc.

217

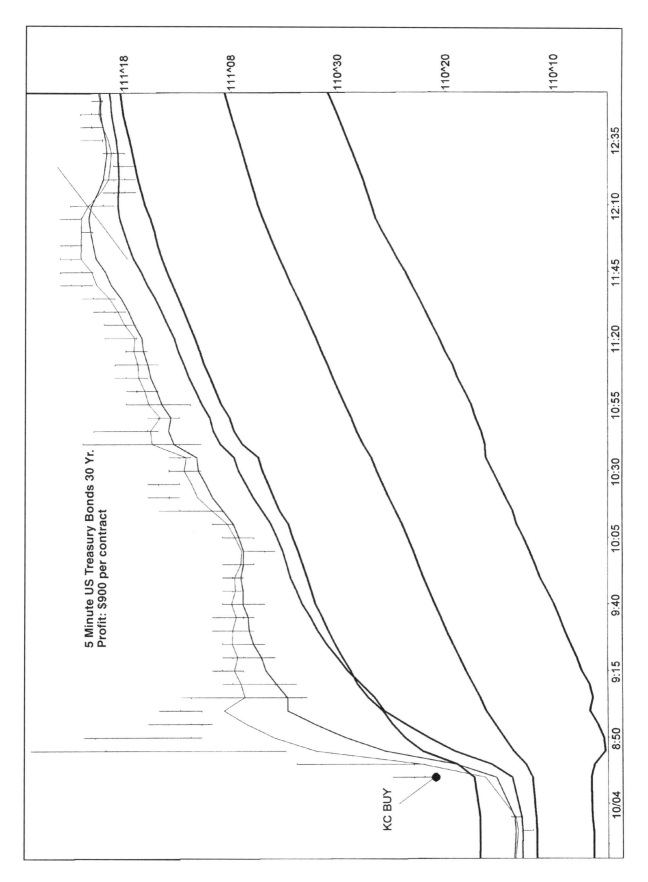

5 Minute US Treasury Bonds 30 Yr.
Profit: $900 per contract

KC BUY

111^18
111^08
110^30
110^20
110^10

10/04   8:50   9:15   9:40   10:05   10:30   10:55   11:20   11:45   12:10   12:35

Chart created with TradeStation™ by Omega Research, Inc.

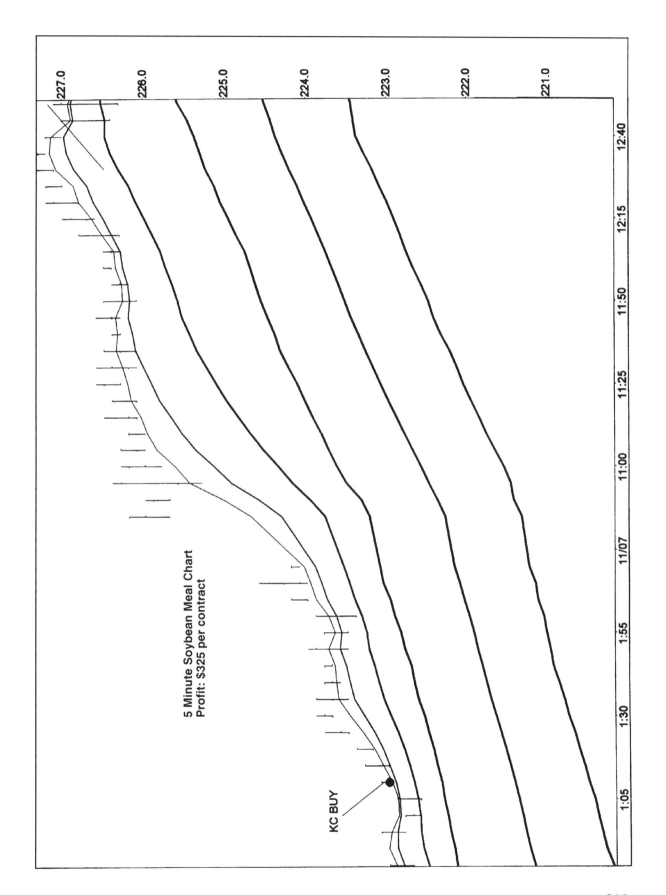

5 Minute Soybean Meal Chart
Profit: $325 per contract

KC BUY

Chart created with TradeStation™ by Omega Research, Inc.

219

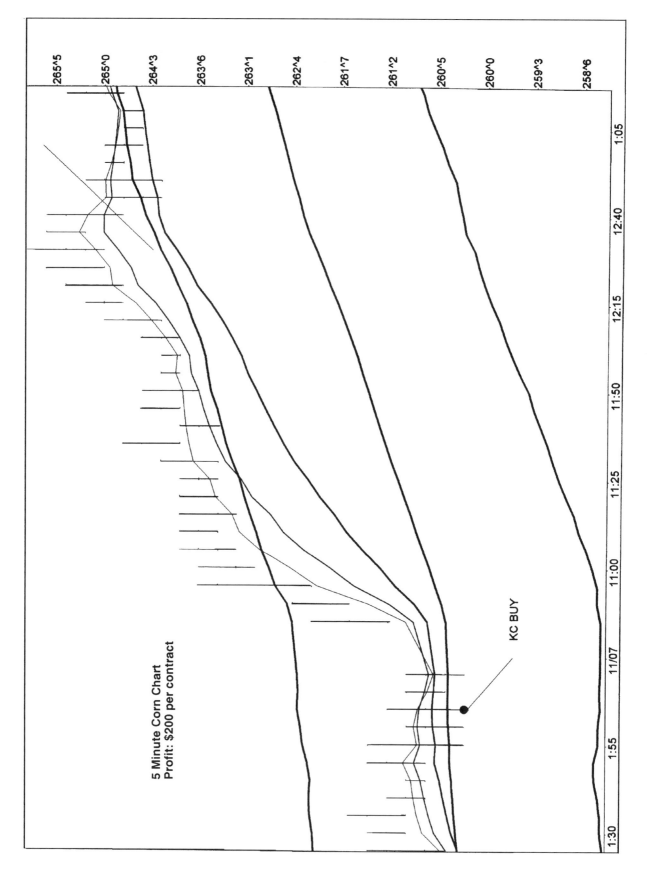

5 Minute Corn Chart
Profit: $200 per contract

KC BUY

Chart created with TradeStation™ by Omega Research, Inc.

220

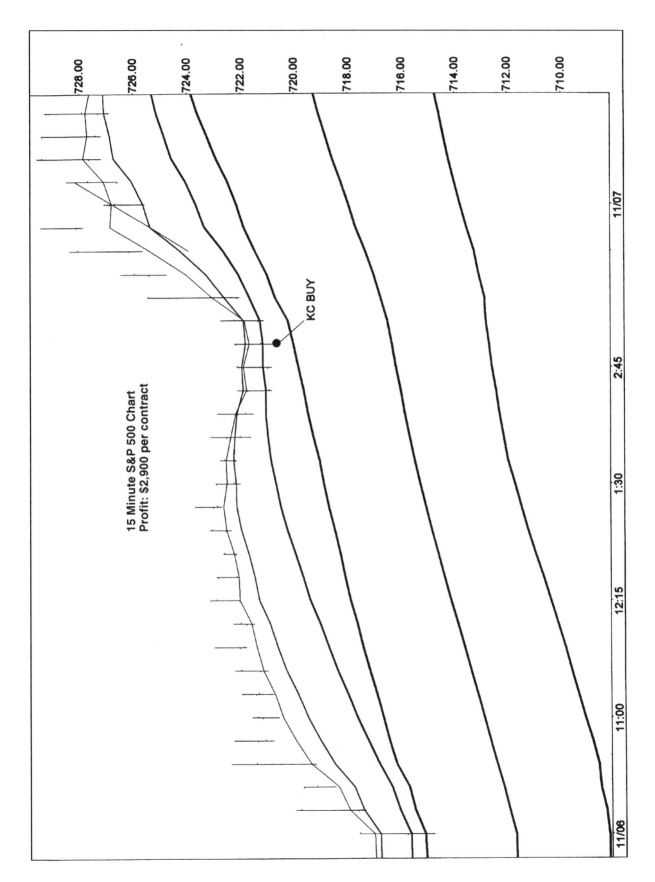

15 Minute S&P 500 Chart
Profit: $2,900 per contract

KC BUY

728.00
726.00
724.00
722.00
720.00
718.00
716.00
714.00
712.00
710.00

11/06    11:00    12:15    1:30    2:45    11/07

Chart created with TradeStation™ by Omega Research, Inc.

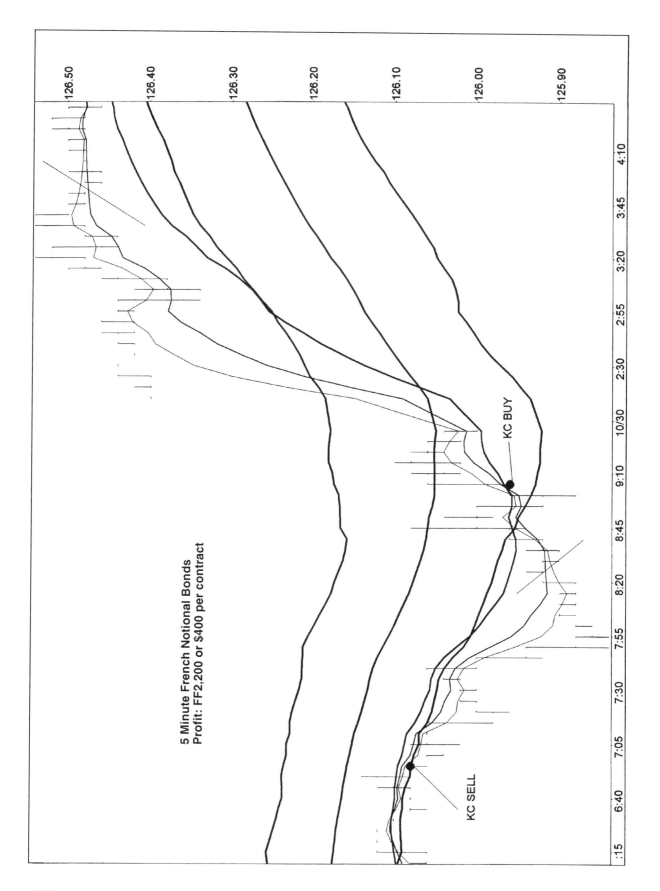

5 Minute French Notional Bonds
Profit: FF2,200 or $400 per contract

126.50
126.40
126.30
126.20
126.10
126.00
125.90

:15  6:40  7:05  7:30  7:55  8:20  8:45  9:10  10/30  2:30  2:55  3:20  3:45  4:10

KC BUY

KC SELL

Chart created with TradeStation™ by Omega Research, Inc.

222

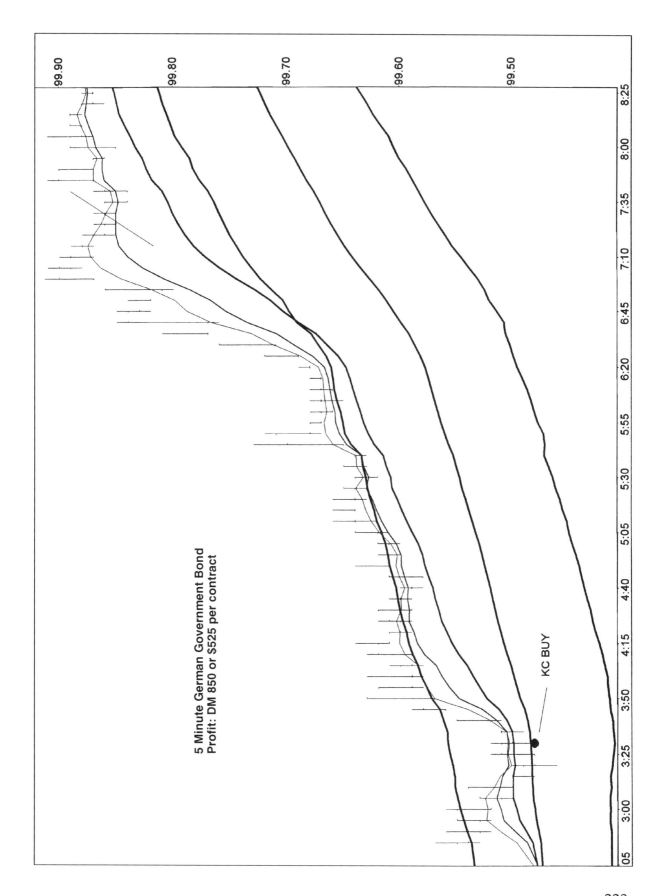

5 Minute German Government Bond
Profit: DM 850 or $525 per contract

KC BUY

Chart created with TradeStation™ by Omega Research, Inc.

223

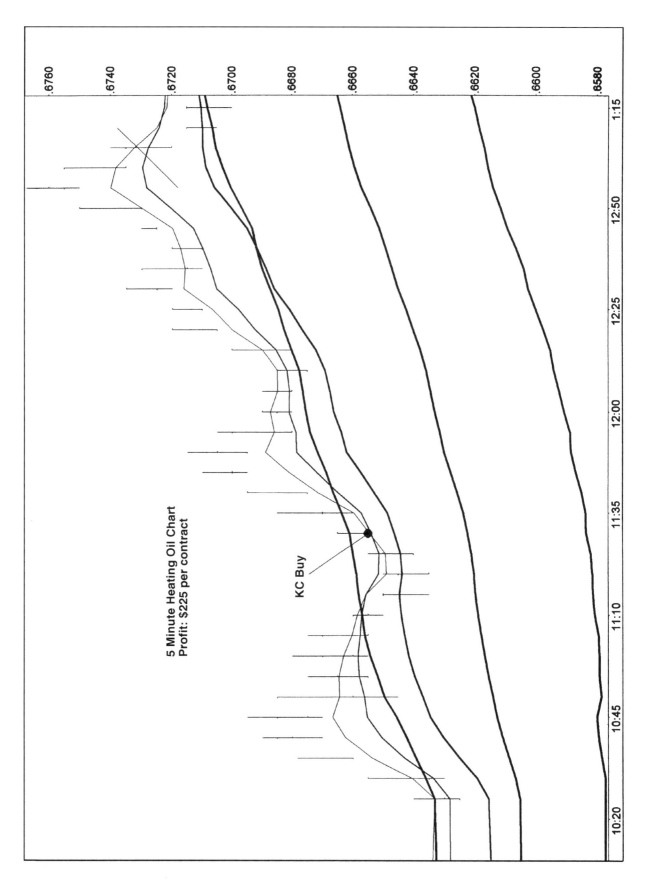

5 Minute Heating Oil Chart
Profit: $225 per contract

KC Buy

.6760 .6740 .6720 .6700 .6680 .6660 .6640 .6620 .6600 .6580

10:20 10:45 11:10 11:35 12:00 12:25 12:50 1:15

Chart created with TradeStation™ by Omega Research, Inc.

224

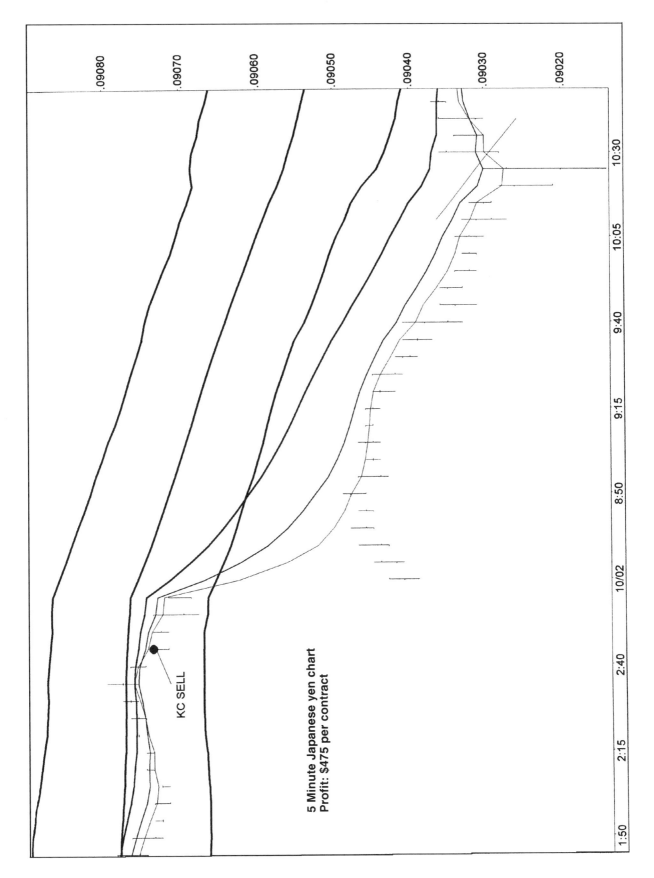

KC SELL

**5 Minute Japanese yen chart**
**Profit: $475 per contract**

.09080
.09070
.09060
.09050
.09040
.09030
.09020

1:50   2:15   2:40   10/02   8:50   9:15   9:40   10:05   10:30

Chart created with TradeStation™ by Omega Research, Inc.

225

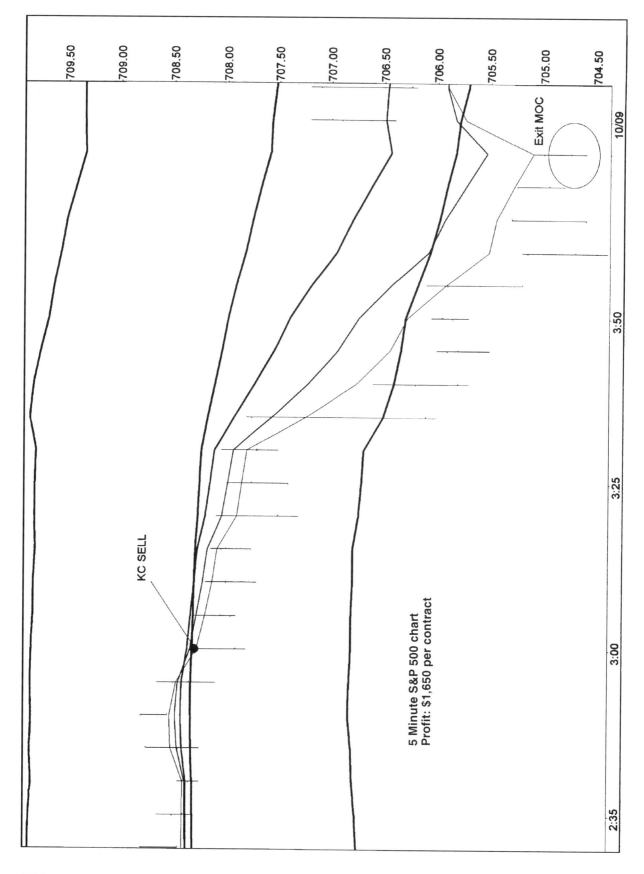

226

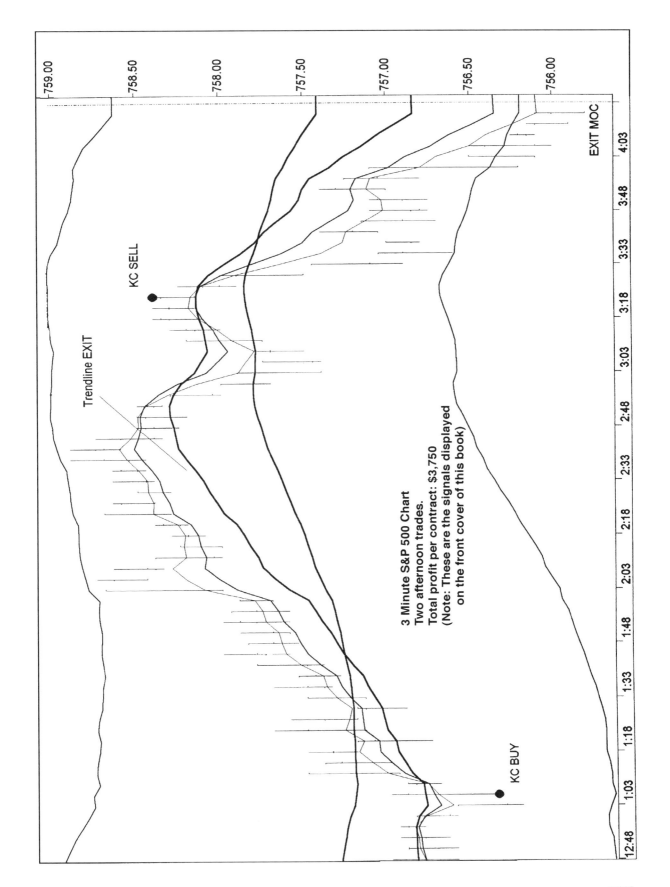

3 Minute S&P 500 Chart
Two afternoon trades.
Total profit per contract: $3,750
(Note: These are the signals displayed
on the front cover of this book)

Chart created with TradeStation™ by Omega Research Inc.

227

# APPENDIX D

## Trading Performance Summaries

# EXAMINING PERFORMANCE SUMMARIES

System reports, which can be automatically generated from within sophisticated charting and testing programs like *Omega TradeStation*, offer a wealth of valuable information to the trader. They can help him to clearly discriminate between a poor to fair system and a spectacular one.

The summaries in this Appendix describe performance results for the *KC Collection,* but the category explanations below will help you to analyze the reports for any software package you may be considering or currently testing.

## INTRADAY SUMMARY

The first summary is a illustration of what can happen when the *KC Collection* is traded intraday for even a short period. The market is the S&P 500 and we are trading with 5 minute bars. For the time period, we chose the last six weeks just prior to going to press with this new guidebook edition.

Immediately evident is the gap between the "largest winning trade" and the "largest losing trade", as well as between the "average winning trade" and the "average losing trade." For a method to be consistently profitable, these numbers must be clearly and strongly skewed to the winning side, as these are. "Avg # bars" is another important comparison. A winning strategy must generate a significantly greater number of bars per each winning trade than it does for each losing trade. The *KC Collection* tends to work well in this category because of its tendency to catch the largest and longest winning moves (i.e., third Elliot Waves).

"Maximum intraday drawdown" is an important factor which must be related to the volatility of the market in question. In general, it should be a small percentage of both the gross and net profit figures. Its dollar amount is used for the "account size required" number. Obviously, the actual account size required to trade depends on the margin requirements for the contract in question, but this purely mathematical view gives us an excellent indication of the overall profitability of the system. The ROA (Return on Account) expresses this profitability as a function of the maximum intraday drawdown (i.e. minimum account size required) and the total net profit.

## DAILY SUMMARIES

The next four summaries illustrate what can happen when the *KC Collection* is traded in the long-term, on daily bars. Each report takes the historical data of a particular contract back a number of decades to when trading began in that commodity. (Please note that the summary reports in this Appendix do not include the costs for broker commissions and trading slippage).

## THE KC COLLECTION

It is important to note that the results on the following pages are considering what happens when only 4 of the 11 elements of the *KC Collection* are employed. These are called the *system elements*. The other 7 elements of the Collection (the *discretionary elements*) are used to filter out many of the losing trades (seen on the Performance Summaries) and thus assist to further increase the overall profitability of the system. (This is explained and illustrated further in Appendix E).

Whatever software package you either decide to purchase or wind-up developing yourself, a careful examination of its performance summaries can clearly help you to determine its potential, and thus its bottom-line value to you.

## Omega TradeStation 4.0 System Report

**KC Collection**          S&P 500-5 Min.          09/12/96 - 10/30/96
**Performance Summary: All Trades**

| | | | |
|---|---|---|---|
| **Total net profit** | $10,720.00 | Open position P/L | $ 0.00 |
| Gross Profit | $16,850.00 | Gross Loss | $-6,125.00 |
| | | | |
| Total # of trades | 67 | Percent Profitable | 48% |
| Number winning trades | 32 | Number losing trades | 35 |
| | | | |
| Largest winning trade | $2,475.00 | Largest losing trade | $-175.00 |
| Average winning trade | $ 526.56 | Average losing trade | $-175.00 |
| Ratio avg. win/avg. loss | 3.01 | Avg trade (win & loss) | $ 160.07 |
| | | | |
| Max consec. winners | 4 | Max consec. losers | 6 |
| Avg #bars in winners | 11 | Avg # bars in losers | 6 |
| | | | |
| Max intraday drawdown | $-1,550.00 | | |
| Profit factor | 2.75 | Max # contracts held | 1 |
| Account size required | $1,550.00 | **Return on Account** | **692%** |

## Omega TradeStation 4.0 System Report

**KC Collection**          CBT CORN - Daily          02/15/68 - 07/31/96
**Performance Summary: All Trades**

| | | | |
|---|---|---|---|
| **Total net profit** | $17,025.00 | Open position P/L | $ 0.00 |
| Gross Profit | $28,956.00 | Gross Loss | $-11,931.25 |
| | | | |
| Total # of trades | 166 | Percent Profitable | 36% |
| Number winning trades | 60 | Number losing trades | 106 |
| | | | |
| Largest winning trade | $6,312.50 | Largest losing trade | $-500.00 |
| Average winning trade | $ 482.60 | Average losing trade | $-112.56 |
| Ratio avg. win/avg. loss | 4.29 | Avg trade (win & loss) | $ 102.56 |
| | | | |
| Max consec. winners | 5 | Max consec. losers | 9 |
| Avg #bars in winners | 19 | Avg # bars in losers | 4 |
| | | | |
| Max drawdown | $-1,812.50 | | |
| Profit factor | 2.43 | Max # contracts held | 1 |
| Account size required | $1,812.50 | **Return on Account** | **939%** |

## Omega TradeStation 4.0 System Report

**KC Collection**    **SOYBEANS - Daily**    02/02/68 - 07/31/96
**Performance Summary: All Trades**

| | | | |
|---|---|---|---|
| **Total net profit** | **$58,956.25** | Open position P/L | $ 0.00 |
| Gross Profit | $95,406.25 | Gross Loss | $-36,450.00 |
| | | | |
| Total # of trades | 173 | Percent Profitable | 46% |
| Number winning trades | 79 | Number losing trades | 94 |
| | | | |
| Largest winning trade | $14,675.00 | Largest losing trade | $-1,000.00 |
| Average winning trade | $1,207.67 | Average losing trade | $-387.77 |
| Ratio avg. win/avg. loss | 3.11 | Avg trade (win & loss) | $ 341.79 |
| | | | |
| Max consec. winners | 6 | Max consec. losers | 9 |
| Avg #bars in winners | 17 | Avg # bars in losers | 6 |
| | | | |
| Max drawdown | $-9,200.00 | | |
| Profit factor | 2.62 | Max # contracts held | 1 |
| Account size required | $9,200.00 | **Return on Account** | **641%** |

## Omega TradeStation 4.0 System Report

**KC Collection**    **COMEX GOLD - Daily**    12/31/74 - 07/31/96
**Performance Summary: All Trades**

| | | | |
|---|---|---|---|
| **Total net profit** | **$60,460.00** | Open position P/L | $ 0.00 |
| Gross Profit | $104,680.00 | Gross Loss | $-44,220.00 |
| | | | |
| Total # of trades | 112366 | Percent Profitable | 40% |
| Number winning trades | 57 | Number losing trades | 66 |
| | | | |
| Largest winning trade | $29,300.00 | Largest losing trade | $-2,500.00 |
| Average winning trade | $1,836.49 | Average losing trade | $-670.00 |
| Ratio avg. win/avg. loss | 2.74 | Avg trade (win & loss) | $ 491.54 |
| | | | |
| Max consec. winners | 4 | Max consec. losers | 5 |
| Avg #bars in winners | 21 | Avg # bars in losers | 9 |
| | | | |
| Max drawdown | $-6,490.00 | | |
| Profit factor | 2.37 | Max # contracts held | 1 |
| Account size required | $6,490.00 | **Return on Account** | **932%** |

## Omega TradeStation 4.0 System Report

**KC Collection**                  COMEX SILVER - Daily                  07/29/71 - 07/31/96
**Performance Summary: All Trades**

| | | | |
|---|---|---|---|
| **Total net profit** | **$66,660.00** | Open position P/L | $ 0.00 |
| Gross Profit | $104,010.00 | Gross Loss | $-37,350.00 |
| | | | |
| Total # of trades | 113 | Percent Profitable | 40% |
| Number winning trades | 45 | Number losing trades | 68 |
| | | | |
| Largest winning trade | $24,950.00 | Largest losing trade | $-2,500.00 |
| Average winning trade | $ 2,311.33 | Average losing trade | $-549.26 |
| Ratio avg. win/avg. loss | 4.21 | Avg trade (win & loss) | $ 589.91 |
| | | | |
| Max consec. winners | 4 | Max consec. losers | 7 |
| Avg #bars in winners | 22 | Avg # bars in losers | 6 |
| | | | |
| Max drawdown | $-5,660.00 | | |
| Profit factor | 2.78 | Max # contracts held | 1 |
| Account size required | $5,660.50 | **Return on Account** | **1178%** |

# APPENDIX E

**System + Discretion =** *Synergy*

# THE SUM OF THE PARTS IS GREATER THAN THE WHOLE

"Synergism" is defined in *Merriam Webster's Collegiate Dictionary* as "the interaction of discrete conditions such that the total effect is *enhanced* (italics mine), and is greater than the sum of the individual effects."

The concept of "trading synergy" appears throughout this guide. We saw it first in the discussion of trading perspectives, where, by combining both technical and fundamental information, the trader can have a clearer vision of the markets than he can by relying exclusively on either perspective alone. We saw it again in the section on multiple time frame trading, where, through analysis of both short- and long-term charts, the trader is able to successfully confirm his short-term signals by trading with the long-term trend, resulting in increased profits.

This principle can prove its great value once again if the technical trader will consider it when he is developing his own trading methodology. As described earlier in this guide, traders are generally categorized to be either system traders (those who strictly follow mechanical signals) or discretionary traders (those who analyze chart patterns and indicators to come to their trading decisions). Each method has its strengths and weaknesses.

In the first case, vendors of purely mechanical trading systems will often describe it as an advantage that the trader does not have to look at charts or really learn how to trade at all. All he has to do is wait for an audible signal to occur, and then just read the order to the broker right off the screen. This certainly sounds wonderful, but unfortunately, in real-time trading, this luxurious picture of a purely "hands-off" scenario can be often quite deceptive. The problem with trading systems like these is that they are often heir to very large drawdowns, and therefore the margin requirements to trade them are usually quite high (whether or not they are actually profitable). Another more subtle point is that they require complete "surrender" to the system, with no chance for the trader to offer any personal input, trading knowledge or creativity. This is especially true in the case of systems that do not utilize charts, but just offer signals generated through their internal algorithms; this can also help to make them especially difficult to trade psychologically after taking a long string of losses.

On the other hand, purely discretionary methods require that your eyes be on those charts — if not glued to the same — throughout the complete morning and afternoon sessions (in real-time trading). Should the trader want to take advantage of all of the best chart and indicator patterns developing throughout the day, and not miss any, there really is no way to find them other than to be there. This ability to recognize the most profitable patterns obviously requires that the trader first learn what they are, through detailed analysis and determined practice.

Of the two perspectives, which trader do you think really learns how to trade? The system trader who (blindly?) takes mechanical signals with no chance for personal analysis, or the discretionary trader who must learn to recognize profitable patterns through serious analysis and practice? I think you can see my bias here. In my opinion, it is the discretionary trader alone who is clearly in the position to really *learn* how to technically trade stocks and futures. I am not saying that there are no profitable mechanical systems out there — there are — it is just that, for me, trading them *exclusively* is frought with both financial and psychological disadvantages.

So how do we capture the advantages and minimize the disadvantages of both mechanical systems and discretionary methods? And come to that most appealing, profitable point of consistent synergy? One way is to design your method to mechanically signal you *when* to apply your discretionary method! This is what the **KC Collection** is designed to do, and I recommend you consider these broad design concepts should you be a developer, or potential developer, of your own trading methodology.

Appendix C contains charts which display **KC Collection** mechanical signals and the market action following those signals. The performance summaries of Appendix D give an idea of what can happen when these signals alone are traded over time. As mentioned there, these signals (seen as black dots on the charts) comprise only four of the eleven elements of the **KC Collection.**

These are the *mechanical system elements.* The other seven are the *discretionary confirming elements.* One way to maximize the profitability of your own system/method is to make sure it uses *both trending and countertrending indicators which complement each other.* This is what we have done with our software.

One of these discretionary elements, our Peak/Valley (P/V) Oscillator, has been added to the charts on the following pages, and the benefit of its use is immediately apparent. Example #1 shows a **KC Collection** mechanical sell signal that has been effectively *filtered out* using the P/V Oscillator (note that the Keltner itself is also one of these discretionary confirming elements). That mechanical signal could have easily appeared on the performance summary as a losing trade (it soon became a loss after the Keltner bounce), but as we successfully filtered it out with both the P/V Ocillator and the Keltner, we didn't take that trade — and our bottom line profit is now that much higher. The sell signal in Example #2, on the other hand, was *confirmed* strongly by the P/V Oscillator and so we can take that one with confidence. Bottom line: the analysis of our discretionary indicators, following the mechanical sell signals, has increased the profitability of the overall method by filtering out losers and confirming winners. See how it works?

It is important to note that the mechanical signals of the *KC Collection* are *trend-following studies,* and the P/V Oscillator, since it is an oscillator, is a *countertrending study.* By combining robust trending studies with complementary countertrending studies we dramatically increase the overall profitability of the method. Examples #3 and #4 show the same methodology in action for *KC Collection* mechanical buy signals.

By programming the appropriate mechanical signal with an audible and visual display, we are alerted — at a very favorable market moment — to immediately concentrate on *analyzing the viability of that signal* with our discretionary elements (for instance, with the higher high peaks on the P/V Oscillator for a buy signal, and lower low valleys for a sell signal). This alert is a major advantage since markets tend to spend most of their time "in the noise", and we really want to be seriously looking at the screen, analyzing our indicators with the greatest concentration, at only the most opportune moments.

We recommend that you consider either developing or acquiring a trading system that works closely with a complementary discretionary method — so that *you* can trade with a strong measure of control. Trading with a discretionary attitude, born of judgement based on your own experience, will help you to become a more knowledgable trader. And *that* — above all — is what is going to really help you to reach your financial goals.

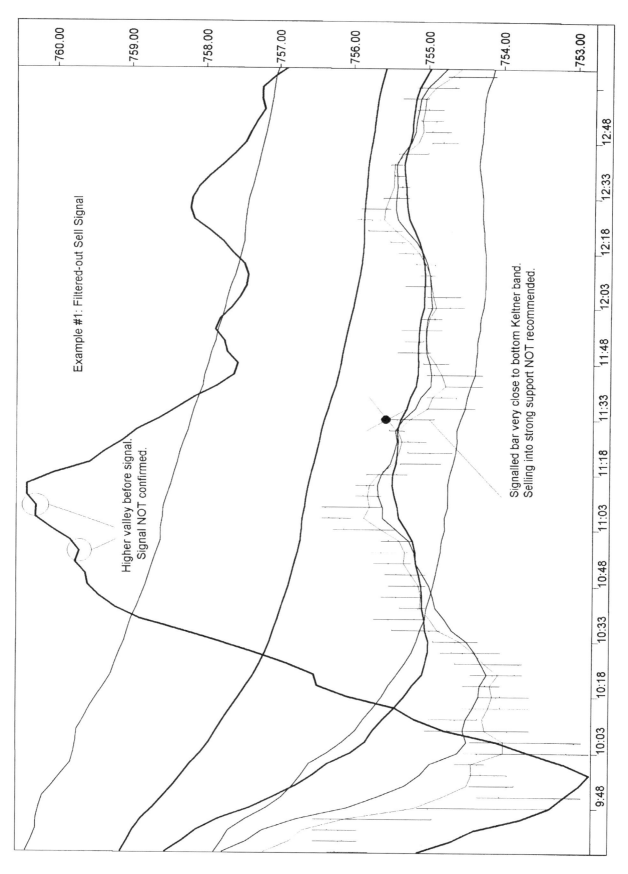

Example #1: Filtered-out Sell Signal

Higher valley before signal.
Signal NOT confirmed.

Signalled bar very close to bottom Keltner band.
Selling into strong support NOT recommended.

Chart created with TradeStation™ by Omega Research, Inc.

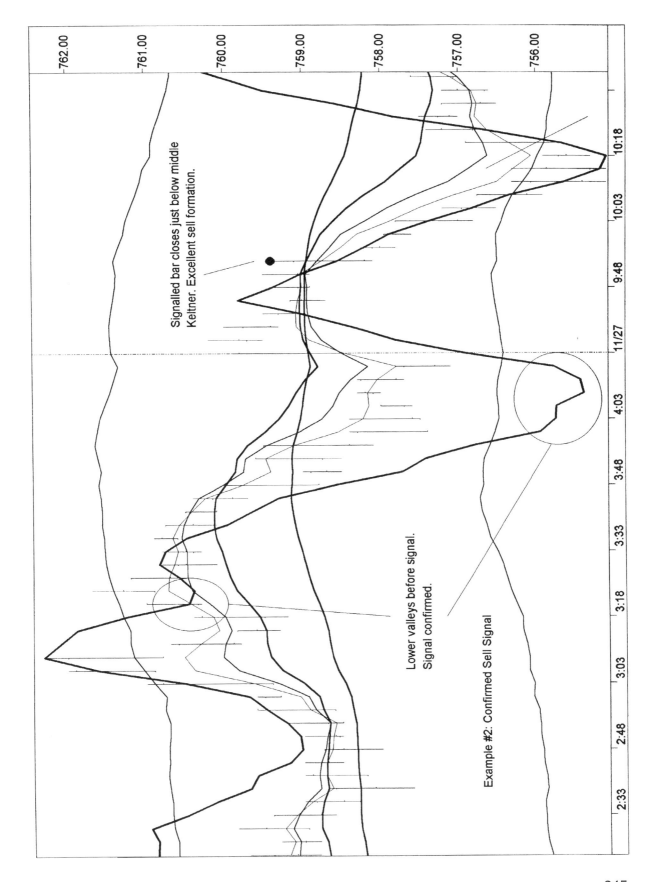

762.00
761.00
760.00
759.00
758.00
757.00
756.00

2:33  2:48  3:03  3:18  3:33  3:48  4:03  11/27  9:48  10:03  10:18

Signalled bar closes just below middle
Keltner. Excellent sell formation.

Lower valleys before signal.
Signal confirmed.

Example #2: Confirmed Sell Signal

Chart created with TradeStation™ by Omega Research, Inc.

245

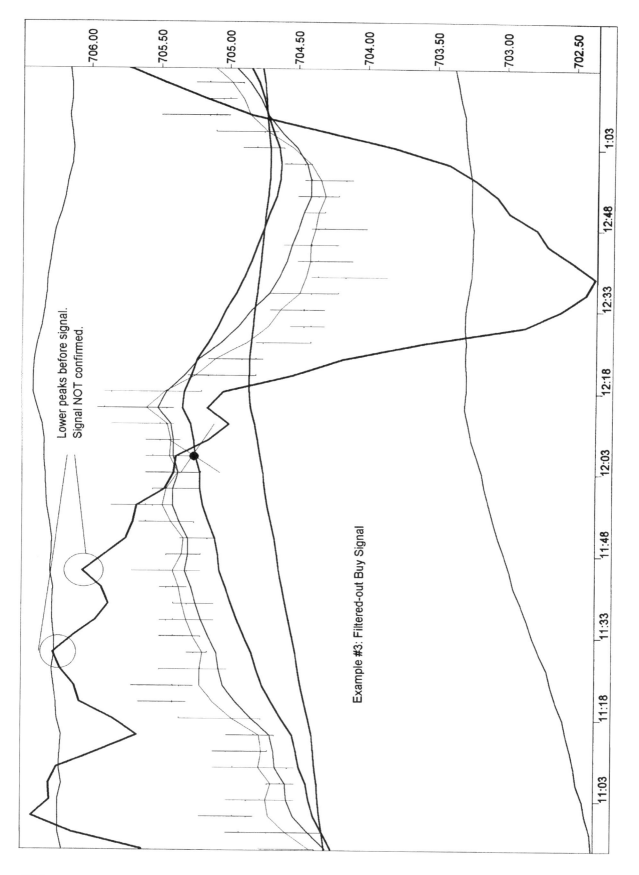

Lower peaks before signal.
Signal NOT confirmed.

Example #3: Filtered-out Buy Signal

Chart created with TradeStation™ by Omega Research, Inc.

246

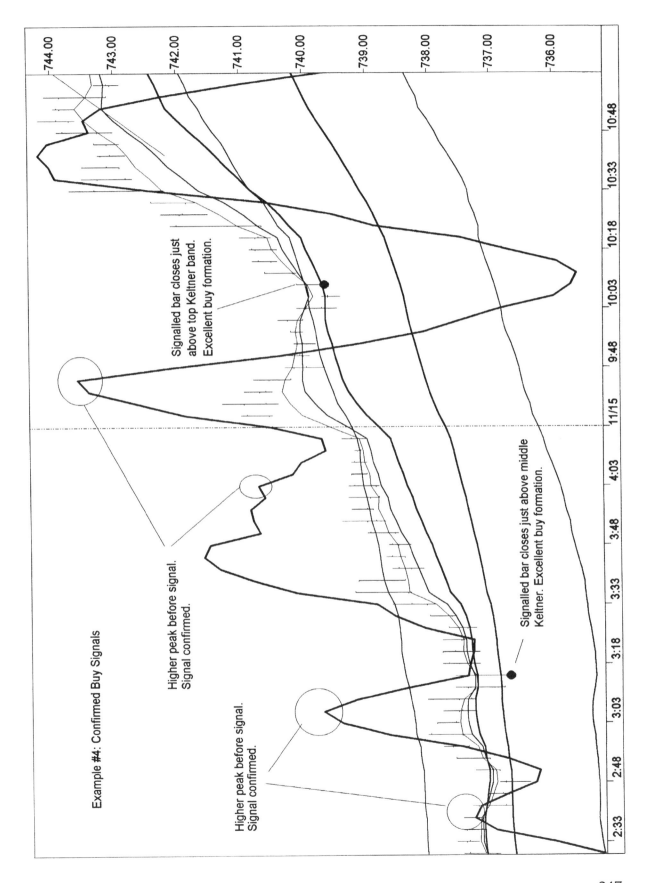

Example #4: Confirmed Buy Signals

Higher peak before signal.
Signal confirmed.

Higher peak before signal.
Signal confirmed.

Signalled bar closes just
above top Keltner band.
Excellent buy formation.

Signalled bar closes just above middle
Keltner. Excellent buy formation.

Chart created with TradeStation™ by Omega Research, Inc.

247

# APPENDIX F

A Guide to Futures and Options
Market Terminology

**Across the board:** All the months of a particular futures contract or futures option contract, for example, if all the copper contracts open limit up, they were limit up "across the board."

**Actuals:** The physical or cash commodity, which is different from a futures contract. *See* Cash commodity.

**Arbitrage:** The purchase of a commodity against the simultaneous sale of a commodity to profit from unequal prices. The two transactions may take place on different exchanges, between two different commodities, in different delivery months, or between the cash and futures markets. *See* Spreading.

**Arbitration:** The procedure available to customers for the settlement of disputes. Brokers and exchange members are required to participate in arbitration to settle disputes. Arbitration is available through the exchanges, the NFA, and the CFTC.

**Assignment:** Options are exercised through the option purchaser's broker, who notifies the clearinghouse of the option's exercise. The clearinghouse then notifies the option seller that the buyer has exercised. When futures options are exercised, the buyer of a call is assigned a long futures contract, and the seller receives the corresponding short. Conversely, the buyer of a put is assigned a short futures contract upon exercise, while the seller receives the corresponding long.

**At the market:** When issued, this order is to buy or sell a futures or options contract as soon as possible at the best possible price. *See* Market order.

**At-the-money:** An option is at-the-money when its strike price is equal, or approximately equal, to the current market price of the underlying futures contract.

**Bar chart:** A graphic representation of price movement disclosing the high, low, close, and sometimes the opening prices for the day. A vertical line is drawn to correspond with the price range for the day, while a horizontal "tick" pointing to the left reveals the opening price, and a tick to the right indicates the closing price. After days of charting, patterns start to emerge, which technicians interpret for their price predictions.

**Basis:** The difference between the cash price and the futures price of a commodity. CASH - FUTURES = BASIS. Basis also is used to refer to the difference between prices at different markets or between different commodity grades.

**Bear call spread:** The purchase of a call with a high strike price against the sale of a call with a lower strike price. The maximum profit receivable is the net premium received (premium received minus premium paid), while the maximum loss is calculated by subtracting the net premium received from the difference between the high strike price and the low strike price (high strike price - low strike price - net premium received). A bear call spread should be entered when lower prices are expected. It is a type of vertical spread.

**Bear market (bear/bearish):** When prices are declining, the market is said to be a "bear market"; individuals who anticipate lower prices are "bears." Situations believed to bring with them lower prices are considered "bearish."

**Bear put spread:** The purchase of a put with a high strike price against the sale of a put with a lower strike price in expectation of declining prices. The maximum profit is calculated as follows: (high strike price - low strike price) - net premium cost. The maximum loss is the net premium paid. A vertical spread.

**Bear Spread:** Sale of a near month futures contract against the purchase of a deferred month futures contract in expectation of a price decline in the near month relative to the more distant month. Example: selling a December contract and buying the more distant March contract.

**Bid:** The request to buy a futures contract at a specified price; the opposite of offer.

**Board of trade:** An exchange or association of persons participating in the business of buying or selling any commodity or receiving it for sale on consignment. Generally, an exchange where commodity futures and/or futures options are traded.

*See also* Contract market and Exchange.

**Bearish:** When market prices tend to go lower, the market is said to be bearish.

**Beta:** A measure correlating stock price movement to the movement of an index. Beta is used to determine the number of contracts required to hedge with stock index futures or futures options.

**Board orders:** *See* Market if touched orders.

**Break:** A sudden price move; prices may break up or down.

**Break-even:** Refers to a price at which an option's cost is equal to the proceeds acquired by exercising the option. The buyer of a call pays a premium. His break-even point is calculated by adding the premium paid to the call's strike price. For example, if you purchase a May 58 cotton call for 2.25¢ per pound when May cotton futures are at 59.48¢/lb., the break-even price is 60.25¢/lb. (58.00¢/lb. + 2.25¢/lb. = 60.25¢/lb.). For a put purchaser, the break-even point is calculated by subtracting the premium paid from the put's strike price. Please note that, for puts, you do not exercise unless the futures price is below the break-even point.

**Broker:** An agent who executes trades (buy or sell orders) for customers. He receives a commission for these services. Other terms used to describe a broker include: a) Account Executive (AE), b) Associated Person (AP), c) Registered Commodity Representative (RCR), d) NFA Associate.

**Bullish:** A tendency for prices to move up.

**Bull call spread:** The purchase of a call with a low strike price against the sale of a call with a higher strike price; prices are expected to rise. The maximum potential profit is calculated as follows: (high strike price - low strike price) - net premium cost, where net premium cost = premiums paid - premiums received. The maximum possible loss is the net premium cost.

**Bull market (bull/bullish):** When prices are rising, the market is said to be a "bull market"; individuals who anticipate higher prices are considered "bulls." Situations arising which are expected to bring higher prices are called "bullish."

**Bull put spread:** The purchase of a put with a low strike price against the sale of a call with a higher strike price; prices are expected to rise. The maximum potential profit equals the net premium received. The maximum loss is calculated as follows: (high strike price - low strike price) - net premium received where net premium received = premiums paid - premiums received.

**Bull spread:** The purchase of near month futures contracts against the sale of deferred month futures contracts in expectation of a price rise in the near month relative to the deferred. One type of bull spread, the limited risk spread, is placed only when the market is near full carrying charges. *See* Limited risk spread.

**Butterfly spread:** Established by buying an at-the-money option, selling 2 out-of-the-money options, and buying an out-of-the-money option. A butterfly is entered anytime a credit can be received; i.e., the premiums received are more than those paid.

**Buy stop/sell stop orders:** *See* Stop orders.

**Buyer:** Anyone who enters the market to purchase a good or service. For futures, a buyer can be establishing a new position by purchasing a contract (going long), or liquidating an existing short position. Puts and calls can also be bought, giving the buyer the right to purchase or sell an underlying futures contract at a set price within a certain period of time.

**Calendar spread:** The sale of an option with a nearby expiration against the purchase of an option with the same strike price, but a more distant expiration. The loss is limited to the net premium paid, while the maximum profit possible depends on the time value of the distant option when the nearby expires. The strategy takes advantage of time value differentials during periods of relatively flat prices.

**Call:** The period at market opening or closing during which futures contract prices are established by auction.

**Call option:** A contract giving the buyer the right to purchase something within a certain period of time at a specified price. The seller receives money (the premium) for the sale of this right. The contract also obligates the seller to deliver, if the buyer exercises his right to purchase.

**Carrying charges:** The cost of storing a physical commodity, consisting of interest on the invested funds, insurance, storage fees, and other incidental costs. Carrying costs are usually reflected in the difference between futures prices for different delivery months. When futures prices for deferred contract maturities are higher than for nearby maturities, it is a carrying charge market. A full carrying charge market reimburses the owner of the physical commodity for its storage until the delivery date.

**Carryover:** The portion of existing supplies remaining from a prior production period.

**Cash commodity/cash market:** The actual or physical commodity. The market in which the physical commodity is traded, as opposed to the futures market, where contracts for future delivery of the physical commodity are traded. *See also* Actuals.

**Cash flow:** The cash receipts and payments of a business. This differs from net income after taxes in that non-cash expenses are not included in a cash flow statement. If more cash comes in than goes out, there is a positive cash flow, while more outgoing cash causes a negative cash flow.

**Cash forward contract:** *See* Forward contract.

**Cash market:** A market in which goods are purchased either immediately for cash, as in a cash and carry contract, or where they are contracted for presently, with delivery occurring at the time of payment. All terms of the contract are negotiated between the buyer and seller.

**Cash price:** The cost of a good or service when purchased for cash. In commodity trading, the cash price is the cost of buying the physical commodity on the current day in the spot market, rather than buying contracts in the futures market.

**Cash settlement:** Instead of having the actuals delivered, cash is transferred upon settlement.

**Certificate of Deposit (CD):** A large time deposit with a bank, having a specified maturity date stated on the certificate. CDs usually are issued with $100,000 to $1,000,000 face values.

**Certificated stock:** Stocks of a physical commodity that have been inspected by the exchange and found to be acceptable for delivery on a futures contract. They are stored at designated delivery points.

**Charting:** When technicians analyze the futures markets, they employ graphs and charts to plot the price movements, volume, open interest, or other statistical indicators of price movement. *See also* Technical analysis and Bar chart.

**Chicago Board of Trade (CBOT):** Founded in 1848 with 82 original members, it had an active cash and forward contracting business at first. Although the records were destroyed in the fire of 1871, it is agreed the CBOT is the largest exchange in the world. It is known for its grain, gold, Treasury Bond, and Major Market Index futures, as well as options on T-Bond futures. The Chicago Board of Trade is located at 141 W. Jackson Blvd., Chicago, IL 60604.

**Chicago Mercantile Exchange (CME):** The second largest futures exchange in the United States. Originally formed in 1874 as the Chicago Produce Exchange, the "Chicago Merc" was primarily a perishable agricultural products market (butter, eggs, poultry, etc.). The name was changed in 1919, and since then the CME has been an innovator in the industry. Important subsidiary divisions have been formed including the International Monetary Market (IMM) and the Index and Options Market (IOM). The IMM deals with financial futures while the IOM handles options and stock index futures contracts. The CME is the largest exchange for futures contracts in live commodities, foreign currencies, and U.S. Treasury bills. Foreign currencies contracts traded on the IMM include: West German Mark, Canadian Dollar, French Franc, Swiss Franc, Dutch Guilder, British Pound, Australian Dollar, and Japanese Yen. Futures contracts on the S&P 500 and S&P 100 Stock Indexes and options on the S&P 500 futures contract are also traded at the IOM. The CME is located at 30 S. Wacker Dr., Chicago, IL 60606.

**Chicago Rice and Cotton Exchange (CRCE):** Founded originally as the New Orleans Commodity Exchange, the CRCE moved to Chicago, where it became a division of the Chicago Board of Trade, and where it continues to trade rice and cotton. The CRCE is located at 141 W. Jackson Blvd., Chicago, IL 60604.

**Churning:** When a broker engages in excessive trading to derive a profit from commissions while ignoring his client's best interests.

**Clearinghouse:** An agency associated with an exchange which guarantees all trades, thus assuring contract delivery and/or financial settlement. The clearinghouse becomes the buyer for every seller, and the seller for every buyer.

**Clearing margin:** Funds deposited by a futures commission merchant with its clearing member.

**Clearing member:** A clearinghouse member responsible for executing client trades. Clearing members also monitor the financial capability of their clients by requiring sufficient margins and position reports.

**Close or closing range:** The range of prices found during the last two minutes of trading. The average price during the "close" is used as the settlement price from which the allowable trading range is set for the following day.

**Coffee, Sugar & Cocoa Exchange:** Founded in 1882 as the Coffee Exchange of the City of New York. In 1916, the exchange changed its name to the New York Coffee and Sugar Exchange,

Inc., and in 1979 to the Coffee, Sugar & Cocoa Exchange, Inc., when it merged with the New York Cocoa Exchange, Inc. Today, it is known for its Coffee, Sugar, and Cocoa contracts and is located at 4 World Trade Center, New York, NY 10048.

**Commercials:** Firms that are actively hedging their cash grain positions in the futures markets; e.g., millers, exporters, and elevators.

**Commission:** The fee which clearinghouses charge their clients to buy and sell futures and futures options contracts. The fee that brokers charge their clients is also called a commission.

**Commission house:** Another term used to describe brokerage firms because they earn their living by charging commissions.

**Commodity:** A good or item of trade or commerce. Goods tradeable on an exchange, such as corn, gold, or soybeans, as distinguished from instruments or other intangibles like T-Bills or stock indexes.

**Commodity Credit Corporation (CCC):** A government-owned corporation established in 1933 to support prices through purchases of excess crops, to control supply through acreage reduction programs, and to devise export programs.

**Commodity Exchange (COMEX):** Formed in 1933, when four different exchanges trading metals, rubber, silk, and hides merged. Today, the COMEX is known for its metals, including gold, silver, aluminum, ew York, NY 10048.

**Commodity Futures Trading Commission (CFTC):** A federal regulatory agency established in 1974 to administer the Commodity Exchange Act. This agency monitors the futures and futures options markets through the exchanges, futures commission merchants and their agents, floor brokers, and customers who use the markets for either commercial or investment purposes.

**Commodity pool:** A venture where several persons contribute funds to trade futures or futures options. A commodity pool is not to be confused with a joint account.

**Commodity Pool Operator (CPO):** An individual or firm who accepts funds, securities, or property for trading commodity futures contracts, and combines customer funds into pools. The larger the account, or pool, the more staying power the CPO and his clients have. They may be able to last through a dip in prices until the position becomes profitable. CPOs must register with the CFTC, and are closely regulated.

**Commodity-Product Spread:** The simultaneous purchase (or sale) of a commodity and the sale (or purchase) of the products derived from that commodity; for example, buying soybeans and selling soybean oil and meal. This is known as a crush spread. Another example is the crack spread, where the crude oil is purchased and gasoline and heating oil are sold.

**Commodity Trading Advisor (CTA):** An individual or firm who directly or indirectly advises others about buying or selling futures or futures options. Analyses, reports, or newsletters concerning futures may be issued by a CTA; he may also engage in placing trades for other people's accounts. CTAs are required to be registered with the CFTC and to belong to the NFA.

**Confirmation statement:** After a futures or options position has been initiated, a statement must be issued to the customer by the commission house. The statement contains the number of contracts bought or sold, and the prices at which the transactions occurred, and is sometimes combined with a purchase and sale statement.

**Congestion:** A charting term used to describe an area of sideways price movement. Such a range is thought to provide support or resistance to price action.

**Contract:** A legally enforceable agreement between two or more parties for performing, or refraining from performing, some specified act; e.g., delivering 5,000 bushels of corn at a specified grade, time, place, and price.

**Contract market:** Designated by the CFTC, a contract market is a board of trade set up to trade futures or option contracts, and generally means any exchange on which futures are traded. *See* Board of trade and Exchange.

**Contract month:** The month in which a contract comes due for delivery according to the futures contract terms.

**Controlled account:** *See* Discretionary account

**Contrarian Theory:** A theory suggesting that the general consensus about trends is wrong. The contrarian takes the opposite position from the majority opinion to capitalize on overbought or oversold situations.

**Convergence:** The coming together of futures prices and cash market prices on the last trading day of a futures contract.

**Conversion:** The sale of a cash position and investment of part of the proceeds in the margin for a long futures position. The remaining money is placed in an interest-bearing instrument. This practice allows the investor/dealer to receive high rates of interest, and take delivery of the commodity if needed.

**Conversion factor:** A figure published by the CBOT used to adjust a T-Bond hedge for the difference in maturity between the T-Bond contract specifications and the T-Bonds being hedged.

**Cover:** Used to indicate the repurchase of previously sold contracts as, he covered his short position. Short covering is synonymous with liquidating a short position or evening up a short position.

**Covered position:** A transaction which has been offset with an opposite and equal transaction; for example, if a gold futures contract had been purchased, and later a call option for the same commodity amount and delivery date was sold, the trader's option position is "covered." He holds the futures contract deliverable on the option if it is exercised. Also used to indicate the repurchase of previously sold contracts as, he covered his short position.

**Crack spread:** A type of commodity-product spread involving the purchase of crude oil futures and the sale of gasoline and heating oil futures.

**Cross-hedge:** A hedger's cash commodity and those traded on an exchange are not always of the same quality or grade. Therefore, a hedger may have to select a similar commodity (one with similar price movement) for his hedge. This is known as a "cross-hedge."

**Crush spread:** A type of commodity-product spread which involves the purchase of soybean futures and the simultaneous sale of soybean meal and soybean oil futures, used primarily by soybean processors.

**Day order:** An order which, if not executed during the trading session the day it is entered, automatically expires at the end of the session. All orders are assumed to be day orders unless specified otherwise.

**Day-trader:** Traders who usually initiate and offset a position during a single trading session.

**Dealer option:** A put or call on a physical good written by a firm dealing in the underlying cash commodity. A dealer option does not originate on, nor is it subject to the rules of an exchange.

**Debt instruments:** 1) Generally, legal IOUs created when one person borrows money from (becomes indebted to) another person; 2) Any commercial paper, bank CDs, bills, bonds, etc.; 3) A document evidencing a loan or debt. Debt instruments such as T-Bills and T-Bonds are traded on the CME and CBOT, respectively.

**Deck:** All orders in a floor broker's possession that have not yet been executed.

**Deep in-the-money:** An option is "deep in-the-money" when it is so far in-the-money that it is unlike to go out-of-the-money prior to expiration. It is an arbitrary term and can be used to describe different options by different people.

**Deep out-of-the-money:** Used to describe an option that is unlikely to go into-the-money prior to expiration. An arbitrary term.

**Default:** Failure to meet a margin call or to make or take delivery. The failure to perform on a futures contract as required by exchange rules.

**Deferred delivery:** Futures trading in distant delivery months.

**Deferred pricing:** A method of pricing where a producer sells his commodity now and buys a futures contract to benefit from an expected price increase. Although some people call this hedging, the producer is actually speculating that he can make more money by selling the cash commodity and buying a futures contract than by storing the commodity and selling it later. (If the commodity has been sold, what could he be hedging against?)

**Delivery:** The transportation of a physical commodity (actuals or cash) to a specified destination in fulfillment of a futures contract.

**Delivery month:** The month during which a futures contract expires, and delivery is made on that contract.

**Delivery notice:** Notification of delivery by the clearinghouse to the buyer. Such notice is initiated by the seller in the form of a "Notice of Intention to Deliver."

**Delivery point:** The location approved by an exchange for tendering and accepting goods deliverable according to the terms of a futures contract.

**Delta:** The correlation factor between a futures price fluctuation and the change in premium for the option on that futures contract. Delta changes from moment to moment as the option premium changes.

**Demand:** The desire to purchase economic goods or services (and the financial ability to do so) at the market price constitutes demand. When many purchasers demand a good at the market price, their combined purchasing power constitutes "demand." As this combined demand increases or decreases, other things remaining constant, the price of the good tends to rise or fall.

**Diagonal spread:** Uses options with different expiration dates and different strike prices; for example, a trader might purchase a 26 December West German Mark put and sell a 28 September West German Mark put when the futures price is $.2600/DM.

**Direct hedge:** When the hedger has (or needs) the commodity (grade, etc.) specified for delivery in the futures contract, he is "direct hedging." When he does not have the specified commodity, he is cross hedging.

**Discount:** 1) Quality differences between those standards set for some futures contracts and the quality of the delivered goods. If inferior goods are tendered for delivery, they are graded below the standard, and a lesser amount is paid for them. They are sold at a discount; 2) Price differences between futures of different delivery months; 3) For short-term financial instruments, "discount" may be used to describe the way interest is paid. Short-term instruments are purchased at a price below the face value (discount). At maturity, the full face value is paid to the purchaser. The interest is imputed, rather than being paid as coupon interest during the term of the instrument; for example, if a T-Bill is purchased for $974,150, the price is quoted at 89.66, or a discount of 10.34% (100.00 - 89.66 = 10.34). At maturity, the holder receives $1,000,000.

**Discount Rate:** The interest rate charged by the Federal Reserve to its member banks (banks which belong to the Federal Reserve System) for funds they borrow. This rate has a direct bearing on the interest rates banks charge their customers. When the discount rate is increased, the banks must raise the rates they charge to cover their increased cost of borrowing. Likewise, when the discount rate is lowered, banks are able to charge lower interest rate on their loans.

**Discretionary accounts:** An arrangement in which an account holder gives power of attorney to another person, usually his broker, to make decisions to buy or to sell without notifying the owner of the account. Discretionary accounts often are called "managed" or "controlled" accounts.

**Downtrend:** A channel of downward price movement.

**Economic good:** That which is scarce and useful to mankind.

**Economy of scale:** A lower cost per unit produced, achieved through large-scale production. The lower cost can result from better tools of production, greater discounts on purchased supplies, production of by-products, and/or equipment or labor used at production levels closer to capacity. A large cattle feeding operation may be able to benefit from economies such as lower unit feed costs, increased mechanization, and lower unit veterinary costs.

**Efficiency:** Because of futures contracts' standardization of terms, large numbers of traders from all walks of life may trade futures, thus allowing prices to be determined readily (it is more likely that someone will want a contract at any given price). The more readily prices are discovered, the more efficient are the markets.

**Elasticity:** A term used to describe the effects price, supply, and demand have on one another for a particular commodity. A commodity is said to have elastic demand when a price change affects the demand for that commodity; it has supply elasticity when a change in price cauity. A commodity has inelastic supply or demand when they are unaffected by a change in price.

**Equity:** The value of a futures trading account with all open positions valued at the going market price.

**Eurodollar Time Deposits:** U.S. dollars on deposit outside the United States, either with a foreign bank or a subsidiary of a U.S. bank. The interest paid for these dollar deposits generally is higher than that for funds deposited in U.S. banks because the foreign banks are riskier — they will not be supported or nationalized by the U.S. government upon default. Furthermore, they may pay higher rates of interest because they are not regulated by the U.S. government.

**Even up:** To close out, liquidate, or cover an open position.

**Exchange:** An association of persons who participate in the business of buying or selling futures contracts or futures options. A forum or place where traders (members) gather to buy or sell economic goods. There are 12 domestic futures exchanges currently operating as non-profit member organizations. See also Board of trade or Contract market.

**Exchange rates:** The price of foreign currencies. If it costs $.42 to buy one Swiss Franc, the exchange rate is .4200. As one currency is inflated faster or slower than the other, the exchange rate will change, reflecting the change in relative value. The currency being inflated faster is said to be becoming weaker because more of it must be exchanged for the same amount of the other currency. As a currency becomes weaker, exports are encouraged because others can buy more with their relatively stronger currencies.

**Expiration date:** The final date when an option may be exercised. Many options expire on a specified date during the month prior to the delivery month for the underlying futures contract.

**Ex-pit transactions:** Occurring outside the futures exchange trading pits. This includes cash transactions, the delivery process, and the changing of brokerage firms while maintaining open positions. All other transactions involving futures contracts must occur in the trading pits through open outcry.

**Exercise:** When a call purchaser takes delivery of the underlying long futures position, or when a put purchaser takes delivery of the underlying short futures position. Only option buyers may "exercise" their options; option sellers have a passive position.

**Expiration:** An option is a wasting asset; i.e., it has a limited life, usually nine months. At the end of its life, it either becomes worthless (if it is at-the-money or out-of-the-money), or is automatically exercised for the amount by which it is in-the-money.

**Federal Reserve Board:** A board of Directors comprised of seven members which directs the federal banking system, is appointed by the President of the United States and confirmed by the Senate. The functions of the board include formulating and executing monetary policy, overseeing the Federal Reserve Banks, and regulating and supervising member banks. Monetary policy is implemented through the purchase or sale of securities, and by raising or lowering the discount rate, the interest rate at which banks borrow from the Federal Reserve.

**Fill or Kill order (FOK):** Also known as a quick order, is a limit order which, if not filled immediately, is canceled.

**Financial futures:** Include interest rate futures, currency futures, and index futures. The financial futures market currently is the fastest growing of all the futures markets.

**First notice day:** Notice of intention to deliver a commodity in fulfillment of an expiring futures contract can be given to the clearinghouse by a seller (and assigned by the clearinghouse to a buyer) no earlier than the first notice day. First notice days differ depending on the commodity.

**Floor broker:** A person who executes orders on the trading floor of an exchange on behalf of other people. They are also known as pit brokers because the trading area has steps down into a "pit" where the brokers stand to execute their trades.

**Floor trader:** Exchange members present on the exchange floor to make trades on their own behalf. They may be referred to as scalpers or locals.

**Forward contract:** A contract entered into by two parties who agree to the future purchase or sale of a specified commodity. This differs from a futures contract in that the participants in a forward contract are contracting directly with each other, rather than through a clearing corporation. The terms of a forward contract are negotiated between the buyer and seller, while exchanges set the terms of futures contracts.

**Forward pricing:** The practice of locking in a price in the future, either by entering into a cash forward contract or a futures contract. In a cash forward contract, the parties usually intend to tender and accept the commodity, while futures contracts are generally offset, with a cash transaction occurring after offset.

**Free market:** A market place where individuals can act in their own best interest, free from outside forces (freedom means freedom from government) restricting their choices, or regulating or subsidizing product prices. Free market also refers to the political system where the means of production are owned by free, non-regulated individuals.

**Full carry:** When the difference between futures contract month prices equals the full cost of carrying (storing) the commodity from one delivery period to the next. Carrying charges include insurance, interest, and storage.

**Fundamental analysis:** The study of specific factors, such as weather, wars, discoveries, and changes in government policy, which influence supply and demand and, consequently, prices in the market place.

**Futures Commission Merchant (FCM):** An individual or organization accepting orders to buy or sell futures contracts or futures options, and accepting payment for his services. FCMs must be registered with the CFTC and the NFA, and maintain a minimum capitalization of $100,000.

**Futures Contract:** A standardized and binding agreement to buy or sell a predetermined quantity and quality of a specified commodity at a future date. Standardization of the contracts enhances their transferability. Futures contracts can be traded only by auction on exchanges registered with the CFTC.

**Futures Industry Association (FIA):** The futures industry's national trade association.

**Gambler:** One who seeks profit by taking noncalculated or manmade risks. If one flips a coin to determine his course of action, he is gambling as to the outcome. If one bets on the horses, the outcome of a sports event, or some other man-made event, he is gambling. A gambler is distinguished from a speculator in that a speculator could profit from price change if he knew enough about the supply and demand factors used to determine price. He also trades economic goods, thus benefitting mankind.

**Gap:** A term used by technicians to describe a jump or drop in prices; i.e., prices skipped a trading range. Gaps are usually filled at a later date.

**Geometric index:** An index in which a 1% change in the price of any two stocks comprising the index impacts on it equally. The Value Line Average index is composed of 1,700 stocks and is a geometric index.

**Give-up:** A customer "give-up" is a trade executed by one broker for the client of another broker and then "given-up" to the regular broker; e.g., a floor broker with discretion must have another broker execute the trade.

**Good till Canceled (GTC):** A qualifier for any kind of order extending its life indefinitely; i.e., until filled or canceled.

**Grantor:** Someone who assumes the obligation, not the right, to buy (for a put) or sell (for a call) the underlying futures contract or commodity at the strike price. *See also* Writer.

**Guarantee Fund:** One of two funds established for the protection of customers' monies; the clearing members contribute a percentage of their gross revenues to the guarantee fund. *See also* Surplus fund.

**Guided account:** An account that has a planned trading strategy and is directed by either a CTA or a FCM. The customer is advised on specific trading positions, which he must approve before an order may be entered. These accounts often require a minimum initial investment, and may use only a predetermined portion of the investment at any particular time. Not to be confused with a discretionary account.

**Hedge ratio:** The relationship between the number of contracts required for a direct hedge and the number of contracts required to hedge in a specific situation. The concept of hedging is to match the size of a positive cash flow from a gaining futures position with the expected negative cash flow created by unfavorable cash market price movements. If the expected cash flow from a $1 million face-value T-Bill futures contract is one-half as large as the expected cash market loss on a $1 million face-value instrument being hedged (for whatever reason), then two futures contracts are needed to hedge each $1 million of face value. The hedge ratio is 2:1.

Hedge ratios are used frequently when hedging with futures options, interest rate futures, and stock index futures, to aid in matching expected cash flows. Generally, the hedge ratio between the number of futures options required and the number of futures contracts is 1:1. For interest rate and stock index futures, the ratios may vary depending on the correlation between price movement of the assets being hedged and the futures contracts or options used to hedge them. Most agricultural hedge ratios are 1:1.

**Hedger:** One who hedges; one who attempts to transfer the risk of price change by taking an opposite and equal position in the futures or futures option market from that position held in the cash market.

**Hedging:** Transferring the risk of loss due to adverse price movement through the purchase or sale of contracts in the futures markets. The position in the futures market is a substitute for the future purchase or sale of the physical commodity in the cash market. If the commodity will be bought, the futures contract is purchased (long hedge); if the commodity will be sold, the futures contract is sold (short hedge).

**High:** The top price paid for a commodity or its option in a given time period, usually a day or the life of a contract.

**Inelasticity:** A statistic attempting to quantify the change in supply or demand for a good, given a certain price change. The more inelastic demand (characteristic of necessities), the less effect a change in price has on demand for the good. The more inelastic supply, the less supply changes when the price does.

**In-the-money:** A call is in-the-money when the underlying futures price is greater than the strike price. A put is in-the-money when the underlying futures price is less than the strike price. In-the-money options have intrinsic value.

**Index:** A specialized average. Stock indexes may be calculated by establishing a base against which the current value of the stocks, commodities, bonds, etc., will change; for example, the S&P 500 index uses the 1941-1943 market value of the 500 stocks as a base of 10.

**Inflation:** The creation of money by monetary authorities. In more popular usage, the creation of money that visibly raises goods prices and lowers the purchasing power of money. It may be creeping, trotting, or galloping, depending on the rate of money creation by the authorities. It may take the form of "simple inflation," in which case the proceeds of the new money issues accrue to the government for deficit spending; or it may appear as "credit expansion," in which case the authorities channel the newly created money into the loan market. Both forms are inflation in the broader sense.

**Initial margin:** When a customer establishes a position, he is required to make a minimum initial margin deposit to assure the performance of his obligations. Futures margin is earnest money or a performance bond.

**Interest:** What is paid to a lender for the use of his money and includes compensation to the lender for three factors: 1) Time value of money (lender's rate) — the value of today's dollar is more than tomorrow's dollar. Tomorrow's dollars are discounted to reflect the time a lender must wait to "enjoy" the money, not to mention the uncertainties tomorrow brings. 2) Credit risk — the risk of repayment varies with the creditworthiness of the borrower. 3) Inflation — as the purchasing power of a dollar declines, more dollars must be repaid to maintain the same purchasing power. Interest is one of the components of carrying charges; i.e., the cost of the money needed to finance the commodity's purchase or storage. The market rate of interest can also be used to establish an opportunity cost for the funds that are tied up in any investment.

**Interest rate futures:** Futures contracts traded on long-term and short-term financial instruments: GNMAs, Treasury debt, and the liabilities of large banking institutions (CDs and Eurodollar Time Deposits).

**Inter-market:** A spread in the same commodity, but on different markets. An example of an inter-market spread would be buying a wheat contract on the Chicago Board of Trade, and simultaneously selling a wheat contract on the Kansas City Board of Trade.

**Intra-market:** A spread within a market. An example of an intra-market spread is buying a corn contract in the nearby month and selling a corn contract on the same exchange in a distant month.

**Intrinsic value:** The amount an option is in-the-money, calculated by taking the difference between the strike price and the market price of the underlying futures contract when the option is "in-the-money." A COMEX 350 gold futures call has an intrinsic value of $10 if the underlying gold futures contract is at $360/ounce.

**Introducing Broker (IB):** An individual or firm who can perform all the functions of a broker except one. An IB is not permitted to accept money, securities, or property from a customer. An IB must be registered with the CFTC, and conduct its business through an FCM on a fully disclosed basis.

**Inverted market:** A futures market in which near-month contracts are selling at prices that are higher than those for deferred months. An inverted market is characteristic of a short-term supply shortage. The notable exceptions are interest rate futures, which are inverted when the distant contracts are at a premium to near-month contracts.

**Kansas City Board of Trade (KCBT):** The first verifiable futures exchange in the United States (1856) was incorporated in 1973. Contracts on wheat and grain sorghum have been traded there for many years. The KCBT was the first exchange to introduce stock index futures (the Value Line Average); they also have an option on that futures contract. They are located at 4800 Main St., Suite 303, Kansas City, MO 64112.

**Last trading Day:** The last day on which a futures contract is traded.

**Law of Demand:** Demand exhibits a direct relationship to price. If all other factors remain constant, an increase in demand leads to an increased price, while a decrease in demand leads to a decreased price.

**Law of Supply:** Supply exhibits an inverse relationship to price. If all other factors hold constant, an increase in supply causes a decreased price, while a decrease in supply causes an increased price.

**Letter of acknowledgment:** A form received with a Disclosure Document intended for the customer's signature upon reading and understanding the Disclosure Document. The FCM is required to maintain all letters of acknowledgment on file. It may also be known as a Third Party Account Controllers form.

**Leverage:** The control of a 1arger sum of money with a smaller amount. By accepting the liability to purchase or deliver the total value of a futures contract, a smaller sum (margin) may be used as earnest money to guarantee performance. If prices move favorably, a large return on the margin can be earned from the leverage. Conversely, a loss can also be large, relative to the margin, due to the leverage.

**Liability:** 1) In the broad legal sense, responsibility or obligation. For example, a person is liable to pay his debts, under the law; 2) In accounting, any debt owed by an individual or organization. Current, or short-term, liabilities are those to be paid in less than one year (wages, taxes, accounts payable, etc.). Long-term, or fixed, liabilities are those that run for one year or more (mortgages, bonds, etc.); 3) In futures, traders deposit margin as earnest money, but they are liable for the entire value of the contract; 4) In futures options, purchasers of options have their liability limited to the premium they pay; option writers are subject to the liability associated with the underlying deliverable futures contract.

**Limit:** *See* Price limit, Position limit, and Variable limit.

**Limit move:** The increase or decrease of a price by the maximum amount allowed for any one trading session. Price limits are established by the exchanges, and approved by the CFTC. They vary from contract to contract.

**Limit orders:** A customer sets a limit on price or time of execution of a trade, or both; for example, a "buy limit" order is placed below the market price. A "sell limit" order is placed above the market price. A sell limit is executed only at the limit price or higher (better), while the buy limit is executed at the limit price or lower (better).

**Limited Risk:** A concept often used to describe the option buyer's position. Because the option buyer's loss can be no greater than the premium he pays for the option, his risk of loss is limited.

**Limited Risk Spread:** A bull spread in a market where the price difference between the two contract months covers the full carrying charges. The risk is limited because the probability of the distant month price moving to a premium greater than full carrying charges is minimal.

**Line-bar chart:** *See* Bar chart.

**Liquidate:** Refers to closing an open futures position. For an

272

open long, this would be selling the contract. For a short position, it would be buying the contract back (short covering, or covering his short).

**Liquidity (liquid market):** A market which allows quick and efficient entry or exit at a price close to the last traded price. The ability to liquidate or establish a position quickly is due to a large number of traders willing to buy and sell.

**Locals:** The floor traders who trade primarily for their own accounts. Although "locals" are speculators, they provide the liquidity needed by hedgers to transfer the risk of price change.

**Long:** One who has purchased futures contracts or the cash commodity, but has not taken any action to offset his position. Also, purchasing a futures contract. A trader with a long position hopes to profit from a price increase.

**Long hedge:** A hedger who is short the cash (needs the cash commodity) buys a futures contract to hedge his future needs. By buying a futures contract when he is short the cash, he is entering a long hedge. A long hedge is also known as a substitute purchase or an anticipatory hedge.

**Long-the-basis:** A person who owns the physical commodity and hedges his position with a short futures position is said to be long-the-basis. He profits from the basis becoming more positive (stronger); for example, if a farmer sold a January soybean futures contract at $6.00 with the cash market at $5.80, the basis is -.20. If he repurchased the January contract later at $5.50 when the cash price was $5.40, the basis would then be -.10. The long-the-basis hedger profited from the 10¢ increase in basis.

**Low:** The smallest price paid during the day or over the life of the contract.

**Maintenance margin:** The minimum level at which the equity in a futures account must be maintained. If the equity in an account falls below this level, a margin call will be issued, and funds must be added to bring the account back to the initial margin level. The maintenance margin level generally is 75% of the initial margin requirement.

**Managed Account:** *See* Discretionary account.

**Margin:** Margin in futures is a performance bond or "earnest money." Margin money is deposited by both buyers and sellers of futures contracts, as well as sellers of futures options. *See* Initial margin.

**Margin call:** A call from the clearinghouse to a clearing member, or from a broker to a customer, to add funds to their margin account to cover an adverse price movement. The added margin assures the brokerage firm and the clearinghouse that the customer can purchase or deliver the entire contract, if necessary.

**Mark-to-market:** The IRS's practice of calculating gains and losses on open futures positions as of the end of the tax year. In other words, taxpayers' open futures positions are marked to the market price as of the end of the tax year and taxes are assessed as if the gains or losses had been realized.

**Market-if-touched order (MIT):** They are similar to stop orders in two ways: 1 ) They are activated when the price reaches the order level; 2) They become market orders once they are activated; however, MIT orders are used differently from stop orders. A buy MIT order is placed below the current market price, and establishes a long position or closes a short position. A sell MIT order is placed above the current market price, and establishes a short position or closes a long position.

**Market order:** An order to buy or sell futures or futures options contracts as soon as possible at the best available price. Time is of primary importance.

**Market-share weighted index:** An index where the impact of a stock price change depends upon the market-share that stock controls. For example, a stock with a large marketshare, such as IBM with over 600 million shares outstanding, would have a greater impact on a market-share weighted index than a stock with a small market-share, such as Foster Wheeler, with approximately 34 million shares outstanding.

**Market-value weighted index:** A stock index in which each stock is weighted by market value. A change in the price of any stock will influence the index in proportion to the stock's respective market value. The weighting of each stock is determined by multiplying the number of shares outstanding by the stock's market price per share; therefore, a high-priced stock with a large number of shares outstanding has more impact than a low-priced stock with only a few shares outstanding. The S&P 500 is a value weighted index.

**Maturity:** The period during which a futures contract can be settled by delivery of the actuals; i.e., the period between the first notice day and the last trading day. Also, the due date for financial instruments.

**Maximum price fluctuation:** *See* Limit move.

**MidAmerica Commodity Exchange (MACE):** Founded in 1868, it was incorporated as the Chicago Open Board of Trade in 1880, and changed its name to MidAmerica Commodity Exchange in 1972. The MidAm is known for its mini-contracts. It has contracts with a smaller commodity quantity deliverable in grains, currencies, metals, interest rate futures, and the meats. It also has options for many of its futures contracts. The MidAm was recently purchased by the Chicago Board of Trade and is located at 141 W. Jackson Blvd., Chicago, IL 60604.

**Minimum price fluctuation:** The smallest allowable fluctuation in a futures price or futures option premium.

**Minneapolis Grain Exchange (MGE):** The largest organized cash grain market in the world, founded in 1881, has futures contracts in wheat, high fructose corn syrup, and oats, as well MGE is located at 400 S. 4th St., Minneapolis, MN 55415.

**Monthly statement:** An account record for each month of activity in a futures and/or futures options account. Quarterly statements are required for inactive accounts.

**Moving average:** An average of prices for a specified number of days. If it is a three (3) day moving average, for example, the first three days' prices are averaged (1,2,3), followed by the next three days' average price (2,3,4), and so on. Moving averages are used by technicians to spot changes in trends.

**Naked:** When an option writer writes a call or put without owning the underlying asset.

**National Association of Futures Trading Advisors (NAFTA):** A national association consisting primarily of Commodity Trade Advisors and Commodity Pool Operators.

**National Futures Association (NFA):** A "registered futures association" authorized by the CFTC in 1982 that requires membership for FCMs, their agents and associates, CTAs, and CPOs. This is a self-regulatory group for the futures industry similar to the National Association of Securities Dealers, Inc. in the securities industry.

**Nearby:** The futures contract month with the earliest delivery period.

**Net position:** The difference between total open long and open short positions in any one or all combined futures contract months held by an individual.

**Neutral calendar spread:** *See* Calendar spread.

**New York Cotton Exchange (NYCE):** Founded in 1870, the state charter restricts trading to cotton, thus associate memberships have been established to trade other items such as orange juice, the U.S. dollar index, 5 year T-Notes, and options on the futures contracts. They are located at 4 World Trade Center, New York, NY 10048.

**New York Futures Exchange (NYFE):** A subsidiary of the New York Stock Exchange, created trading in financial futures contracts. Today, the NYFE has stock index futures contracts based on the New York Stock Exchange Composite (NYSEC) Index, the Commodity Research Bureau (CRB) Index, the Russell 2000 Index, and the Russell 3000 Index. They also have an option on the NYSEC index and the CRB index. The NYFE is located at 20 Broad St., New York, NY 10005.

**New York Mercantile Exchange (NYME):** Founded in 1872 to trade cheese, butter, and eggs, it changed its emphasis to cover futures contracts for platinum, palladium, and energy (crude oil, gasoline, etc.), as well as options on some of their contracts. They are located at 4 World Trade Center, New York, NY 10048.

**Nominal price (or nominal quotation):** The price quotation calculated for futures or options for a period during which no actual trading occurred. These quotations are usually calculated by averaging the bid and asked prices.

**Normal market:** The deferred months' prices for futures contracts are normally higher than the nearby months' to reflect the costs of carrying a contract from now until the distant delivery date. Thus, a "normal market," for non-interest rate futures contracts, exists when the distant months are at a premium to the nearby months. For interest rate futures, just the opposite is true. The yield curve dictates that a "normal market" for interest rate futures occurs when the nearby months are at a premium to the distant months.

**Notice of intention to deliver:** During the delivery month for a futures contract, the seller initiates the delivery process by submitting a "notice of intention to deliver" to the clearinghouse, which, in turn, notifies the oldest outstanding long of the seller's intentions. If the long does not offset his position, he will be called upon to accept delivery of the goods.

**Offer:** To show the desire to sell a futures contract at an established price.

**Offset:** *See* Offsetting.

**Offsetting:** Eliminating the obligation to make or take delivery of a commodity by liquidating a purchase or covering a sale of

277

futures. This is affected by taking an equal and opposite position: either a sale to offset a previous purchase, or a purchase to offset a previous sale in the same commodity, with the same delivery date. If an investor bought an August gold contract on the COMEX, he would offset this obligation by selling an August gold contract on the COMEX. To offset an option, the same option must be bought or sold; i.e., a call or a put with the same strike price and expiration month.

**Offsetting positions:** 1) Taking an equal and opposite futures position to a position held in the cash market. The offsetting futures position constitutes a hedge; 2) Taking an equal and opposite futures position to another futures position, known as a spread or straddle; 3) Buying a futures contract previously sold, or selling a futures contract previously bought, to eliminate the obligation to make or take delivery of a commodity. When trading futures options, an identical option must be bought or sold to offset a position.

**Omnibus account:** An account carried by one Futures Commission Merchant (FCM) with another. The transactions of two or more individual accounts are combined in this type of account. The identities of the individual account holders are not disclosed to the holding FCM. A brokerage firm may have an omnibus account including all its customers with its clearing firm.

**One Cancels Other (OCO):** A qualifier used when multiple orders are entered and the execution of one order cancels a second or alternate order.

**Open:** 1) The first price of the day for a contract on a securities or futures exchange. Futures exchanges post opening ranges for daily trading. Due to the fast-moving operation of futures markets, this range of closely related prices allows market participants to fill contracts at any price within the range, rather than be restricted to one price. The daily prices that are published are approximate medians of the opening range; 2) When markets are in session, or contracts are being traded, the markets are said to be "open."

**Open interest:** For futures, the total number of contracts not yet liquidated by offset or delivery; i.e., the number of contracts outstanding. Open interest is determined by counting the number of transactions on the market (either the total contracts bought or sold, but not both). For futures options, the number of calls or puts outstanding; each type of option has its own open interest figure.

**Open outcry:** Oral bids and offers made in the trading rings, or pits. "Open outcry" is required for trading futures and futures options contracts to assure arms-length transactions. This method also assures the buyer and seller that the best available price is obtained.

**Open trade equity:** The gain or loss on open positions that has not been realized.

**Opening range:** Upon opening of the market, the range of prices at which transactions occurred. All orders to buy and sell on the opening are filled within the opening range.

**Opportunity cost:** The price paid for not investing in a different investment. It is the income lost from missed opportunities. Had the money not been invested in land, earning 5%, it could have been invested in T-Bills, earning 10%. The 5% difference is an opportunity cost.

**Option seller:** *See* Grantor and Writer.

**Option contract:** A unilateral contract giving the buyer the right, but not the obligation, to buy or sell a commodity, or a futures contract, at a specified price within a certain time period. It is unilateral because only one party (the buyer) has the right to demand performance on the contract. If the buyer exercises his right, the seller (writer or grantor) must fulfill his obligation at the strike price, regardless of the current market price of the asset.

**Order:** 1) In business and trade, making a request to deliver, sell, receive, or purchase goods or services; 2) In the securities and futures trade, instructions to a broker on how to buy or sell.

The most common orders in futures markets are market orders and limit orders (which see).

**Original margin:** *See* Initial margin.

**Out-of-the-money:** A call is out-of-the-money when the strike price is above the underlying futures price. Arlying futures price.

**Overbought:** A technician's term to describe a market in which the price has risen relatively quickly too quickly to be justified by the underlying fundamental factors.

**Oversold:** A technical description for a market in which prices have dropped faster than the underlying fundamental factors would suggest.

**Pit:** The area on the trading floor of an exchange where futures trading takes place. The area is described as a"pit" because it is octagonal with steps descending into the center. Traders stand on the various steps, which designate the contract month they are trading. When viewed from above, the trading area looks like a pit.

**Pit broker:** A person on the exchange floor who trades futures contracts in the pits. *See also* Floor broker.

**Point:** *See* Minimum price fluctuation.

**Point and figure chart:** A graphic representation of price movement using vertical rows of "x"s to indicate significant up ticks and "o"s to reflect down ticks. Such charts do not reveal minute price fluctuations, only trends once they have established themselves.

**Portfolio:** The group of investments held by an investor.

**Position limit:** The maximum number of futures contracts permitted to be held by speculators or spreaders. The CFTC establishes some position limits, while the exchanges establish others. Hedgers are exempt from position limits.

**Position trader:** A trader who establishes a position (either by purchasing or selling) and holds it for an extended period of time.

**Power of attorney:** An agreement establishing an agent-principal relationship. The "power of attorney" grants the agent authority to act on the principal's behalf under certain designated circumstances. In the futures industry, a power of attorney must be in writing and must be renewed every year.

**Premium:** The price paid by a buyer to purchase an option. Premiums are determined by "open outcry" in the pits.

**Price:** A fixed value of something. Prices are usually expressed in monetary terms. In a free market, prices are set as a result of the interaction of supply and demand in a market; when demand for a product increases and supply remains constant, the price tends to decline. Conversely, when the supply increases and demand remains constant, the price tends to decline; if supply decreases and demand remains constant prices tend to rise. Today's markets are not purely competitive; prices are affected by government controls and supports that create artificial supplies and demand and inhibit free trade, thus making price predictions more difficult for those not privileged with inside government information.

**Price discovery mechanism:** The method by which the price for a particular shipment of a commodity is determined. Factors taken into account include quality, delivery point, and size of the shipment. For example, if the price of corn is $3.50 per bushel on the CBOT, the local price of corn per bushel can be discovered by taking into consideration the distance from Chicago that corn would have to be shipped, the difference in quality between local and Chicago corn, and the amount of corn to be transported. Once these factors are considered, both the buyer and seller can arrive at reasonable price for their area.

**Price limit:** The maximum price rise or decline permitted by an exchange in its commodities. The limit varies from commodity to commodity and may change depending on price volatility (variable price limits). Not all exchanges have limits; those that do set their limits relative to the prior day's settlement, for example, the CBOT may set its limit at 10¢ for corn. On day 2, corn may trade up or down 10¢ from the previous day's close of $3.00 per bushel; i.e., up to $3.10 or down to $2.90 per bushel.

**Price weighted index:** A stock index weighted by adding the price of 1 share of each stock included in the index, and dividing this sum by a constant divisor. The divisor is changed when a stock split or stock dividend occurs because these affect the stock prices. The MMI is a price weighted index.

**Primary markets:** The principal market for the purchase and sale of physical commodities.

**Purchase and sale statement:** A form required to be sent to a customer when a position is closed; it must describe the trade, show profit or loss and the commission.

**Purchaser:** Anyone who enters the market as a buyer of a good, service, futures contract, call, or put.

**Pure hedging:** A technique used by a hedger who holds his futures or option position without exiting and re-entering the position until the cash commodity is sold. Pure hedging also is known as conservative or true hedging, and is used largely by inexperienced traders wary of price fluctuation, but interested in achieving a target price.

**Put:** An option contract giving the buyer the right to sell something at a specified price within a certain period of time. A put is purchased in expectation of lower prices. If prices are expected to rise, a put may be sold. The seller receives the premium as compensation for accepting the obligation to accept delivery, if the put buyer exercises his right to sell.

**Pyramiding:** Purchasing additional contracts with the profits earned on open positions.

**Quotation:** Often referred to as a "quote." The actual, bid or asked price of futures, options or cash commodities at a certain time.

**Rally:** An upward price movement. *See* Recovery.

**Ratio writing:** When an investor writes more than one option to hedge an underlying futures contract. These options usually are written for different delivery months. Ratio writing expands the profit potential of the investor's option position. Example: an investor would be ratio writing if he is long one August gold contract and he sells (writes) two gold calls, one for February delivery, the other for August.

**Recovery:** Rising prices following a decline.

**Registered Commodity Representative**: A person registered with the exchange(s) and the CFTC who is responsible for soliciting business, "knowing" his/her customers, collecting margins, submitting orders, and recommending and executing trades for customers. A registered commodity representative is sometimes called a"broker" or "account exchanges executive."

**Regulations (CFTC):** The guidelines, rules, and regulations adopted and enforced by the Commodity Futures Trading Commision (the CFTC is a federal regulatory agency established in 1974) in administration of the Commodity Exchange Act.

**Reparations:** Parties that are wronged during a futures or options transaction may be awarded compensation through the CFTC's claims procedure. This compensation is known as reparations because it "repairs" the wronged party.

**Reportable positions:** Positions where the reporting level has been exceeded. *See also* Reporting level.

**Reporting level:** An arbitrary number of contracts held by a trader that must be reported to the CFTC and the exchange. Reporting levels apply to all traders; hedgers, speculators, and spreaders alike. Once a trader has enough contracts to exceed the reporting level, he has a "special account," and must report and changes in his positions.

**Resistance:** A horizontal price range where price hovers due to selling pressure before attempting a downward move.

**Retender:** The right of a futures contract holder, who has received a notice of intention to deliver from the clearinghouse, to offer the notice for sale on the open market, thus offsetting his obligation to take delivery under the contract. This opportunity is only available for some commodities and only within a certain period of time.

**Ring:** A designated area on the exchange floor where traders stand while executing trades. Instead of rings, some exchanges use pits.

**Risk Disclosure Document:** A document outlining the risks involved in futures trading. The document includes statements to the effect that: you may lose your entire investment; you may find it impossible to liquidate a position under certain market conditions; spread positions may not be less risky than simple "long" or "short" positions; the use of leverage can lead to large losses as well as large profits; stop-loss orders may not limit your losses; managed commodity accounts are subject to substantial management and advisory charges.

There is a separate risk disclosure document for options which warns of the risks of loss in options trading. This statement includes a description of commodity options, margin requirements, commissions, profit potential, definitions of various terms, and a statement of the elements of the purchase price.

**Rolling hedge:** Changing a futures hedge from one contract month to another. Rolling a short hedge may be advisable when more time is needed to complete the cash transaction to avoid delivery on the futures contract. Hedge rolling may also be considered to keep the hedge in the less active, more distant months, thus reducing the liklihood of swift price movements and the resulting margin calls.

**Round turn:** A complete futures transaction (both entry and exit); for example, a sale and covering purchase, or a purchase and liquidating sale. Commissions are usually charged on a "round-turn" basis.

**Scalper:** A floor trader who buys and sells quickly to take advantage of small price fluctuations. Usually a scalper is ready to buy at the bid and sell at the asked price, providing liquidity to the market. The term "scalper" is used because these traders attempt to "scalp" a small amount on a trade.

**Security deposit:** *See* Margin.

**Segregated account:** An account separate from brokerage firm accounts. Segregated accounts hold customer funds so that if a brokerage house becomes insolvent, the customers' funds will be readily recognizable and will not be tied up in litigation for extended periods of time.

**Selective Hedging:** The technique of hedging where the futures or option position may be lifted and re-entered numerous times before the cash market transaction takes place. A hedge "locks-in" a target price to minimize risk. Lifting the hedge lifts the risk protection (increasing the possibility of loss), but also allows the potential for gain.

**Sell stop order:** *See* Stop orders.

**Selling hedge:** *See* Short hedge.

**Settlement:** The clearinghouse practice of adjusting all futures accounts daily according to gain or loss from price movement is generally called settlement.

**Settlement price:** Established by the clearinghouse from the closing range of prices (the last 2 minutes of the day). The settlement price is used to determine the next day's allowable trading range, and to settle all accounts between clearing members for each contract month. Margin calls and invoice prices for deliveries are determined from the settlement prices. In addition to this, settlement prices are used to determine account values and determine margins for open positions.

**Short:** Someone who has sold actuals or futures contracts, and has not yet offset the sale; the act of selling the actuals or futures contracts, absent any offset.

**Short covering:** Buying by shorts to liquidate existing positions.

**Short hedge:** When a hedger has a long cash position (is holding an inventory or growing a crop) he enters a short hedge by selling a futures contract. A sell or short hedge is also known as a substitute sale.

**Short-the-basis:** When a person or firm needs to buy a commodity in the future, he can protect himself against price increases by making a substitute purchase in the futures market. The risk this person now faces is the risk of a change in basis (cash price - futures price). This hedger is said to be short-the-basis because he will profit if the basis becomes more negative (weaker); for example, if a hedger buys a corn futures contract at 325¢ when cash corn is 312¢, the basis is -.13. If this hedge is lifted with futures at 320¢ and cash at 300¢, the basis is -.20, and the hedger has profited by the $.07 decrease in basis.

**Sideways:** A market with a narrow price range; i.e., little upward or downward price movement.

**Special account:** An account which has a reportable position in either futures or futures options. *See also* Reporting levels.

**Speculation:** An attempt to profit from commodity price changes through the purchase and/or sale of commodity futures. In the process, the speculator assumes the risk that the hedger is transferring, and provides liquidity in the market.

**Speculator:** One who buys and sells stocks, land, etc., risking his capital with the goal of earning a profit from price changes. In contrast to gamblers, speculators understand and evaluate existing market risks on the basis of data and experience, while gamblers are those who seek out man-made risks or "invest" in a  roll of the dice.

**Spot:** The market in which commodities are available for immediate delivery. It also refers to the cash market price of a specific commodity.

**Spread:** 1) Positions held in two different futures contracts, taken to profit from the change in the difference between the two contract's prices; e.g., long a January Soybean contract and short a March Soybean contract would be a bull spread, used to profit from a narrowing in the difference between the two prices; 2) The difference between the prices of two futures contracts. If January beans are $6.15 and March beans are $6.28, the spread is -.13, or 13¢ under ($6.15 - 6.28 = -.13)

**Spreading:** The purchase of one futures contract and the sale of another in an attempt to profit from the change in price differences between the two contracts . Inter-market, inter-commodity, inter-delivery, and commodity-product are examples of spreads.

**Stock Index Futures:** Based on stock market indexes, including Standard and Poor's 500, Value Line, NYSE Composite, the Major Market Index, and the Over-the-Counter Index, these instruments are used by investors concerned with price changes in a large number of stocks, or with major long-term trends in stock market indexes. Stock index futures are settled in cash and are generally quoted in ticks of .05. To determine the contract value, the quote is generally multiplied by $500.

**Stop orders:** An order which becomes a market order once a certain price level is reached. These orders are often placed with the purpose of limiting losses. They are also used to initiate positions. Buy stop orders are placed at a price above the current market price. Sell stop orders are placed below the market price; for example, if the market price for December corn is 320¢, a buy stop order could be placed at 320 1/4¢ or higher, and a sell stop could be placed at 319 3/4¢ or lower. A buy stop order is activated by a bid or trade at or above the stop price. A sell stop is triggered by a trade or offer at or below the stop price.

**Stopped out:** When a stop order is activated and a position is offset, the trader has been "stopped out."

**Storage:** The cost to store commodities from one delivery month to another. Storage is one of the "carrying charges" associated with futures.

**Straddle:** For futures, the same as spreading. In futures options, a straddle is formed by going long a call and a put of the same strike price (long straddle), or going short a call and a put of the same strike price (short straddle) .

**Strangle spread:** Makes maximum use of the premium's time value decay. To utilize a strangle most profitably, choose a market that is trading within a given range (volatility peaking), and sell an out-of-the-money call and an out-of-the-money put.

**Strike price:** The specified price at which an option contract may be exercised. If the buyer of the option exercises (demands performance), the futures contract positions will be entered at the strike price.

**Strong basis:** A relatively small difference between cash prices and futures prices. A strong basis also can be called a "narrow basis," or a "more positive basis": for example, a strong basis usually occurs in grains in the spring before harvest when supplies are low. Buyers must raise their bids to buy. As the cash prices rise, relative to futures prices, the basis strengthens. A strong basis indicates a good selling market, but a poor buying market.

**Summary suspension:** Occurs when a  member fails to pay NFA levied fines after seven days written notice. One may also be summarily suspended from membership (and trading) when the President and the NFA Board of Directors or Executive Committee have reason to believe that summary suspension is necessary (an emergency) to protect the futures industry, customers, NFA members, etc.  Notice of such action is given to the CFTC. NFA members are prohibited from conducting business while under suspension or with a suspended firm.

**Supply:** The quantity of a good available to meet demand. Supply consists of inventories from previous production, current production, and expected future production. Because resources are scarce, supply creates demand. Only price must be determined.

**Support:** A horizontal price range where price hovers due to buying pressure before attempting an upward move.

**Surplus fund:** A fund established for the protection of customers' monies; a portion of all clearing fees are set aside for this fund.

**Synthetic position:** A hedging strategy combining futures and futures options for price protection and increased profit potential; for example, by buying a put option and selling (writing) a call option, a trader can construct a position that is similar to a short futures position. This position is known as a synthetic short futures position, and shows a profit if the futures prices decline, and receives margin calls if prices rise. Synthetic positions are a form of arbitrage.

**Systematic risk:** The risk affecting a market in general; for example, if the government's monetary and fiscal policies create inflation, price levels rise, affecting the entire market in much the same way, thus creating a systematic risk. Stock index futures can be used to substantially reduce systematic risk. Compare with unsystematic risk.

**Technical Analysis:** Technical analysis uses charts to examine changes in price patterns, volume of trading, open interest, and rates of change to predict and profit from trends. Someone who follows technical rules (called a technician) believes that prices will anticipate changes in fundamentals.

**Technician:** One who uses technical analysis to forecast price movements.

**Terms:** The components, elements, or parts of an agreement. The "terms" of a futures contract include: which commodity, its quality, the quantity, the time and place of delivery, and its price. All the terms of futures and futures option contracts are standardized except for price, which is determined through "open-out-cry" in the exchanges' trading pits.

**Tick:** The minimum allowable price fluctuation (up or down) for a futures contract. Different contracts have different size ticks. Ticks can be stated in terms of price per unit of measure, or in dollars and cents. *See also* Point.

**Time value:** The premium of an out-of-the money option reflecting the probability that an option will move into-the-money before expiration constitutes the time value of the option. There also may be some time value in the premium of an in-the-money option, which reflects the probability of the option moving further into the money. To determine the time value of an in-the-money option, subtract the amount by which the option is in-the-money (intrinsic value) from the total premium.

**Trading range:** The prices between the high and the low for a specific time period (day, week, life of the contract).

**Trend:** A significant price movement in one direction or another. Trends may go either up or down.

**Underlying futures contract:** The futures contract covered by an option; for example, a 300 Dec. corn call's underlying futures contract is the December corn futures contract.

**Unsystematic risk:** The risk of price change for an individual stock, commodity, or industry. Anything from an oil discovery to a change in management could affect this sort of risk. Unsystematic risks are reduced or eliminated through diversification of holdings, not by hedging with index futures. Compare with systematic risk.

**Uptrend:** A channel of upward price movement.

**Value:** The importance placed on something by an individual. Value is subjective and may change according to the circumstances. Something that may be valued highly at one time may be valued less at another time.

**Variable limits:** Most exchanges set limits on the maximum daily price movement of some of the contracts traded on their floors. They also retain the right to expand these limits if the price moves up- or down-limit for one, two, or three trading days in a row. If the limits automatically change after repeated limit moves, they are known as variable limits.

**Variation margin call:** A margin call from the clearinghouse to a clearing member. These margin calls are issued when the clearing member's margin has been reduced substantially by unfavorable price moves. The variation margin call must be met within one hour.

**Vertical spreads:** Also known as a price spread, is constructed with options having the same expiration months. This can be done with either calls or puts. *See* Bear call spread, Bull call spread, Bear put spread, and Bull put spread.

**Volatile:** A market which often is subject to wide price fluctuations is said to be volatile. This volatility is often due to a lack of liquidity.

**Volume:** The number of futures contracts, calls, or puts traded in a day. Volume figures use the number of longs or shorts in a day, not both. Such figures are reported on the following day.

**Wash sales:** An illegal process in which simultaneous purchase and sales are made in the same commodity futures contract, on the same exchange, and in the same month. No actual position is taken, although it appears that trades have been made. It is hoped that the apparent activity will induce legitimate trades, thus increasing trading volume and commissions.

**Wasting asset:** A term often used to describe an option because of its limited life. Shortly before its expiration, an out-of-the-money option has only time value, which declines rapidly. For an in-the-money option, only intrinsic value is left upon expiration. For futures options, this is either automatically exercised or cashed out. At the end of its life, an option that has no intrinsic value becomes worthless; i.e., it wastes away.

**Weak basis:** A relatively large difference between cash prices and futures prices. A weak basis also can be called a "wide basis," or a "more negative basis": for example, a weak basis usually occurs in grains at harvest time when supplies are abundant. Buyers can lower their bids to buy. As the cash prices decline, relative to futures prices, the basis weakens (gets wider). A weak basis indicates a poor selling market, but a good buying market.

**Writer:** One who sells an option. A "writer" (or grantor) obligates himself to deliver the underlying futures position to the option purchaser, should he decide to exercise his right to the underlying futures contract position. Option writers are subject to margin calls because they may have to produce the long or short futures position. A call writer must supply a long futures position upon exercise, and thus receive a short futures position. A put writer must supply a short futures position upon exercise, and thus receive a long futures position.

**Yield:** 1) The production of a piece of land; e.g., his land yielded 100 bushels per acre. 2) The return provided by an investment; for example, if the return on an investment is 10%, the investment yields 10%.

# Appendix G

## Sources and Resources

## ADVISORY SERVICES

All-Star Trader's Hotline:  1-900-288-2262
(Call costs $2.95 per minute. Must be 18 years or older)

Commodity Traders Consumer Report (CTCR) Products
1731 Howe Avenue, Suite 149
Sacramento, CA 95825
(916) 677-7562

## BROKERS

Trader-oriented magazines, such as the two referenced for you in this Appendix, are sources you can research to find out names of Futures Commission Merchants. Rather than list the scores of current FCM's that would love to have your business, I direct you instead to an excellent source designed to help you pick the right one:

Davis, Robert N., *Choosing a Futures Broker,* Cedar Falls, Iowa: Center for Futures Education, 1983 (to obtain this, see Center for Futures Education address under "Industry Information" in this appendix)

## DATA VENDORS

Bloomberg, L.P.    (Offers in-house news services as well)
499 Park Avenue, New York, NY 10022
(212) 318 2000
London:  071-330-7500
Frankfurt: 69-92041-0
Singapore:  65-226-3000
Sydney:  2-241-1133
Tokyo:  03-3578-1625

BMI
3 Triad Center, Suite 100
Salt Lake City, UT 84810
Attn: Mindy Schroeder
(800) 815-8248   E-mail: mschroeder@dbc.com

CQG
PO Box 758
Glenwood Springs, CO 81601
(800) 525-7082

Data Broadcasting Corp.
1900 S. Norfolk Street
Suite 150
San Mateo, CA 94403
USA: (800) 367-4670
England: 44-171-626-6101

DTNstant
9110 W. Dodge Road
Omaha, NE 68114
(800) 397-7000

Future Source
955 Parkview Blvd.
Lombard, IL 60148
(800) 621-2628

Reuters America     (Offers in-house news services as well)
311 S. Wacker Drive
Chicago, IL 60606
(312) 408-8500
Contact Chicago for their worldwide locations.

S & P Comstock
600 Mamaroneck Avenue
Harrison, NY 10528
(800) 431-5019

# FINANCIAL PUBLISHERS

## Contact them for free catalogs

Financial Trading Seminars
PO Box 20555
Columbus Circle Station
New York, NY 10023
(800) 458-0939

Futures Learning Center
219 Parkade
Box 6
Cedar Falls, IA 50613
(319) 277-6341

Irwin Professional Publishers
1333 Burr Ridge Parkway
Burr Ridge, IL 60521
800-634-3966

New York Insitute of Finance
2 Broadway
5th Floor
New York, NY 10004
(800) 227-NYIF

Probus Publishing
1925 N. Clybourne Avenue
Suite 401
Chicago, IL 60614
(800) 776-2871

Trader's Press
PO Box 6206
Greenville, SC 29606
(800) 927-8222

John Wiley & Sons
605 Third Avenue
New York, NY 10158
(212) 850-6000

Windsor Books
PO Box 280
Brightwaters, NY 11718
(516) 321-7831

# GENERAL PURPOSE
# REAL-TIME CHARTING SOFTWARE

Aspen Research Group
710 Cooper Avenue
Suite 300
Glenwood Springs, CO 81601
(800) 359-1121

Equis International
3950 South 700 East
Suite 100
Salt Lake City, UT 84107
(800) 882-3040

Omega Research
8700 West Flagler Street, Suite 250
Miami, FL 33174-2428
Attn: Kevin Feuerlicht
(800) 292-3453
E-mail: kevin.f@omegaresearch.com

Roberts-Slade
619 North 500 West
Provo, UT 84601
(800) 375-6850

## INDUSTRY INFORMATION
Many of these organizations publish literature,
some of it free for the asking

Bolsa Brasileira de Futuros (BBF)
Praça XV de Novembro, 20-5th Fl.
20010-010 Rio de Janeiro-RJ, BRAZIL
5521 + 271-1086; FAX 5521 + 224-5718
Internet: http://www.bbf.com.br

Bolsa de Derivados do Porto (BDP)
Av. da Boavista, n°3433
4100 Porto, PORTUGAL
351-2-618-58 58; FAX 351-2-618 55 66
E-mail: bvp@telepac.pt

Center for Futures Education, Inc. (CFE)
401 Erie St., P.O. Box 309
Grove City, PA 16127
412-458-5860; FAX 412-458-5962
Internet: http://www.thectr.com

Chicago Board of Trade (CBT)
LaSalle at Jackson (141 W. Jackson Blvd.)
Chicago, IL 60604
312-435-3500, 800-THE-CBOT
FAX 312-341-3168 (Market and Product Development)
Internet: http://www.cbot.com

Chicago Mercantile Exchange (CME)
30 S. Wacker Drive
Chicago, IL 60606
312-930-1000; FAX 312-466-4410 (Office Services)
Internet: http://www.cme.com

Coffee, Sugar & Cocoa Exchange, Inc. (CSCE)
4 World Trade Center
New York, Ny 10048
(212) 742-6100; (800) HEDGE-IT
FAX (212) 748-4321; Internet: http://www.csce.com

Commodity Futures Trading Commission (CFTC)
3 Lafayette Centre, 1155 21st Street, NW
Washington, DC 20581
202-418-5080, FAX 202-418-5525
Internet: http://www.cftc.gov

Deutsche Börse AG (DTB)
60284 Frankfurt (postal address)
Schillerstr. 19-25 (street address)
60313 Frankfurt am Main, GERMANY
49 69 2101-4897; FAX 49 69 2101-3941
Internet: http://www.exchange.de

Hong Kong Futures Exchange (HKFE)
Suites 605-608, Asia Pacific Finance Tower
Citibank Plaza, 3 Garden Rd., Central, HONG KONG
852-2842-9333; FAX 852-2845-2043
Internet: http://www.hkfe.com

International Petroleum Exchange of London Ltd. (IPE)
International House, 1 St. Katharine's Way
London, ENGLAND E1 9UN
44 171 481 0643, FAX 44 171 481-8485
Internet: http://www.ipe.uk.com

Kansas City Board of Trade (KCBT)
4800 Main Street, Suite 303
Kansas City, MO 64112
800-821-5228; 816-753-7500; FAX 816-753-3944
Internet: http://www.kcbt.com

The London International Financial Futures and
Options Exchange (LIFFE)
Cannon Bridge
London EC4R 3XX, ENGLAND
44 171 623 044; FAX 44 171 588-3624
Internet: http://www.liffe.com

The London Metal Exchange Ltd. (LME)
56 Leadenhall Street
London EC3A 2BJ, ENGLAND
44 171 264-5555; FAX 44 171 680-0505
Internet:http://www.lme.co.uk

Marché à Terme International de France (MATIF)
115, Rue Réaumur
75083 Paris, FRANCE
33-1-40-28-82-82; FAX 33-1-40-28-8001
Internet: http://www.matif.fr

MidAmerica Commodity Exchange (MACE)
141 W. Jackson Blvd.
Chicago, IL 60604
312-341-3000, 800-572-3276, Marketing 312-435-7239
FAX 312-341-3392, Internet: http://www.midam.com

Minneapolis Grain Exchange (MPLS)
400 S. 4th Street, 130 Grain Exchange Building
Minneapolis, MN 55415
800-827-4746; 612-321-7101
FAX 612-339-1155
Internet: http://www.mgex.com

Montreal Exchange (ME)
The Stock Exchange Tower
800 Square Victoria, 4th Floor, P.O. Box 61
Montreal, Quebec H4Z 1A9 CANADA
514-871-2424, FAX 514-871-3531
Internet: http://www.me.org

National Futures Association (NFA)
200 W. Madison Street, Ste. 1600
Chicago, IL 60606-3447
312-781-1300, 800-621-3570, 800-572-9400 IL
FAX 312-781-1467; Internet: http://www.nfa.futures.org

New York Cotton Exchange (CTN)
4 World Trade Center, New York, NY 10048
212-742-5050; 800-NY-COTTON; FAX 212-748-1241
Internet: http://www.nyce.com

New York Futures Exchange (NYFE)
4 World Trade Celnter, New York, NY 10048
212-742-5061; 800 THE-NYFE; FAX 212-742-5026
Internet: http://www.nyce.com

New York Mercantile Exchange
NYMEX Division (NYM) and COMEX Division (CMX)
4 World Trade Center; New York, NY 10048
212-748-3341; FAX 212-748-3365
Internet: http://www.nymex.com

New Zealand Futures and Options Exchange Ltd. (NZFOE)
P.O. Box 6734, Wellesley Street; Auckland, NEW ZEALAND
64-9-309-8308, FAX 64-9-309-8817
Internet: http://www.phlx.com

Philadelphia Board of Trade (PBOT)
1900 Market Street; Philadelphia, PA 19103-3584
800-843-7459, 215-496-5200: FAX 215-496-5460
Internet: http://www.phlx.com

Singapore Commodity Exchange Ltd. (SICOM)
111 N. Bridge Rd., #23-04/05, Peninsula Plaza
Singapore 179098
65 338-5600; FAX 65 338-9116
Internet: http://www.sicom.com.sg

Singapore International Monetary Exchange Ltd. (SIMEX)
1 Raffles Place, #07-00 OUB Centre
Singapore 048616
65 53507382, FAX 65 535-7282
Internet: http://www.simex.com

Sydney Futures Exchange Ltd. (SFE)
30-32 Grosvenor Street; Sydney, NSW 2000
AUSTRALIA
61 2 9256-0555; FAX 61 2 9256-0666
Internet: http://www.sfe.com.au

The Tokyo Commodity Exchange (TOCOM)
14th Fl. Riverside Yomiuri Bldg.
36-2, Nihonbashi-Hakozakicho
Chuo-ku, Tokyo 103, JAPAN
813-3661-9191; FAX 813-3661-7568

Tokyo International Financial Futures Exchange (TIFFE)
1-3-1 Marunouchi, Chiyoda-ku
Tokyo 100, JAPAN
81-3-5223-2415, FAX 81-3-5223-2450
Internet: http://www.tiffe.or.jp

Toronto Futures Exchange (TFE)
Exchange Tower, 2 First Canadian Place
Toronto, ONT. M5X 1J2 CANADA
416-947-4487, FAX 416-947-4272

U.S. Department of Agriculture
Bulletin Board Inquiries: 800-999-6779. E-mail
Report Inquiries: 607-255-5406
Internet: http://www.usda.gov/fas.

U.S. Department of Commerce
National Technical Information Service (NTIS)
Technology Administration
Springfield, VA 22161
703-487-4630; FAX 703-321-8547

Warenterminbörse Hannover AG (WTB)
Rathenaustr. 2, D-30159 Hannover, GERMANY
49-511-32 76 61; FAX 49-511-32- 49 15
E-mail: BurgWarberg@T-online.de

Winnipeg Commodity Exchange (WPG)
500 Commodity Exchange Tower, 360 Main Street
Winnipeg, Man., CANADA R3C 3Z4
204-925-5000, FAX 204-943-5448
Internet: http://www.wce.mb.ca

## INTERMARKET ANALYSIS

Ruggiero Associates
18 Oregon Avenue
East Haven, CT 06512
(800) 211-9785

## JAPANESE CANDLESTICKS

Nison, Steve,
Japanese Candlestick Charting Techniques - A Contemporary
Guide to the Ancient Investment Techniques of the Far East
New York: New York Institute of Finance, 1991

Nison, Steve,
Beyond Candlesticks
New York: New York Institute of Finance, 1994

## MAGAZINE PUBLISHERS

*Futures* by Oster Communications: (800) 635-3931

*Technical Analysis of Stocks and Commodities* by Technical Analysis:
(800) 832-4642

## SATELLITE NEWS SERVICE

Futures World News
219 Parkade, PO Box 6
Cedar Falls, IA 50613
(319) 277-1271
Now also available through the Data Broadcasting Corporation's
BMI division (see under "Data Vendors") along with their data feed.

# INDEX